Scott Foresman - Addison Wesley

MATH

Enrichment Masters

Extend Your Thinking

Grade 2

Scott Foresman - Addison Wesley

Editorial Offices: Menlo Park, California • Glenview, Illinois
Sales Offices: Reading, Massachusetts • Atlanta, Georgia • Glenview, Illinois
Carrollton, Texas • Menlo Park, California

http://www.sf.aw.com

ISBN 0-201-31261-1

Copyright © Addison Wesley Longman, Inc.

All rights reserved. The blackline masters in this publication are designed to be used with appropriate equipment to reproduce copies for classroom use only. Addison Wesley Longman grants permission to classroom teachers to reproduce these masters.

Printed in the United States of America

3 4 5 6 7 8 9 10 – BW – 02 01 00 99 98

Contents

Chapter 1: Numbers and Graphing

Chapter 2: Addition and Subtraction: Patterns and Concepts

Chapter 3: Addition and Subtraction Facts and Strategies

Chapter 4: Using Addition and Subtraction

Chapter 5: Place Value and Patterns to 100

Chapter 6: Money

Chapter 7: Time

Chapter 8: Two-Digit Addition

Overview

Extend Your Thinking *(Enrichment Masters)* enhance student learning by actively involving students in different areas of mathematical reasoning. These masters consist of four types of motivating and challenging activities that focus on higher-order thinking skills. The categories are Patterns, Critical Thinking, Visual Thinking, and Decision Making.

Patterns activities encourage students to develop skills in recognizing patterns that exist in all facets of mathematics. The study of patterns allows students to gain an appreciation for the inter-relatedness and beauty in the structure of mathematics. These activities cover data, numbers, algebra and geometry, and allow students to find interesting solutions to sometimes difficult problems.

Critical Thinking activities challenge students to examine and evaluate their own thinking about math and about related content areas. The strategies students will use include: Classifying and Sorting, Ordering and Sequencing, Using Logic, Drawing Conclusions, Using Number Sense, Making Generalizations, Reasoning with Graphs and Charts, Explaining Reasoning/Justifying Answers, Developing Alternatives, Evaluating Evidence and Conclusions, and Making and Testing Predictions.

Visual Thinking activities focus on students' ability to perceive and mentally manipulate visual images. Emphasis is placed on spatial perception and visual patterns.

Decision Making activities present real-world situations that require students to make a decision. In most cases, there are no clearly right or wrong answers. This gives students the opportunity to carefully weigh alternate courses of action–as well as consider their personal experiences. You may wish to encourage students to use these decision-making steps as they make and evaluate their decisions:

Understand Encourage students to define the problem. They need to consider why a decision is needed, what goal they wish to meet, and what tools and techniques they can use to reach their decision.

Plan and Solve Have students identify the information that is relevant to the decision-making process.

Make a Decision After students evaluate the data and consider the consequences, they decide which choice is best.

Present the Decision Students explain why they made the choice that they did.

Name ________________________________

Extend Your Thinking
1-1

Visual Thinking

Count the number of objects in each box.
Then follow the direction.

Draw fewer  in the box.

Draw more  in the box.

Draw an equal number of  .

Draw fewer  in the box.

Notes for Home Your child counted objects and drew more, less, or an equal number of objects.
Home Activity: Ask your child to count the number of windows in the room and decide if that number is more, fewer, or equal to the number of people in the room.

Name ______________________________

Extend Your Thinking
1-2

Decision Making

Jamal's family is going on a camping trip.
Do they need more or less of each thing?

more

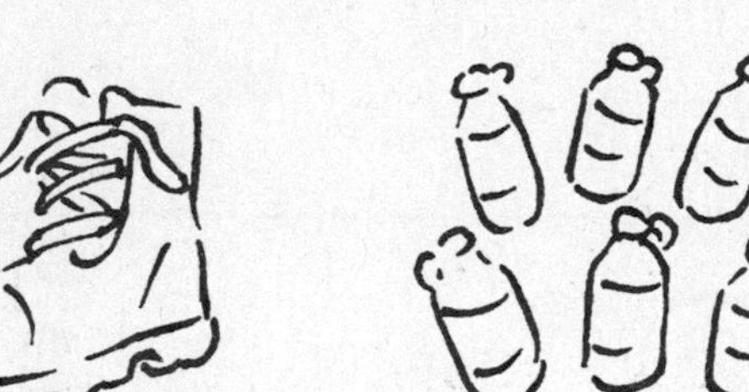

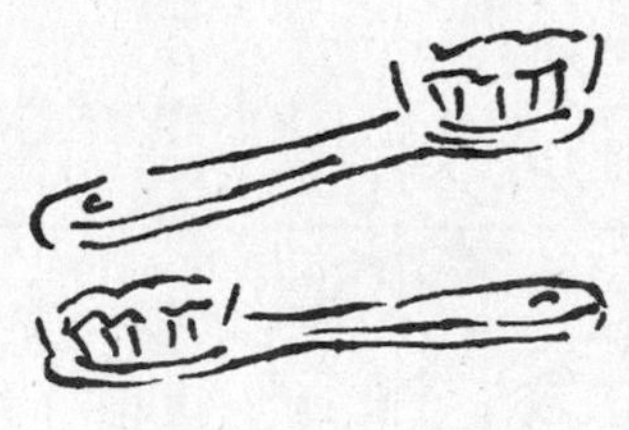

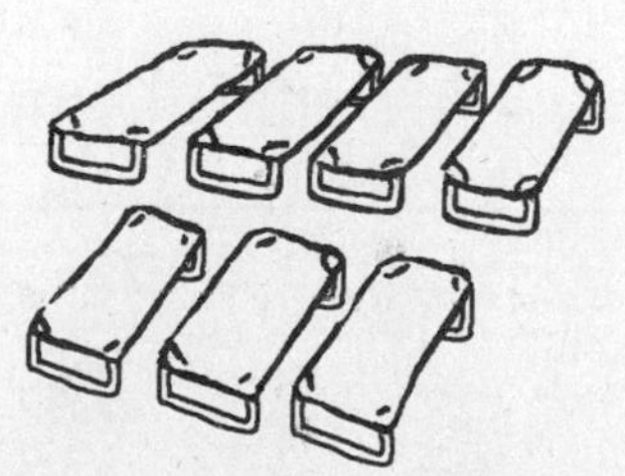

Notes for Home Your child decided whether a family preparing to go camping needed to pack more or less items for their trip. *Home Activity:* Ask your child exactly how many of each item would be needed for the trip. (4 of each)

Name ______________________________________

Extend Your Thinking
1-3

Patterns in Numbers

Bus 2 stops at small houses with numbers used in counting by 2 in order.
Bus 5 stops at big buildings with numbers used in counting by 5 in order.
Draw the paths of the buses from where they are to the school.

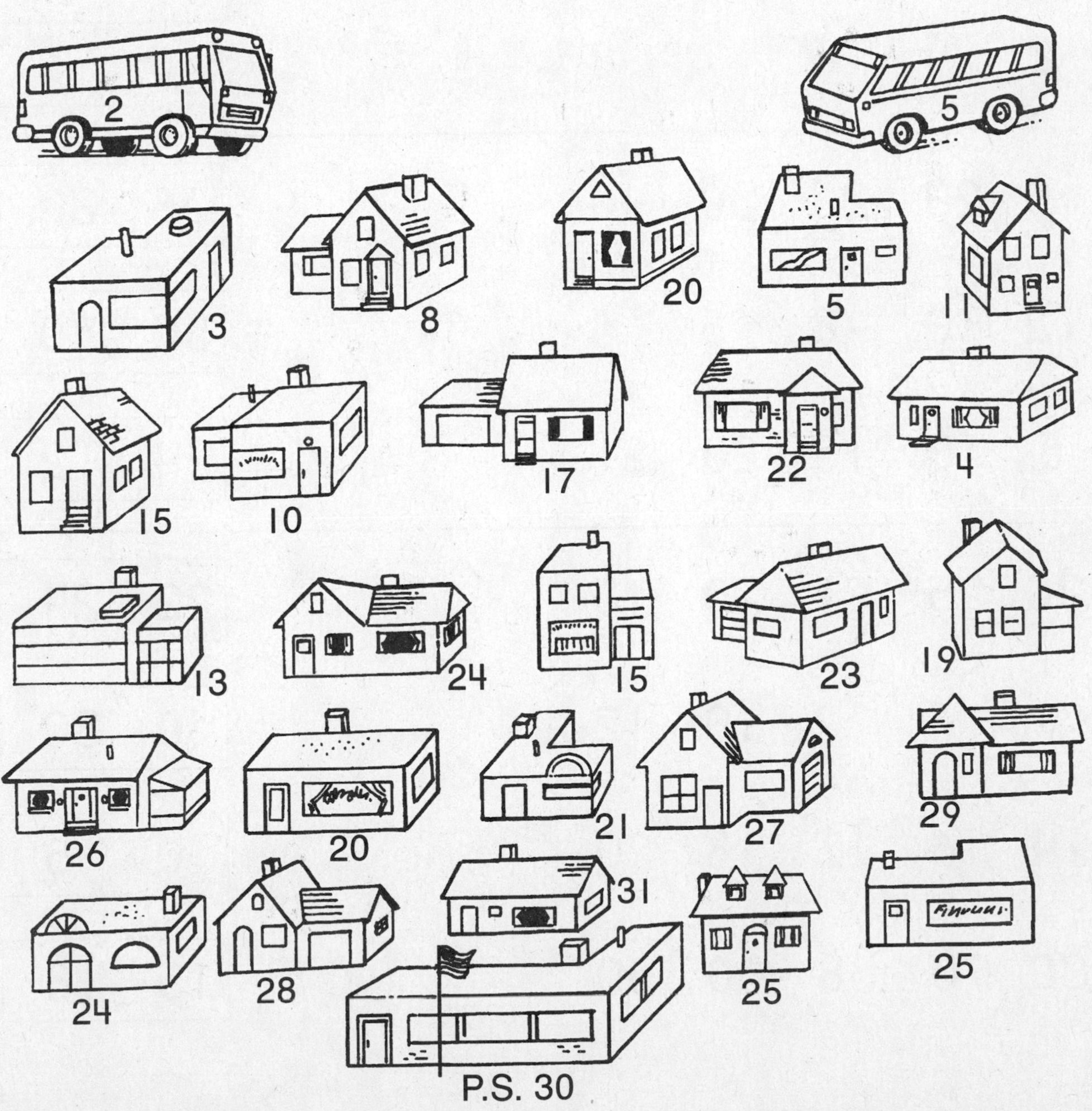

Notes for Home Your child counted by 2s and by 5s to mark the correct houses and apartment buildings the buses stop at. *Home Activity:* Ask your child to state the first ten numbers named counting by 2s, and then the first ten numbers named by counting by 5s. Have him or her compare the final numbers.

Name ______________________________

Extend Your Thinking
1-4

Patterns in Numbers

Cross out the one that does not belong.
Draw a line to what comes next.

1	2	3	~~7~~	4		10	12
2	4	6	7	8		5	6

10	20	23	30	40		25	30
12	10	8	5	6		50	60
5	10	15	20	21		4	2

30	25	21	20	15		22	24
3	6	9	10	12		40	30
14	16	17	18	20		10	5
80	70	68	60	50		15	18

Notes for Home Your child completed a number pattern in each row by drawing a line to the two numbers that come next in the pattern. He or she also indicated the number that does not belong in each pattern. *Home Activity:* Ask your child to explain the reasoning for his or her decisions.

Name ______________________________

Extend Your Thinking
1-5

Critical Thinking

Put each thing with others that are like it.
Write its number on the line.
Some things go on more than one list.

Round things

______

______

______

Things to eat

______

______

______

Loud things

______

______

______

Toys

______

______

______

Cubes

______

______

Notes for Home Your child identified objects that belong in five different categories. *Home Activity:* Ask your child to find objects in the home that can go with each of the listed categories. See if he or she can find anything that falls into two categories.

Name ______________________________

Extend Your Thinking
1-6

Decision Making

Study the November weather graphs from two schools.
Then think about how the objects are used.
Draw a line to match each object with the school that needs it more.

Abraham Lincoln School

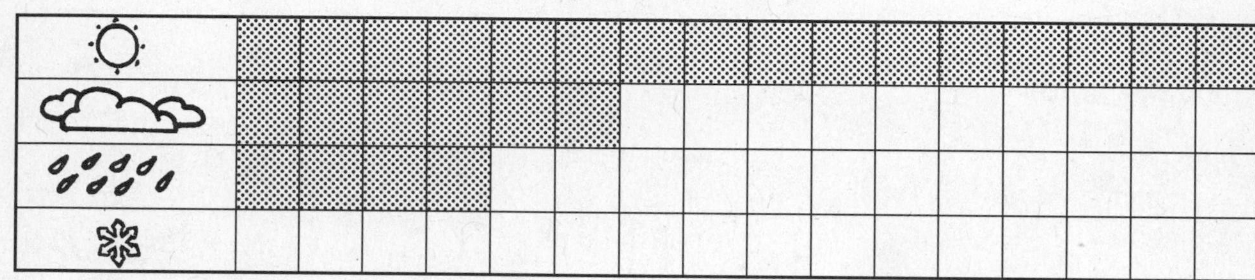

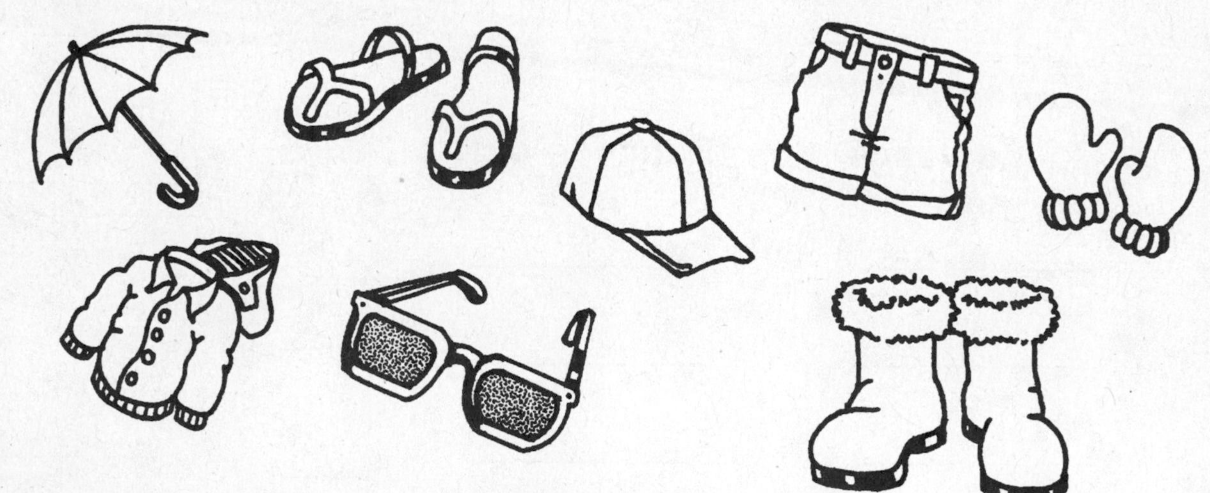

Martin Luther King School

Notes for Home Your child used information provided in graphs to compare weather conditions in two areas and to decide which weather-related items were useful in each area. *Home Activity:* For the next week, assist your child in keeping a record of local weather on a graph like the one shown.

Name ______________________________

Extend Your Thinking
1-7

Visual Thinking

This is the same shape, flipped different ways.

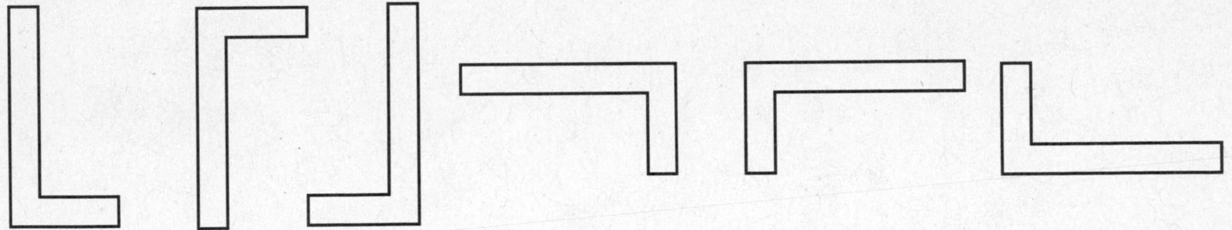

Cross out the shape that is different from the first one in the row.

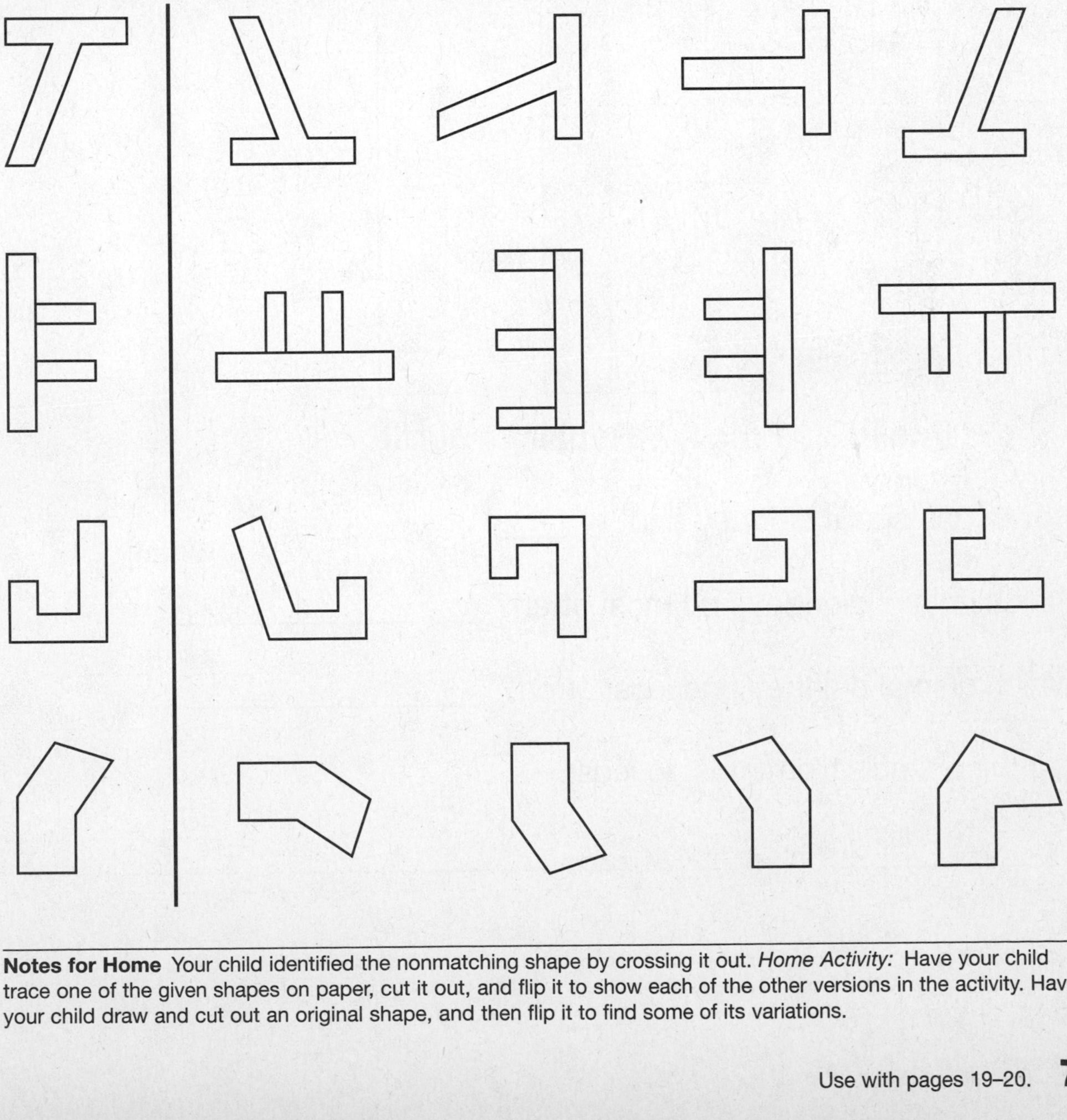

Notes for Home Your child identified the nonmatching shape by crossing it out. *Home Activity:* Have your child trace one of the given shapes on paper, cut it out, and flip it to show each of the other versions in the activity. Have your child draw and cut out an original shape, and then flip it to find some of its variations.

Name ______________________________

Extend Your Thinking
1-8

Critical Thinking

One class went to the lake.

They found these animals.

They made this graph.

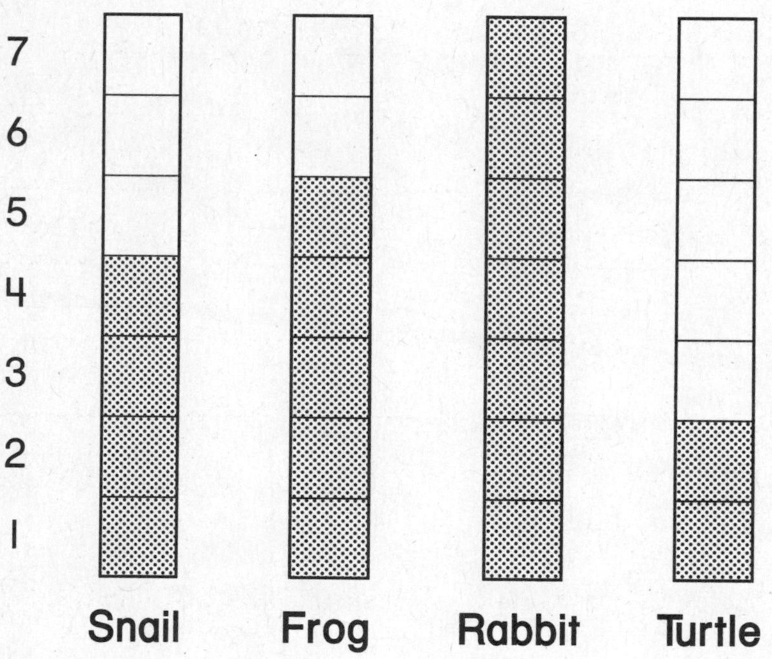

How many snails did they find? _____

Which animal did they find most often? ______________

Which animal did they find least often? ______________

List the animals from most to least.

__________ __________ __________ __________

Notes for Home Your child read a bar graph and compared quantities it described. *Home Activity:* Ask your child to explain how the graph would change if the class saw 6 turtles, or no frogs.

Name ______________________________

Extend Your Thinking
1-9

Patterns in Numbers

A zookeeper bought food for four kinds of zoo animals on May 1.
At the end of each week, she weighs the food that is left.
This chart shows what she found at the end of three weeks.
How much will be left at the end of the fourth week?
Write the amounts you think will be left.

Animal	Pounds of Food Left at the End of			
	Week 1	Week 2	Week 3	Week 4
monkeys	30	20	10	
lions	200	150	100	
elephants	400	300	200	
birds	16	12	8	

How much food did the zookeeper have at the beginning of Week 1?

She had __________ pounds for the monkeys.

She had __________ pounds for the lions.

She had __________ pounds for the elephants.

She had __________ pounds for the birds.

Notes for Home Your child found number patterns and used them to identify the numbers missing from the chart. Then he or she used the numbers to complete the statements. *Home Activity:* Ask your child to explain each of the number patterns to you.

Name ___________________________________

Extend Your Thinking 2-1

Patterns in Geometry

Which shape comes next for each pattern? Circle it.

Notes for Home Your child identified patterns. *Home Activity:* Ask your child to choose one pattern and to draw the shape that comes next.

Name ______________________________

Extend Your Thinking 2-2

Critical Thinking

Four classes voted for an animal for the school flag.
Circle the winning votes in each class.

Class 1	IIII	III	II
Class 2	III	IIII	I
Class 3	II	II	IIII
Class 4	III	IIII	III

Color a box on this graph for every class each animal won in.

In how many classes did win? ______

In how many classes did win? ______

In how many classes did win? ______

The animal on the school flag is

Notes for Home Your child created and interpreted a bar graph. *Home Activity:* Ask your child to decide if looking at the chart of tally marks or at the bar graph makes it easier to know which animal won.

Name ______________________________

Visual Thinking

Use this calendar to make plans for Tim.

Tim's birthday is November 4. Circle that date.

NOVEMBER						
S	M	T	W	T	F	S
	1	2	3	4	5	6
7	8	9	10	11	12	13
14	15	16	17	18	19	20
21	22	23	24	25	26	27
28	29	30				

Tim will visit a friend two days later.

What date will that be? November _____

Tim will go to a park one day after he sees his friend.

What date will that be? November _____

Grandma is coming three days after the park visit.

What date will that be? November _____

Notes for Home Your child used a calendar to count on 1, 2, and 3 days from a given date. *Home Activity:* Show your child the calendar for a month with a special day or holiday. Ask your child to point out 1, 2, and 3 days after that special day or holiday.

Name ______________________________

Extend Your Thinking
2-4

Decision Making

Every fact below stands for a letter.
Think of a secret word.
Then write the related fact for each letter of your word.
The related fact stands for the same letter.

A	9 + 3 = 12	P	7 + 5 = 12
E	9 + 2 = 11	O	7 + 4 = 11
H	8 + 4 = 12	S	7 + 3 = 10
I	8 + 3 = 11	T	6 + 5 = 11
M	8 + 2 = 10	Y	6 + 4 = 10

Ask a classmate to find your secret word by writing the letter above each fact.

Example:
H: 4 + 8 = 12
I: 3 + 8 = 11

Write the related facts here.

Notes for Home Your child discovered a coded message by matching related addition facts. *Home Activity:* Help your child create a new coded message using the same facts and letters.

Name ______________________________

Critical Thinking

Extend Your Thinking 2-5

Cross out the set that does not belong in each group.
Write a fact telling how many things are similar in each group.

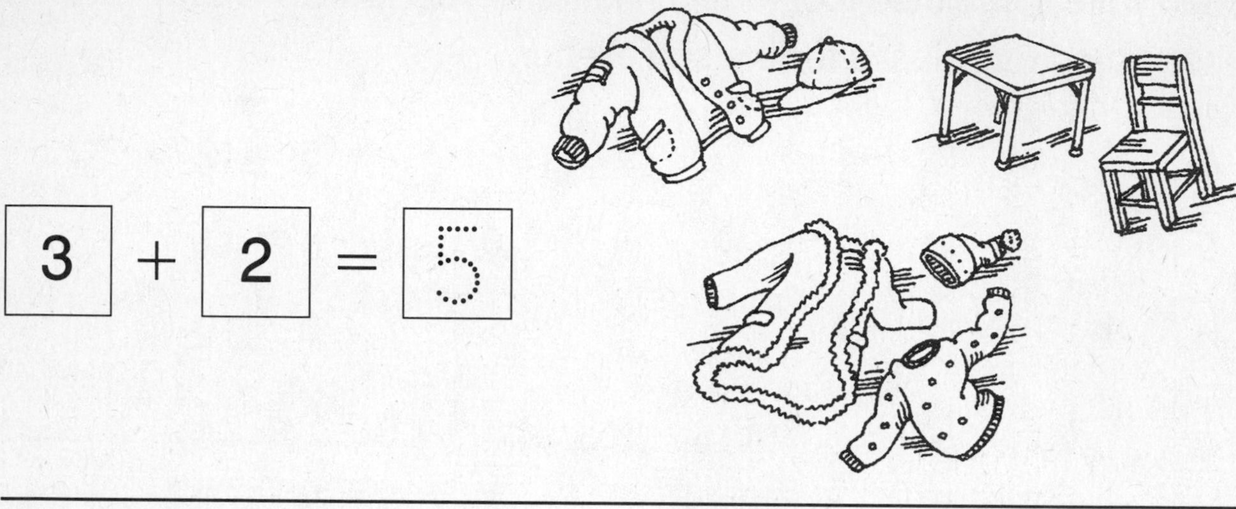

Notes for Home Your child wrote addition facts describing groups of similar items. *Home Activity:* Ask your child to explain why he or she crossed out certain items in each group.

Name ______________________________

Visual Thinking

Begin with the numbers in the center circle.
Add the number in the ring to each number.
Write the answer in the next ring.
Color parts with odd numbers red.

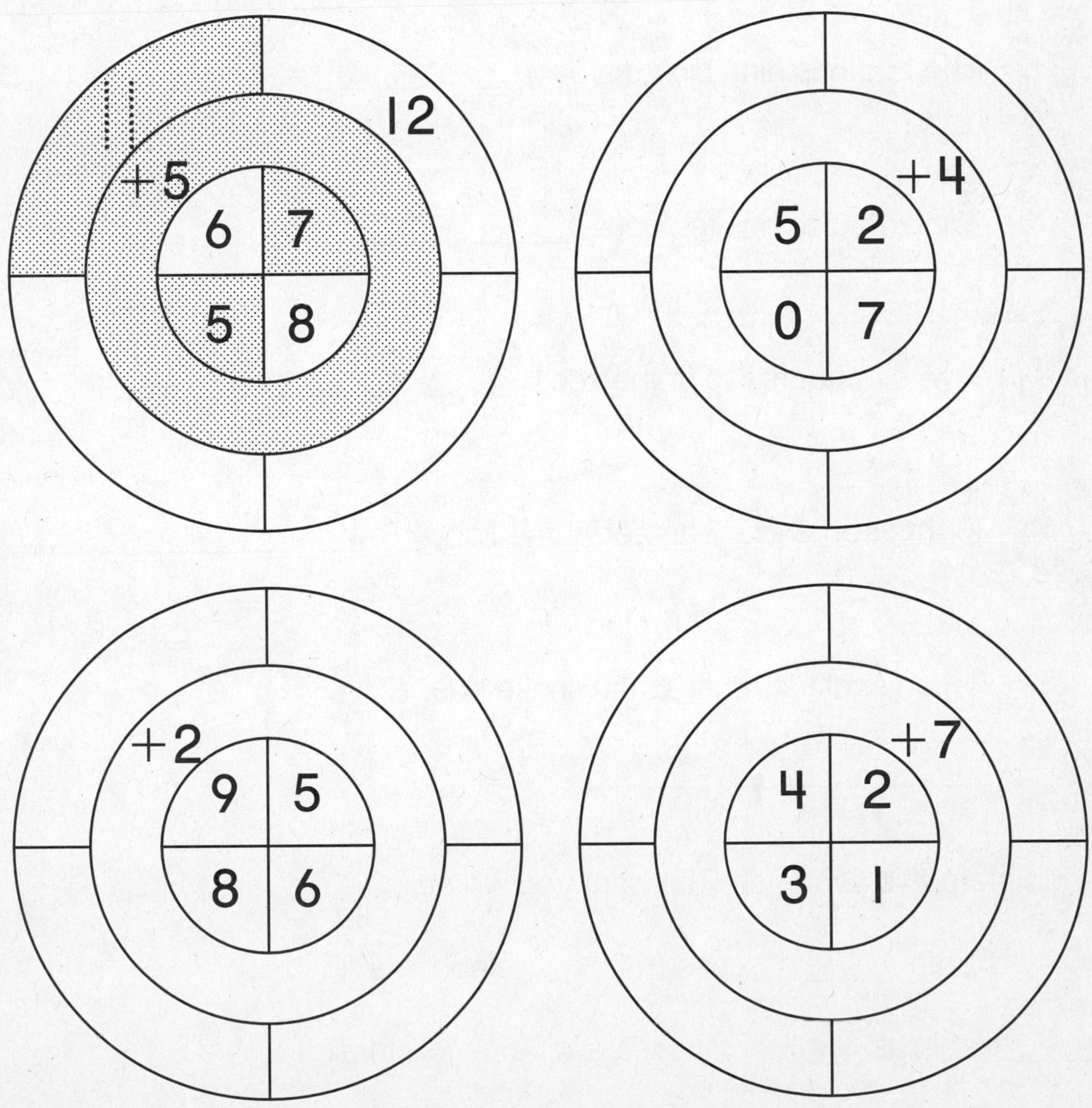

Notes for Home Your child completed addition facts through 12, and identified odd and even numbers. *Home Activity:* Ask your child to tell what the answers would be if you changed the number in the ring of one of the circles to 3.

Name ______________________________

Extend Your Thinking
2-7

Decision Making

The city zoo must sell 10 animals in all to another zoo.
Decide how many animals to sell from each group.
Write 5 subtraction sentences to show your choices.

The zoo has nine big cats. 9 – _____ = _____

The zoo also has ten apes. _____ – _____ = _____

Five elephants live at the zoo. _____ – _____ = _____

Eight zebras live together at the zoo. _____ – _____ = _____

Seven snakes slither in the snake house.

_____ – _____ = _____

Complete this sentence. Tell what you will sell.

_____ cats + _____ apes + _____ elephants +

_____ zebras + _____ snakes = 10 animals in all

Notes for Home Your child wrote subtraction sentences and completed an addition sentence to show that his or her answers were correct. *Home Activity:* Ask your child to explain his or her choices.

Name ______________________________

Extend Your Thinking
2-8

Patterns in Numbers

Count back by 1s from 12 to 0 across each column.
Then connect the dots of the numbers with a pencil.

12•	12•	12•	12•	12•	12•	12•	12•	12•	12•	12•	12•	12•
11•	11•	11•	11•	11•	11•	11•	11•	11•	11•	11•	11•	11•
10•	10•	10•	10•	10•	10•	10•	10•	10•	10•	10•	10•	10•
9•	9•	9•	9•	9•	9•	9•	9•	9•	9•	9•	9•	9•
8•	8•	8•	8•	8•	8•	8•	8•	8•	8•	8•	8•	8•
7•	7•	7•	7•	7•	7•	7•	7•	7•	7•	7•	7•	7•
6•	6•	6•	6•	6•	6•	6•	6•	6•	6•	6•	6•	6•
5•	5•	5•	5•	5•	5•	5•	5•	5•	5•	5•	5•	5•
4•	4•	4•	4•	4•	4•	4•	4•	4•	4•	4•	4•	4•
3•	3•	3•	3•	3•	3•	3•	3•	3•	3•	3•	3•	3•
2•	2•	2•	2•	2•	2•	2•	2•	2•	2•	2•	2•	2•
1•	1•	1•	1•	1•	1•	1•	1•	1•	1•	1•	1•	1•
0•	0•	0•	0•	0•	0•	0•	0•	0•	0•	0•	0•	0•

Begin at the same spot. Count back by 2s from 12 to 0. Connect the dots of the numbers with a red crayon.

Which line is longer? ______________________________

____

Notes for Home Your child compared the patterns made on a grid while counting back by 1s and 2s.
Home Activity: Ask your child to use two more colors to mark the lines formed while counting back by 3s and by 4s. Compare the lines.

Name ___________________________

Extend Your Thinking 2-9

Visual Thinking

These children were at a fair.

They hit a mark with a big hammer to ring the bell.

Circle the answer to each question.

1. How much higher did Jim score than Tom?

   3 4 5

2. How much higher did Tia score than Lucy?

   5 7 6

3. How much higher did Sam score than Noah?

   5 8 7

4. Who had the lowest score?

   Tom Tia Noah

Notes for Home Your child used a picture to answer questions. *Home Activity:* Read the most recent scores for a sports event to your child. Ask him or her to calculate how many points the winning team scored over the losing team.

Name ______________________________

Extend Your Thinking
2-10

Decision Making

Draw a path to the beach.

Solve the problems on your path.

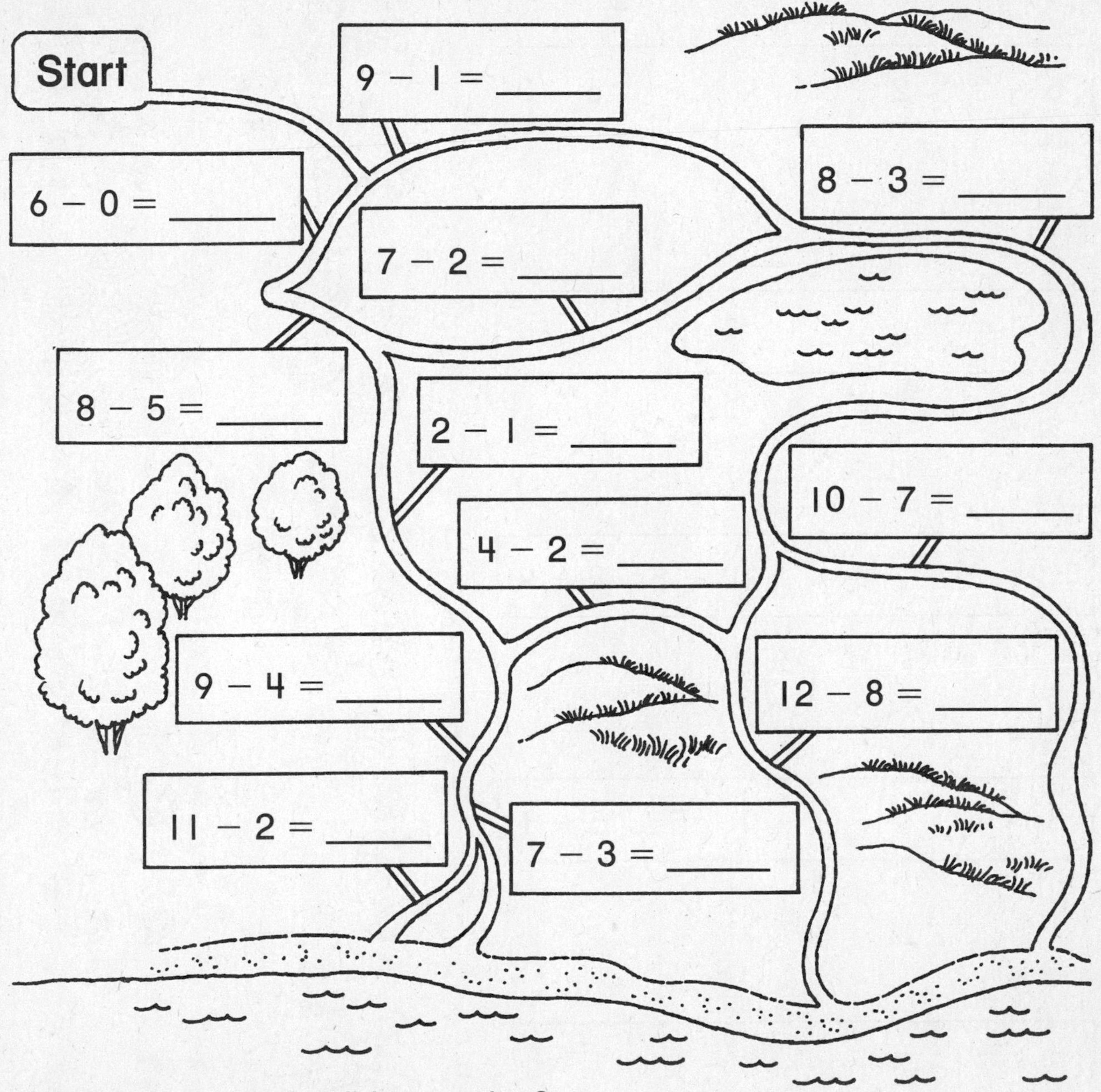

How many problems did you solve? ______

Notes for Home Your child chose a path and solved subtraction problems along the way. *Home Activity:* Ask your child to write three subtraction problems for you to solve. Ask him or her to check your work.

Name ______________________________

Critical Thinking

Extend Your Thinking
2-11

Cross out the one that does not belong.
Match the others with a drawing.

5 − 2	2 + 3	4 + 1	5 − 3

7 − 5	2 + 5	7 − 2	6 + 4

12 − 4	7 + 4	12 − 8	8 + 4

5 + 4	9 − 4	4 + 5	5 − 1

8 − 7	7 − 1	8 − 1	7 + 1

Notes for Home Your child identified related addition and subtraction facts, and matched them to drawings. *Home Activity:* Ask your child to think of a story problem for each picture.

Name ___________________________

Extend Your Thinking
2-12

Critical Thinking

Read the problem.
Solve the number sentence that goes with the problem.

1. One pirate put 8 gold pieces into a chest. Another put in 4 gold pieces. How many gold pieces are there all together?

   $8 - 4 =$ ____ $8 + 4 =$ 12

2. The pirates sailed on 5 ships. Then 2 ships sank. How many ships are left?

   $5 - 2 =$ ____ $5 + 2 =$ ____

3. One pirate saw 9 trees on the island. The other saw 3 trees. How many more did the first pirate see?

   $9 - 3 =$ ____ $9 + 3 =$ ____

4. One pirate dug a hole 5 feet deep. The next pirate dug it 2 feet deeper. How deep was the hole all together?

   $5 - 2 =$ ____ $5 + 2 =$ ____

Notes for Home Your child chose and completed operations to solve story problems. *Home Activity:* Ask your child to explain the reasoning behind his or her choices.

Name ______________________________

Extend Your Thinking
3-1

Patterns in Data

Which award is better?

Award A: You get $3 each day for 4 days.

Award B: You get $1 the first day. On each of the next 3 days, the award is double what it was the day before.

Award A: $3 per day

	Day 1	Day 2	Day 3	Day 4
Today's Award	$3	$3	$	$
Total So Far	$3	Yesterday's Total + Today: $6	Yesterday's Total + Today: $	Yesterday's Total + Today: $

Award B: Doubling yesterday's award

	Day 1	Day 2	Day 3	Day 4
Today's Award	$1	$2	$4	$
Total So Far	$1	Yesterday's Total + Today: $3	Yesterday's Total + Today: $	Yesterday's Total + Today: $

Which award is better, A or B? __________

Notes for Home Your child extended two number patterns to determine quantity. *Home Activity:* Help your child to extend both patterns one more day. (Award A: Day 4 - $15; Award B: Day 4 - $31.)

Name ______________________________

Extend Your Thinking 3-2

Critical Thinking

Help the children in each problem share equally.
Write a new fact using doubles.

Tonya has 5 apples. Richard has 3 apples.

$5 + 3 = 8$ $\quad$ [4] + [4] = 8

Arthur has 8 baseballs. Maria has 6 baseballs.

$8 + 6 =$ ____ $\quad$ [ ] + [ ] = ____

Tawana has 2 pencils. Suli has 4 pencils.

$2 + 4 =$ ____ $\quad$ [ ] + [ ] = ____

Anna has 7 blocks. Laura has 5 blocks.

$7 + 5 =$ ____ $\quad$ [ ] + [ ] = ____

Notes for Home Your child matched addition facts with related doubles facts and solved both problems. *Home Activity:* Arrange 6 objects on a table, with 2 in one pile and 4 in another. Ask your child to rearrange the objects to represent a doubles fact (3 + 3). Repeat the process with 8 and 10 objects. (4 + 4; 5 + 5)

Name ______________________

Visual Thinking

Extend Your Thinking 3-3

First finish the number sentence on each birdhouse roof to tell you how many birds belong.
Then match the birds to the house where they belong.

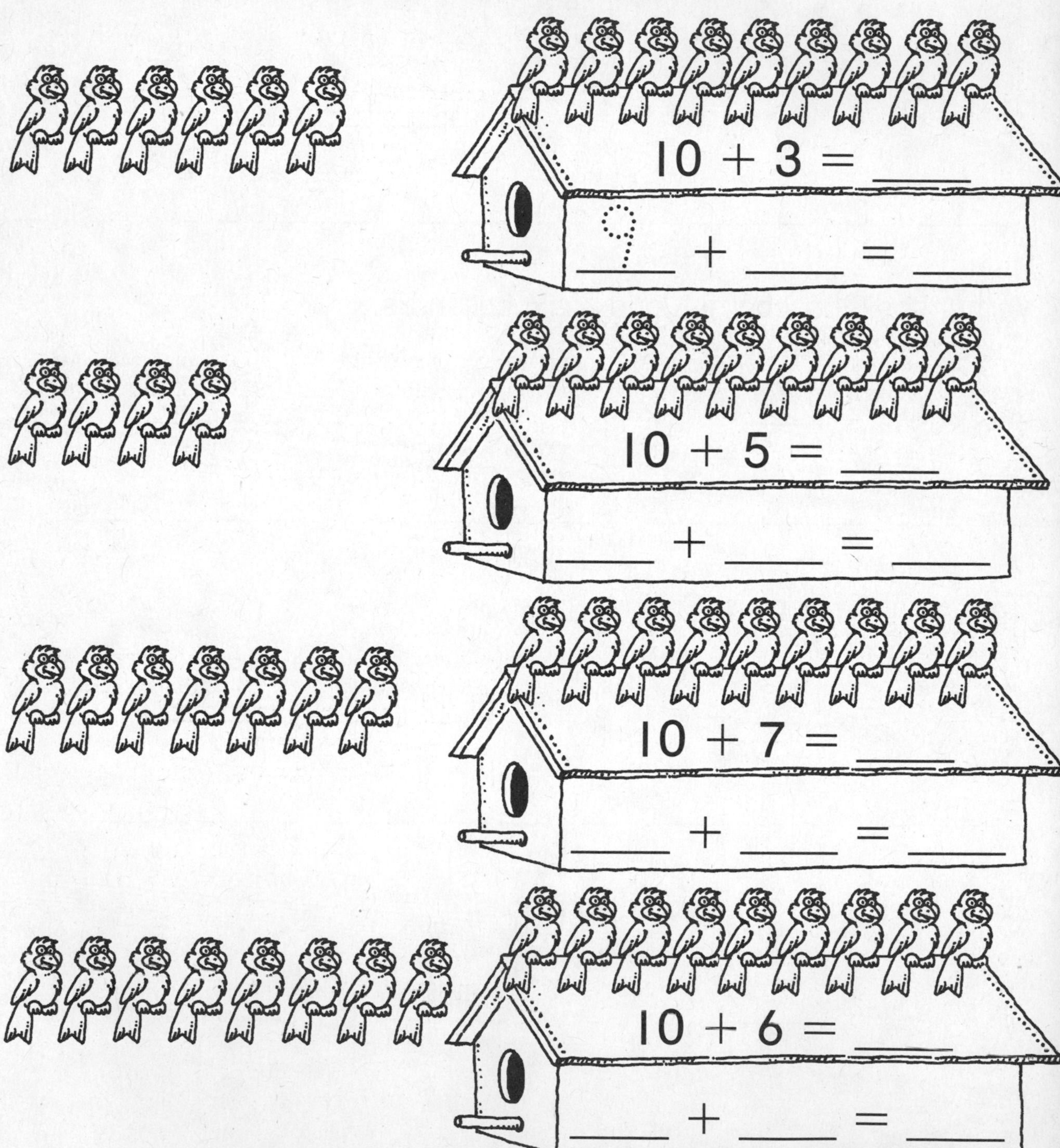

Notes for Home Your child practiced adding with 10 in problems where one addend is 9. *Home Activity:* Try some mental math with your child. Ask him or her for the answers to these problems: 9 + 4 (13), 9 + 7 (16), 9 + 6 (15), and 9 + 2 (11).

Name ______________________________

Extend Your Thinking
3-4

Decision Making

Solve every problem.

Then balance each scale by writing a fact on its other side.

7 + 4 = 11

9 + 4 = 13

10 + 3 = 13 9 + 4 = 13

7 + 6 = ____

3 + 9 = ____

10 + 2 = ____

2 + 9 = ____

3 + 7 = ____

10 + 1 = ____

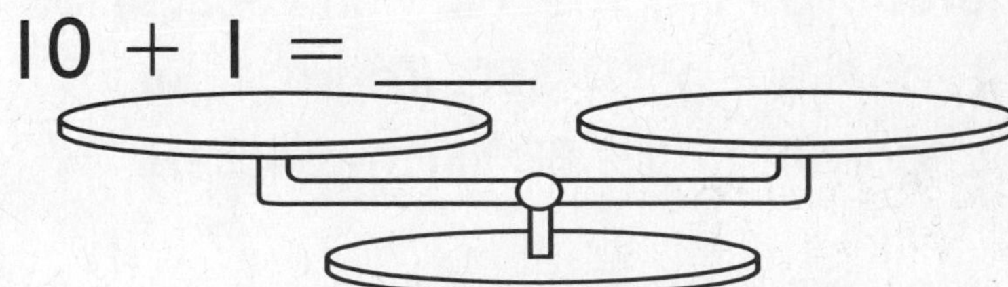

9 + 5 = ____

7 + 8 = ____

10 + 4 = ____

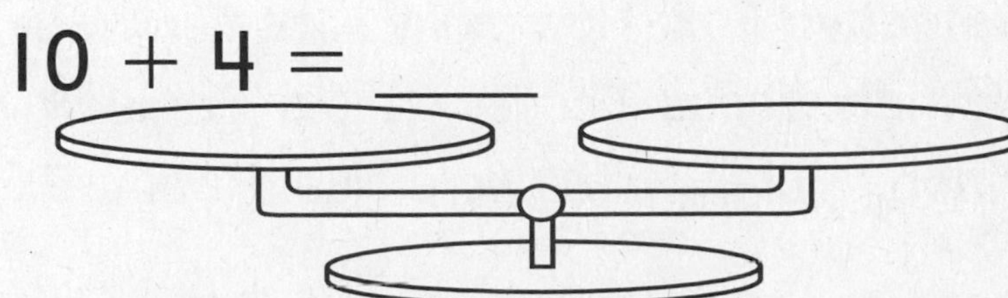

Notes for Home Your child practiced adding with 10 when one of the numbers in an addition problem is 9.
Home Activity: Ask your child to balance a scale with a number fact using 10 and a number fact using 9.

Name ______________________________

Extend Your Thinking
3-5

Critical Thinking

Solve these problems.
Write a number sentence for each.

Detective Fox: Your bucket is gone. How many fish were in it?
Bear: I fished for 5 hours. **Otter:** I put 7 fish in the bucket.
Bear: I put 6 fish in the bucket. **Wildcat:** I was here at 9 A.M.

Detective Fox: My answer is ______________________.

Detective Fox: The safe won't open. How much is in it?
Crocodile: I put in $50. **Zebra**: I put in $10.
Kangaroo: I have $30 in my pocket.

Detective Fox: My answer is ______________________.

Detective Fox: How many birds flew away?
Ostrich: These 2 cages are old. **Eagle**: 9 were in this cage.
Finch: 6 of the birds were blue. **Robin**: 5 were in that cage.

Detective Fox: My answer is ______________________.

Notes for Home Your child solved word problems by identifying necessary information. *Home Activity:* Ask your child to make up another word problem for you to solve.

Name ______________________________

Extend Your Thinking
3-6

Decision Making

Solve these problems.
On the last line of each problem write the addition and subtraction number sentences your used.

Mark has 8 dollars. How much will 2 caps cost? ______

How much money will he have left if he only buys 1 cap? ______

____

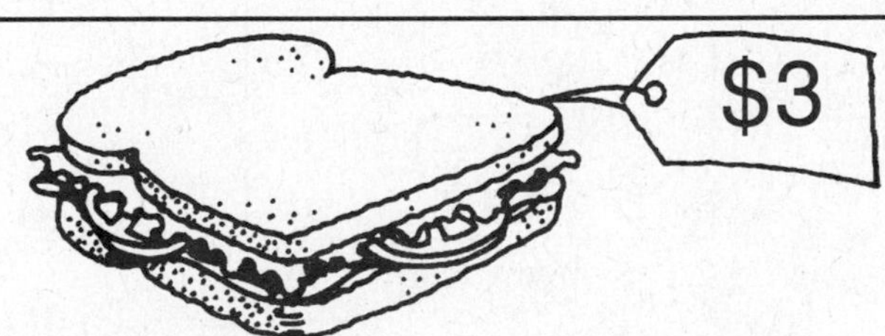

Kris and Carol have 6 dollars. How much will 2 sandwiches cost? ______

How much money will they have left if they only buy 1? ______

____

Tracy has 19 dollars. How much will 2 dolls cost? ______

How much money will she have left if she only buys 1? ______

____

Notes for Home Your child used addition doubles facts to help subtract. *Home Activity:* While in a store, ask your child to double the price of an item. Round each price to a dollar figure from $1 to $9.

Name ______________________________

Visual Thinking

Extend Your Thinking 3-7

Rachel folded pieces of paper.

Then she cut out a shape on each fold.

How will the papers look when they are unfolded?

Match each folded paper with an unfolded paper.

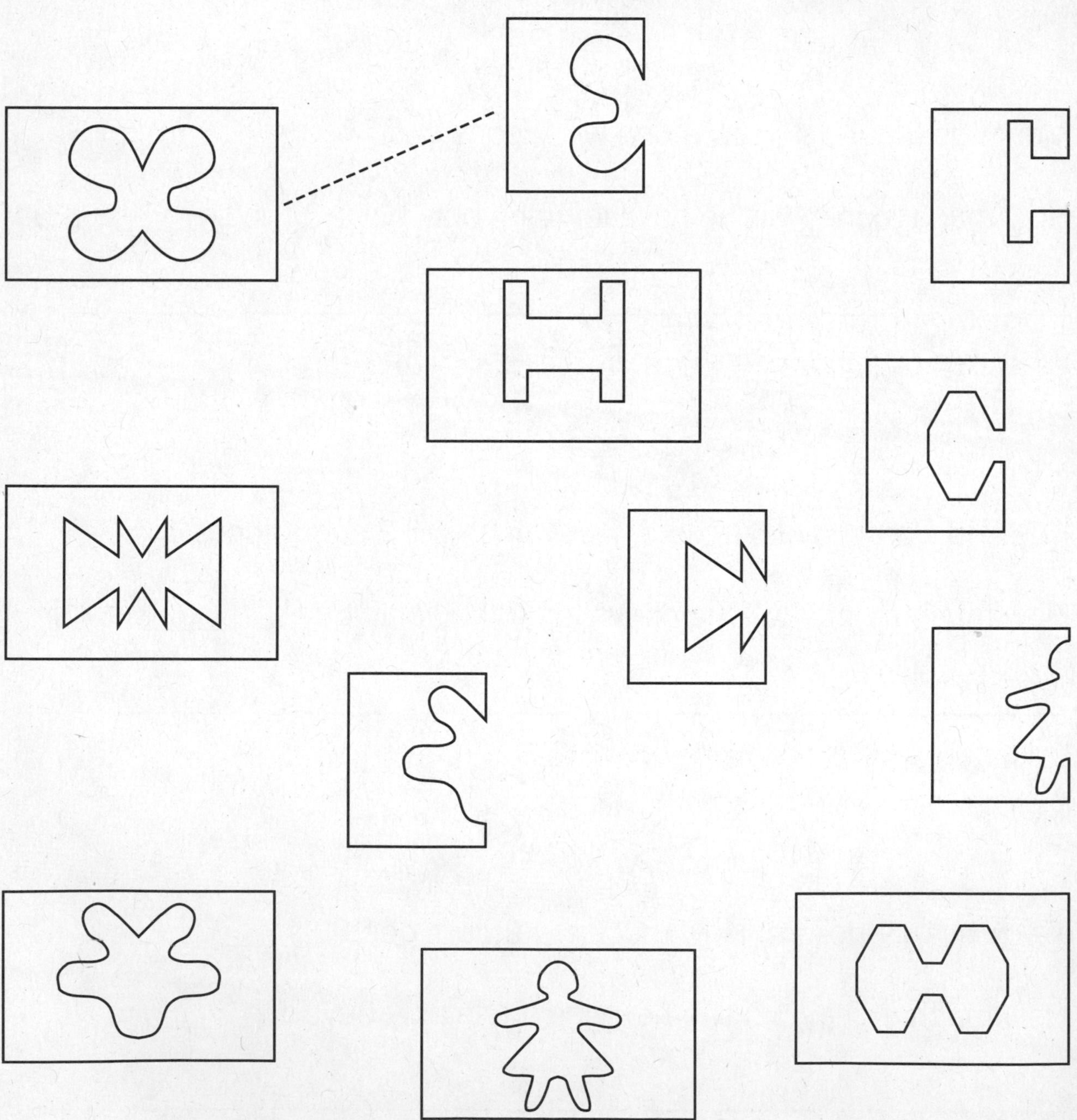

Notes for Home Your child matched shapes. *Home Activity:* Help your child to cut out an original shape from folded paper. Predict the entire shape before unfolding the paper.

Name ______________________________

Extend Your Thinking
3-8

Visual Thinking

Search across for hidden addition facts.

Search down for hidden subtraction facts.

Circle each fact. There are 9 in all.

4	6	10	7	9	16
1	5	4	8	7	15
3	7	6	13	2	23
5	9	14	4	5	8

Write the addition facts you found.

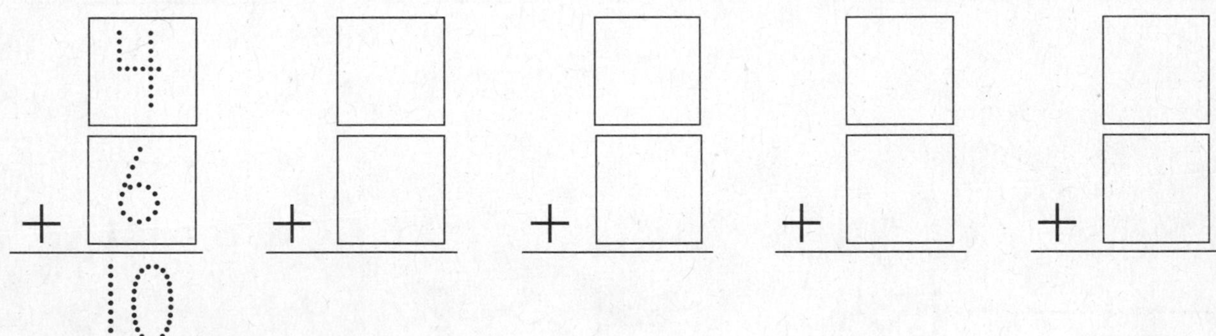

Write the subtraction facts you found.

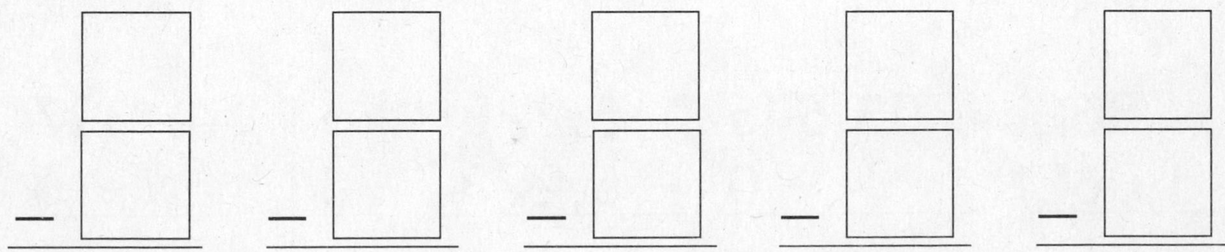

Notes for Home Your child found hidden addition and subtraction facts in a puzzle. *Home Activity:* Ask your child to write one more addition fact and one more subtraction fact.

Name ______________________

Extend Your Thinking
3-9

Critical Thinking

Solve all the problems.

Circle the problems in which you subtract 0.

Draw a box around the problems in which you subtract all.

Examples

5,689	5,689	15
− 0	− 5,689	− 4
5,689	0	11

573	762	3,751	29	42,809
− 573	− 267	− 0	− 29	− 42,809

6,555	1,345	481	27,594	46
− 0	− 1,345	− 31	− 27,594	− 23

4,862	703,645	5,228	11	16,397
− 1,062	− 0	− 5,228	− 11	− 0

Notes for Home Your child identified and solved problems involving subtraction of 0 and of all. *Home Activity:* Ask your child to use mental math and answer a problem in which a very large number is subtracted from itself, such as 87,546 - 87,546.

Name ___________________________________

Patterns in Geometry

Circle the shape that comes next in each pattern.

Notes for Home Your child identified and continued patterns of shapes. *Home Activity:* Ask your child to explain which details helped him or her identify the next shape.

Name ______________________________

Extend Your Thinking
4-1

Visual Thinking

Keep the  fact families together.

Draw lines to match mothers to their children.

8 − 2 =

10 − 7 =

6 + 2 =

7 + 3 =

10 − 3 =

2 + 6 =

8 − 6 =

3 + 7 =

2 + 8 =

10 − 2 =

4 + 5 =

10 − 8 =

8 + 2 =

9 − 4 =

9 − 5 =

5 + 4 =

Notes for Home Your child identified and connected fact families. *Home Activity:* Ask your child to think of two fact families that include the number 10, such as (6 + 4 =10, 10 – 6 =4, 10 – 4 = 6, 4 + 6 = 10.)

Name ______________________________

Extend Your Thinking
4-2

Critical Thinking

Where did Sam leave his glasses? Find the clue in the 3 code words. Then circle the answer at the bottom of the page.

5–B	6–R	7–K
8–P	9–H	10–W
12–O	15–E	18–S

$15 - 5 = 10$ $\quad 10 + 5 = 15$ $\quad$ W E

$15 - 8$ $\quad 7 + 8$ $\quad 8 + 7$ $\quad 15 - 7$

___ ___ ___ ___

$12 - 7$ $\quad 5 + 7$ $\quad 7 + 5$ $\quad 12 - 5$ $\quad 9 + 9$

___ ___ ___ ___ ___

$15 - 6$ $\quad 9 + 6$ $\quad 15 - 9$ $\quad 6 + 9$

___ ___ ___ ___

Where are the glasses? bed car shelf hall kitchen

Notes for Home Your child used his or her knowledge of fact families to solve a puzzle. *Home Activity:* Ask your child to use the code and fact families to develop a one-word message.

Name ______________________

Extend Your Thinking 4-3

Visual Thinking

Complete each number sentence.
Then draw lines to match the shapes that fit together.
Make sure you have all 4 facts in each family.

3 + 9 = ____
9 + 3 = ____

6 + 7 = ____
7 + ____ = ____

13 − 7 = ____
13 − 6 = ____

7 + 8 = ____
8 + ____ = ____

12 − 9 = ____
12 − ____ = ____

7 + ____ = 16
____ + 7 = 16

15 − ____ = 7
____ − ____ = 8

16 − ____ = ____
____ − ____ = 7

Notes for Home Your child completed number sentences and matched fact families. *Home Activity:* Ask your child to make up a story problem for one of the fact families.

Name ______________________

Extend Your Thinking
4-4

Critical Thinking

Read the story.

Circle the fact that solves the problem.

1. 5  live in a cave. 4 can fly.

   How many cannot fly?

   $5 + 4 = 9$ $5 - 4 = 1$

2. 6 came to visit the 5 .

   How many friends were at the cave then?

   $6 + 5 = 11$ $6 - 5 = 1$

3. The friends ate 12 pies. 7 of the pies were apple.

   How many pies were different?

   $12 + 7 = 19$ $12 - 7 = 5$

4. 2 of the 6 went home.

   How many stayed?

   $6 + 2 = 8$ $6 - 2 = 4$

Notes for Home Your child solved story problems by identifying the fact that solved each problem. *Home Activity:* Ask your child to choose one of the circled facts and state the three other addition and subtraction facts related to it. For example, for the fact 5 – 4 = 1, the related facts are 5 – 1 = 4, 4 + 1 = 5, and 1 + 4 = 5.

Name ______________________

Extend Your Thinking
4-5

Critical Thinking

Find the mystery numbers.

	Fact 1	Fact 2	Mystery Numbers
1.	7 + □ = 16	5 + □ = 14	□
2.	□ + 6 = 14	□ + 3 = 11	□
3.	5 + □ = 12	□ + △ = 8	□ △
4.	□ + △ = 17	□ − △ = 1	□ △
5.	□ + □ = 10	□ + △ = 12	□ △

Notes for Home Your child identified the missing number(s) in pairs of facts. *Home Activity:* Ask your child to explain how he or she found the missing numbers in one of the rows.

Name ______________________________

Extend Your Thinking
4-6

Decision Making

Show 2 steps to solve each problem.

Circle the way that is best for you.

		Step I	Step 2	
1.	6 2 + 3 11	2 + 3 (5)	(5) + 6 11	make ten look for doubles (easy fact first)
2.	5 2 + 8	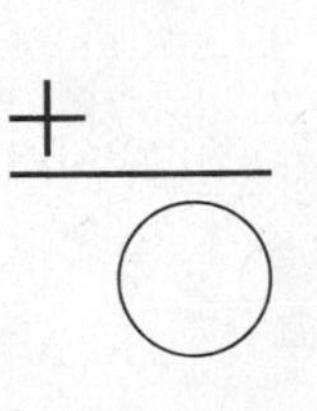		make ten look for doubles easy fact first
3.	7 7 + 2		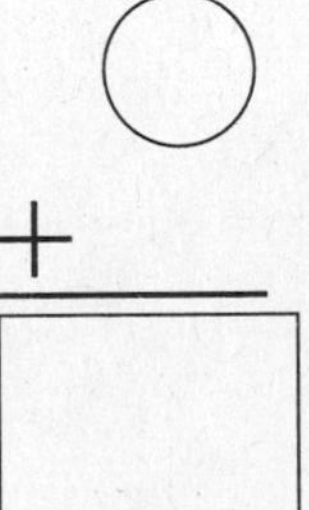	make ten look for doubles easy fact first

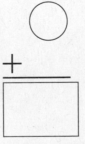

Notes for Home Your child chose the best way to solve addition problems with 3 addends. *Home Activity:* Ask your child to explain his or her choices.

Name ____________________

Patterns in Numbers

This is a function machine. It changes numbers by adding 7.

Fill in the missing numbers going in and coming out.

Notes for Home Your child followed a rule being applied to numbers. *Home Activity:* Ask your child to design a function machine and create a new rule. Work together to apply the rule to the numbers used in this activity.

Name ________________________________

Patterns in Numbers

Help Dino decide how each pattern was made.
Match each pattern with its rule.

Patterns				Rules
3	6	9	12	+5
1	6	11	16	+3
14	12	10	8	−5
3	5	7	9	−4
18	14	10	6	+2
17	12	7	2	−2

Use one of the rules to make your own pattern below.

Notes for Home Your child identified and applied the rules used to create number patterns. *Home Activity:* Ask your child to explain his or her new pattern and its rule.

Name ______________________

Decision Making

Make your own problems.
Circle what happens in each step.
Write number sentences to match.

1. Kim has 3 mice.

Step 1	She buys 2 more.	or	One runs away.
	______________		3 - 1 = 2
Step 2	She finds 3 more.	or	She gives them all away.
	______________		______________

How many does Kim have now? _____

2. Tom put 8 flowers in a vase.

Step 1	He put in 4 more.	or	He put in 6 more.
	______________		______________
Step 2	He took out 2.	or	He put in 2 more.
	______________		______________

How many flowers are in the vase now? _____

Notes for Home Your child created and solved word problems by writing number sentences. *Home Activity:* Ask your child to solve one of the problems again, this time making different choices.

Name ______________________________

Visual Thinking

Read the 2 addition problems.
Which sum will be greater?
Color the ☐ to show each number.
Which set has more colored ☐? Circle that problem.

A

25	red
42	blue
+ 21	green
??	

B

44	red
13	blue
+ 22	green
??	

A

Tens

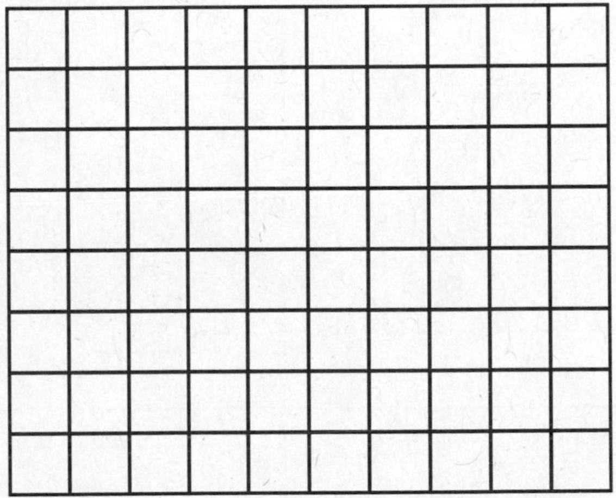

Ones

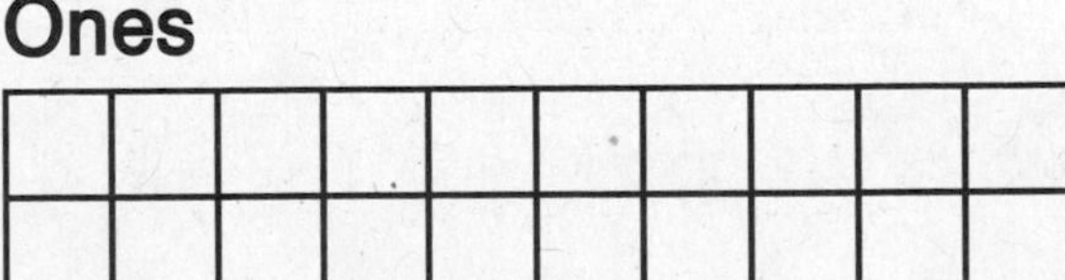

B

Tens

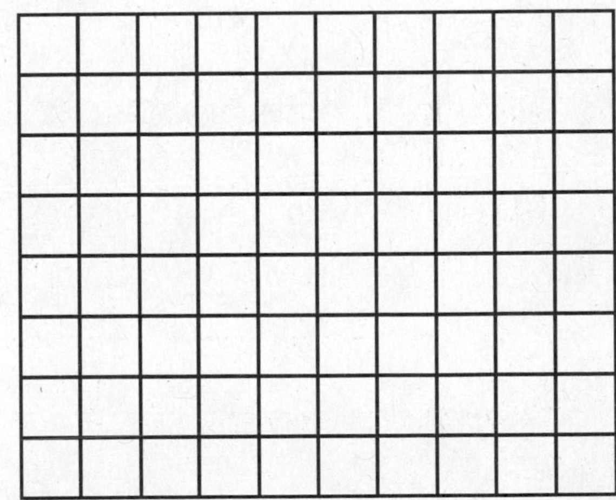

Ones

Notes for Home Your child compared the sums for problems and then colored the ☐ to show the numbers.
Home Activity: Help your child find the sum for 11 + 26 + 45. (82)

Name ______________________________

Extend Your Thinking
5-2

Patterns in Numbers

Find the pattern in each row.
Then draw the picture and write the number in the box to continue the pattern.

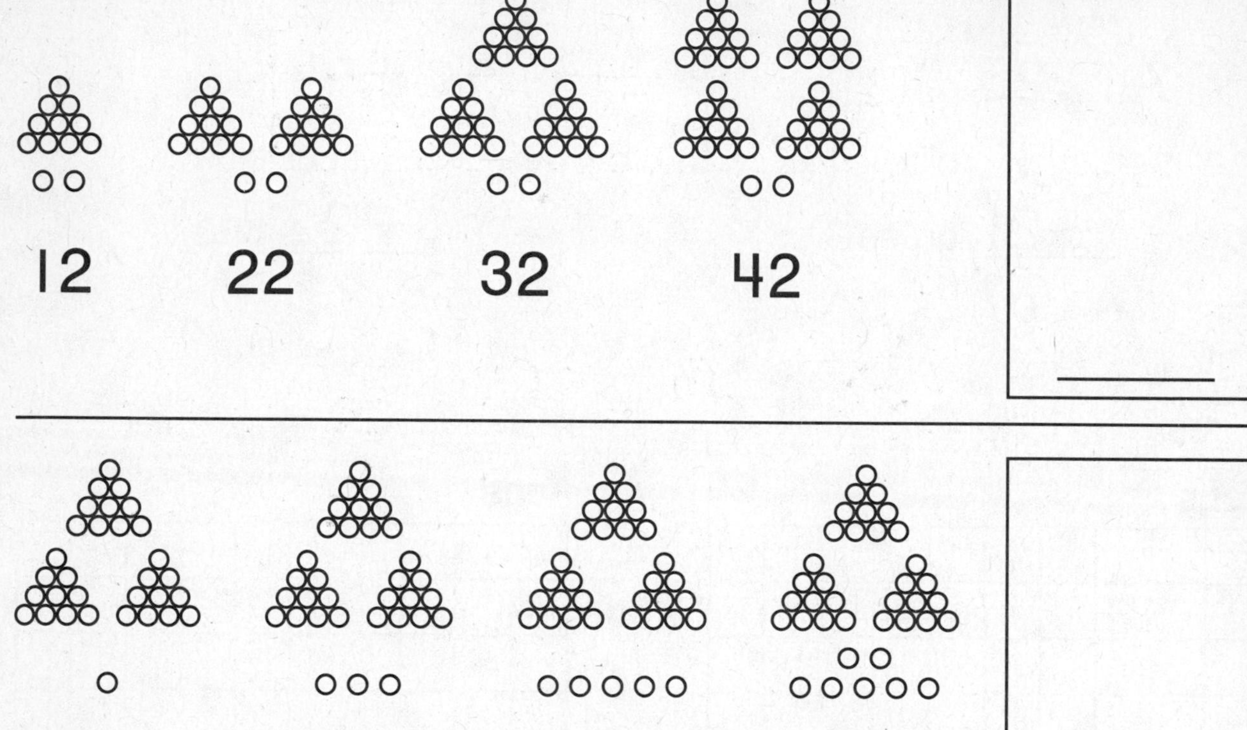

31 33 35 37

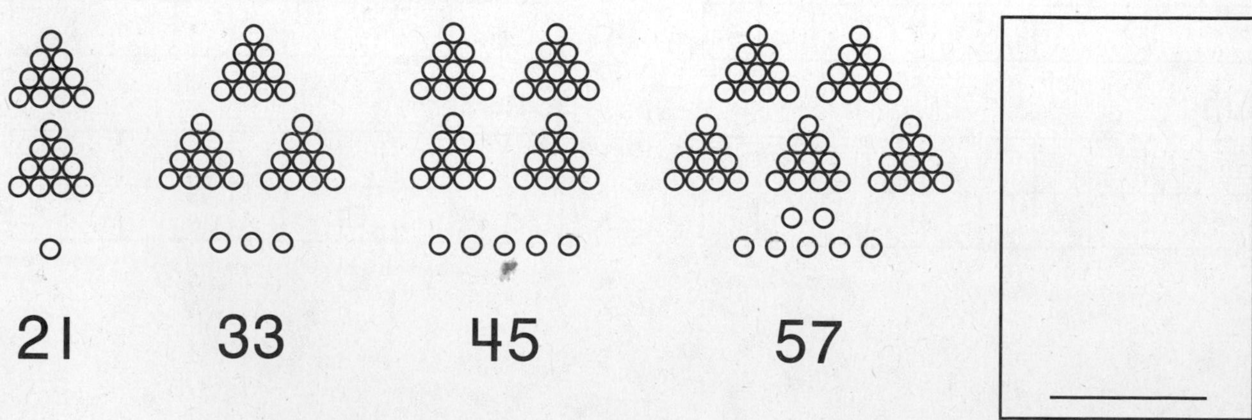

Notes for Home Your child identified number patterns and showed the next step in each pattern.
Home Activity: Ask your child to explain each of the patterns.

Name ______________________________

Extend Your Thinking
5-3

Visual Thinking

Complete the crossword puzzle.
Write the number word for each numeral.
Leave out hyphens (-).

Across	Down
2. 12	1. 70
4. 9	2. 35
5. 13	3. 80
7. 61	6. 4

Notes for Home Your child completed a crossword puzzle, writing number words for numerals.
Home Activity: Ask your child to find a numeral in the newspaper and write the number word for it. Then ask him to find a number word and write the numeral.

Name ________________________________

Decision Making

Circle the things you might buy in groups of 100.

Circle the things you are likely to see in groups of 100.

Notes for Home Your child showed an awareness of the concept of 100 by identifying objects that would be likely to be bought in groups of 100 or seen in groups of 100. *Home Activity:* Ask your child to explain his or her choices.

Name ________________________________

Extend Your Thinking
5-5

Critical Thinking

This graph shows how far children live from school.

Each [figure] stands for 10 children.

Read the graph and then circle the answer to each question.

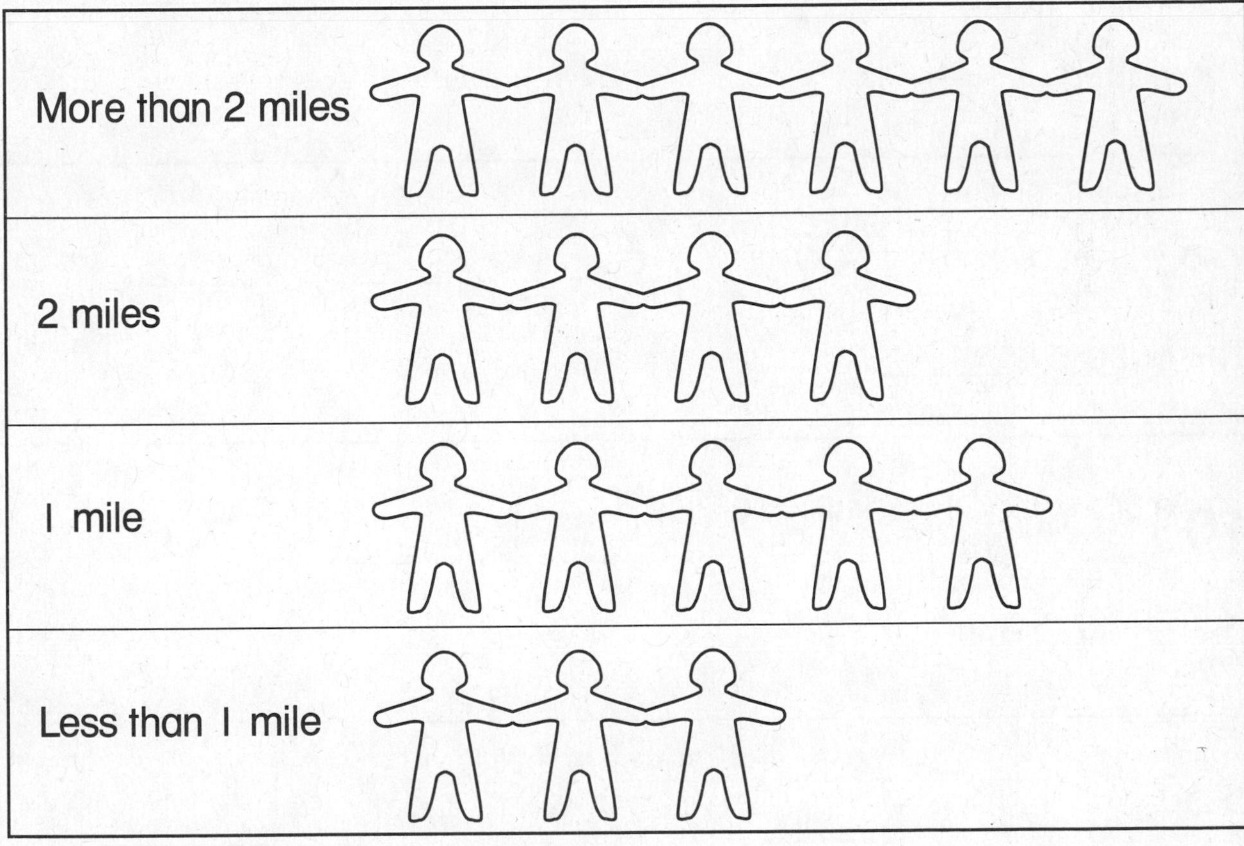

How far do most students live from school?

2 miles or more   I mile or less

How many students live less than a mile from school? 50   30

The children who live more than I mile from school ride the bus.
How many children ride the bus?   100   50

How many children must get to school in other ways? 30 80

Notes for Home Your child used information in a pictograph to answer questions. *Home Activity:* Work with your child to create a pictograph that describes your family in some way. Each symbol should represent ten items. The pictograph could show how many shoes each person has, or how many rocks each person collected on a recent trip to the park.

Name ______________________________

Extend Your Thinking 5-6

Patterns in Numbers

Identify each pattern.

Then write the missing numbers in each pattern.

10 18 26 ____ 42 ____

The pattern is _____.

75 71 67 63 ____ ____

The pattern is _____.

100 94 88 ____ ____ 70

The pattern is _____.

99 91 ____ 75 67 ____

The pattern is _____.

7 ____ 19 25 31 ____

The pattern is _____.

Notes for Home Your child identified and completed patterns involving adding or subtracting 4, 6, or 8.
Home Activity: Ask your child to make an original pattern similar to the ones on this page for you to solve.

Name ______________________________

Extend Your Thinking
5-7

Critical Thinking

Some children tried to guess the number that was in the hat.
Write **A** under each guess that is after 58.
Write **B** under each guess that is before 58.
Circle the guess that is closest to 58.

Beth 36	Sanji 67	Lou 15	Nancy 13
_____	_____	_____	_____
Able 92	Frances 29	Sue 38	James 74
_____	_____	_____	_____
Carl 60	Maria 57	Steve 86	Dawn 41
_____	_____	_____	_____

Each phrase below tells about a number above. Write it.

between 28 and 30	_____	just before 42	_____
between 37 and 39	_____	just after 73	_____
just before 14	_____	just after 14	_____
between 59 and 61	_____	just before 37	_____
between 66 and 68	_____	just after 91	_____

Notes for Home Your child identified numbers that are between, before, or after given numbers. *Home Activity:* Say a number. Have your child tell the number that is immediately before and immediately after that number.

Name ______________________________

Extend Your Thinking
5-8

Visual Thinking

Color each part that is close to 10 red.
Color each part that is close to 20 blue.
Color each part that is close to 30 green.
Color each part that is close to 40 yellow.
Color each part that is close to 50 purple.

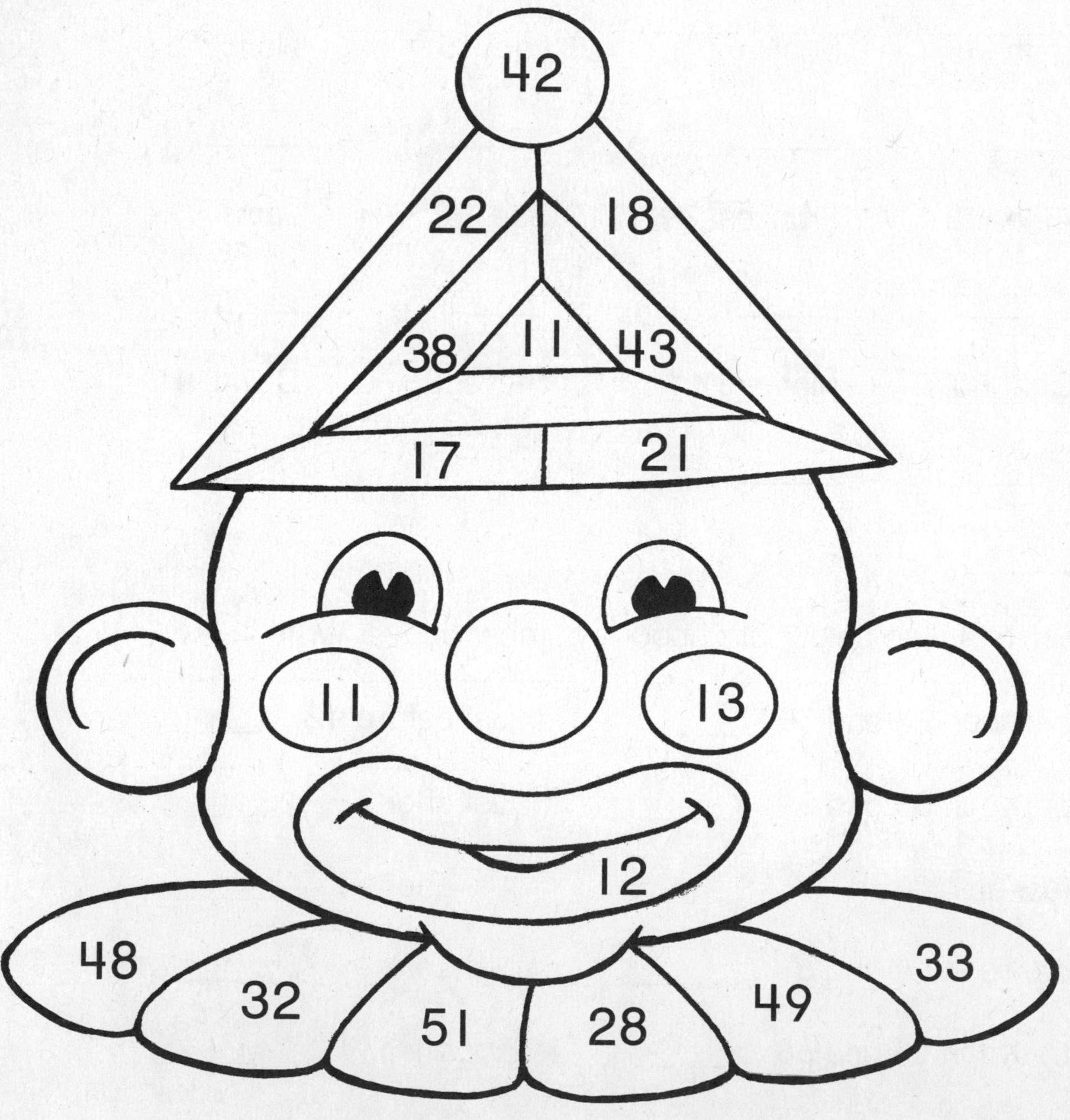

Notes for Home Your child decided whether each number was closer to the decade number before or after it.
Home Activity: With your child, look at newspaper ads and decide whether each price is closer to the decade number before or after it.

Name ___________________________

Critical Thinking

What food does Rex want?

Find the answer below in Morse code.

If the first number is **less than** the second, draw a ●.

If the first number is **greater than** the second, draw a ▬.

A ●▬	I ●●	N ▬●
E ●	M ▬▬	T ▬

38, 52 19, 21	88, 90	35, 36 81, 67	40, 29
● ●			
I	______	______	______

62, 57 90, 89	18, 45	39, 56 50, 33	64, 46
______	______	______	______

Rex says,

"______ ______ ______ ______ ______ ______ ______ ______."

Notes for Home Your child compared pairs of numbers to determine whether the first number in each pair was less than or greater than the second number. *Home Activity:* Say a number such as 25. Ask your child to say a number that is less than 25; then greater than 25. Continue with other numbers.

Name ______________________________

Extend Your Thinking 5-10

Critical Thinking

Draw lines to match children with their names.

Child	Place in line
Minna	fourth
Jack	second
Paul	twelfth
Gerry	sixth
Neil	eighteenth
Lisa	thirteenth
Billy	eighth
Sal	twentieth

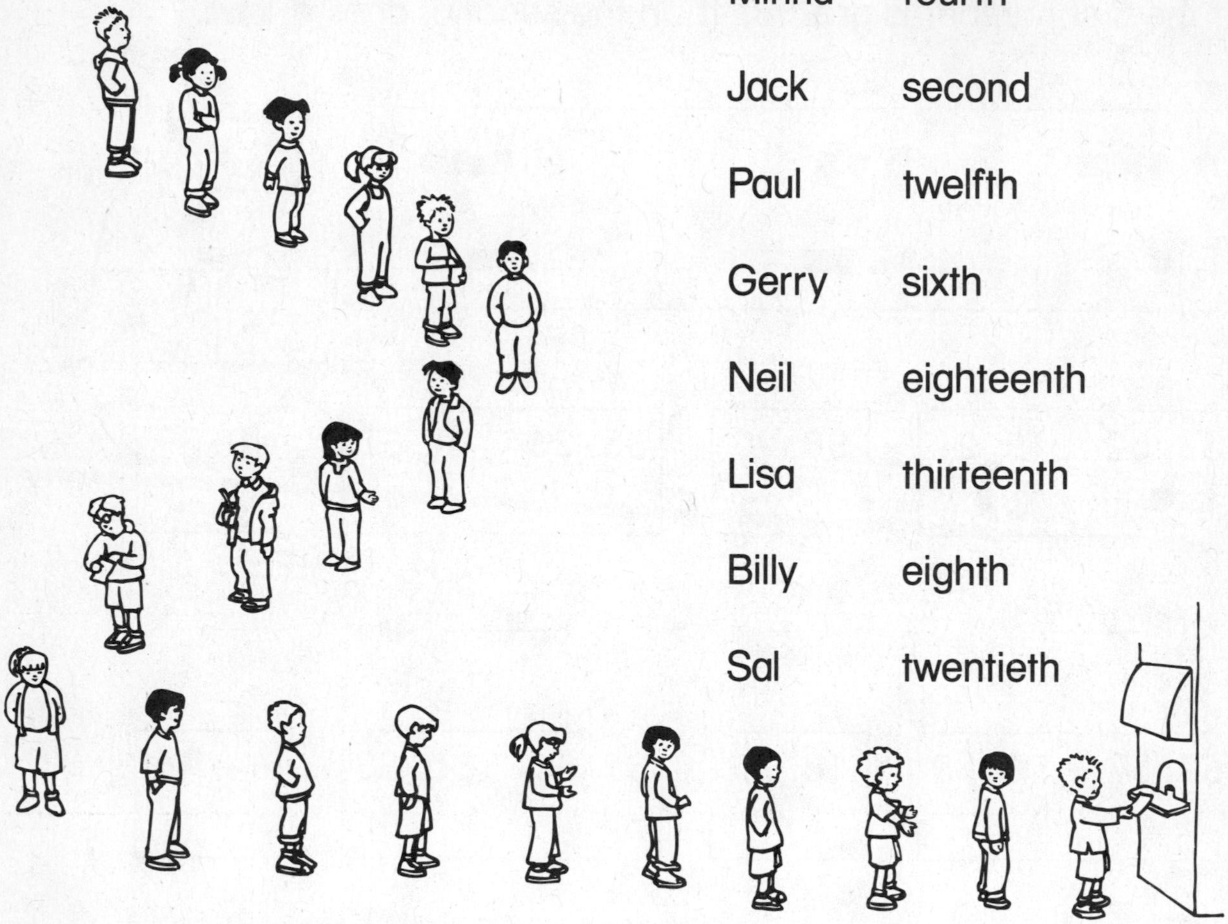

Write where these children stand in line.

Max comes right after Gerry. Max is ______________________.

Tina comes right before Neil. Tina is ______________________.

Notes for Home Your child identified and used ordinal numbers through twentieth. *Home Activity:* Ask your child to point out children in the first, ninth, fifteenth, and nineteenth positions in line.

Name ___________________________________

Extend Your Thinking
5-11

Critical Thinking

The dial on this meter goes around like the hand on a clock.
For each event, write where the hand stops.
Then circle the letter or letters that end each sentence below.

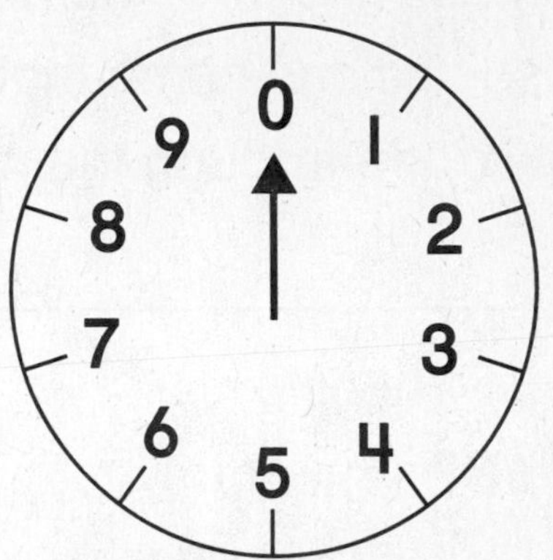

Event:	A	B	C	D
The dial begins at this number:	1	2	3	4
At each move, it goes forward this many notches:	4	4	5	5
It moves this many times:	3	3	3	3
It ends here:				

1. The dial starts and ends on an even number in event A B C D

2. The dial starts on an even number and ends on an odd number in event A B C D

3. The dial starts on an odd number and ends on an even number in event A B C D

Notes for Home Your child followed patterns and identified even and odd numbers. *Home Activity:* Ask your child to extend each event one more turn. Where does the dial end each time? (7, 8, 3, 4)

Name ______________________

Extend Your Thinking
5-12

Critical Thinking

Each box has three names for the same number.
It also has one name that does not belong.
Draw a line through the name that does not belong.

1. forty-nine 39 4 tens 9 ones 49	2. 27 2 tens 7 ones 29 twenty-seven
3. 75 57 7 tens 5 ones seventy-five	4. ninety-three 93 3 tens 9 ones 9 tens 3 ones
5. eighteen 8 tens 0 ones 18 1 ten 8 ones	6. 5 tens 4 ones 54 forty-five fifty-four
7. 6 tens 2 ones sixty-two 2 tens 6 ones 62	8. ninety-eight 8 tens 9 ones 89 eighty-nine

Notes for Home Your child identified three names for the same number. *Home Activity:* Ask your child to write another name for the number he or she crossed out in each box.

Name ______________________________

Extend Your Thinking
6-1

Visual Thinking

Tina and Joe put their money together to buy a gift.
Circle the coins that Tina may have put in.
Draw an X on the coins that Joe may have put in.

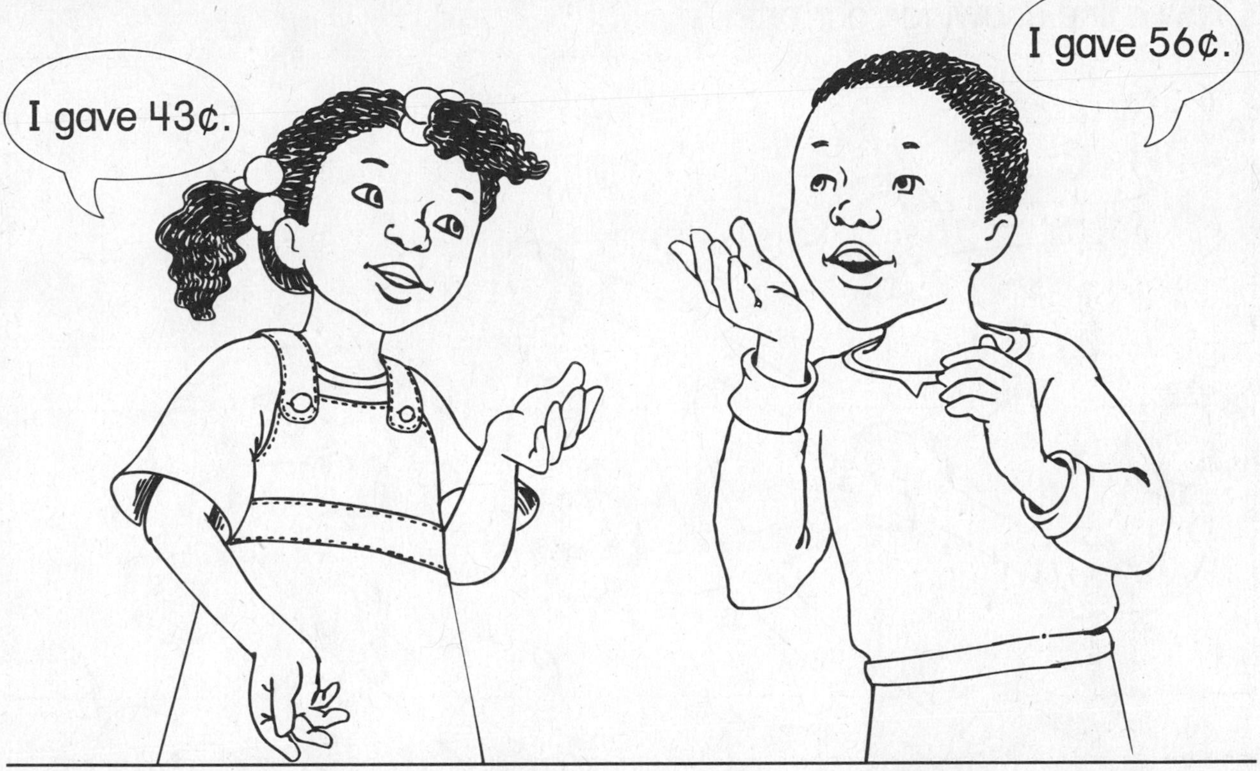

I gave 43¢.
I gave 56¢.

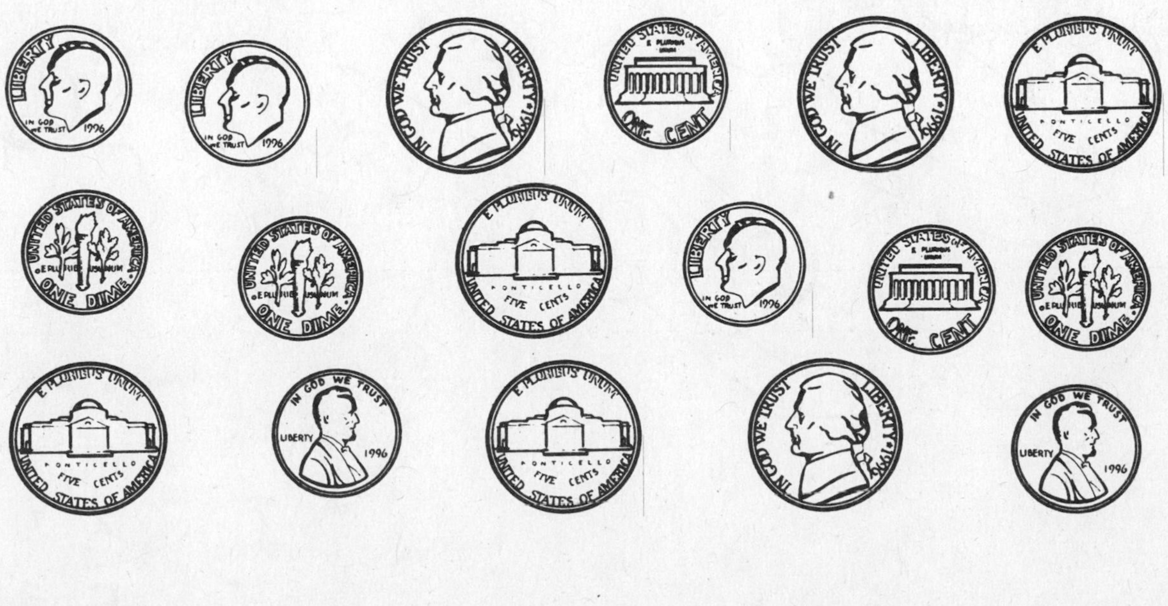

Notes for Home Your child selected coins that together equaled given amounts of money. *Home Activity:* Ask your child to count the dimes, nickels, and pennies in your change purse or pocket.

Name ______________________

Visual Thinking

Many paths lead through the woods.
You need to find exactly 99¢.
Which path will you take?
Draw a line showing your path.

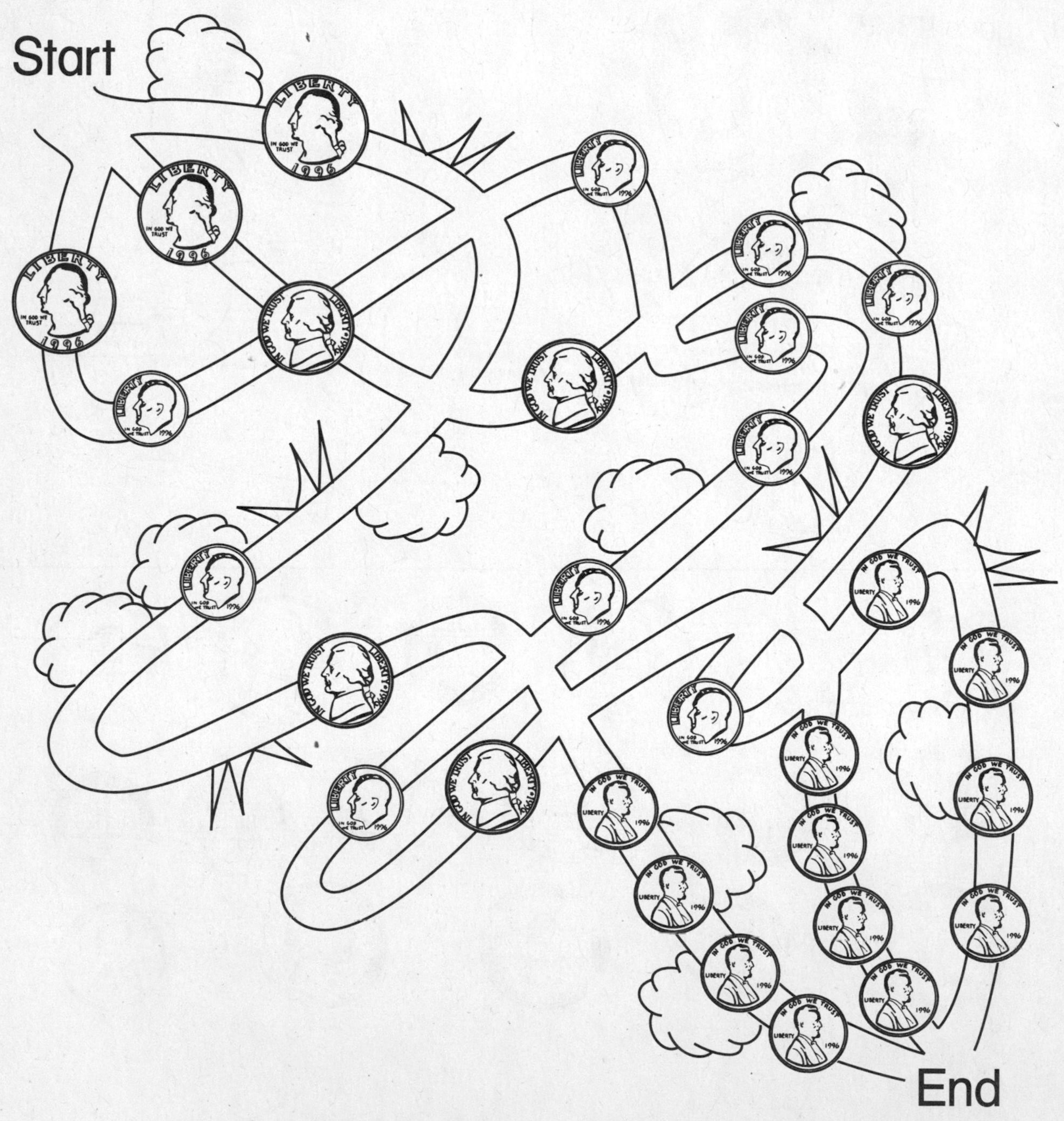

Notes for Home Your child counted quarters, dimes, nickels, and pennies totaling 99¢. *Home Activity:* Ask your child to figure out how 99¢ can be made with the least number of quarters, dimes, nickels, and pennies. Supply a variety of coins to help him or her to discover the answer. (9 coins—3 quarters, 2 dimes, 4 pennies)

Name ______________________________

Patterns in Numbers

Look at each row. Count to find out how much each group of coins is worth. Then write the value in each box. What is the pattern in each row?

The pattern is ______¢.

The pattern is ______¢.

The pattern is ______¢.

Notes for Home Your child counted to find the value of groups of coins in each row, then identified the pattern in each row. *Home Activity:* Ask your child to count one of the groups of coins aloud, starting with the most valuable coins and going to the least valuable.

Name ____________________

Decision Making

You have earned 77¢ Here are 4 ways you can be paid.

A B C D

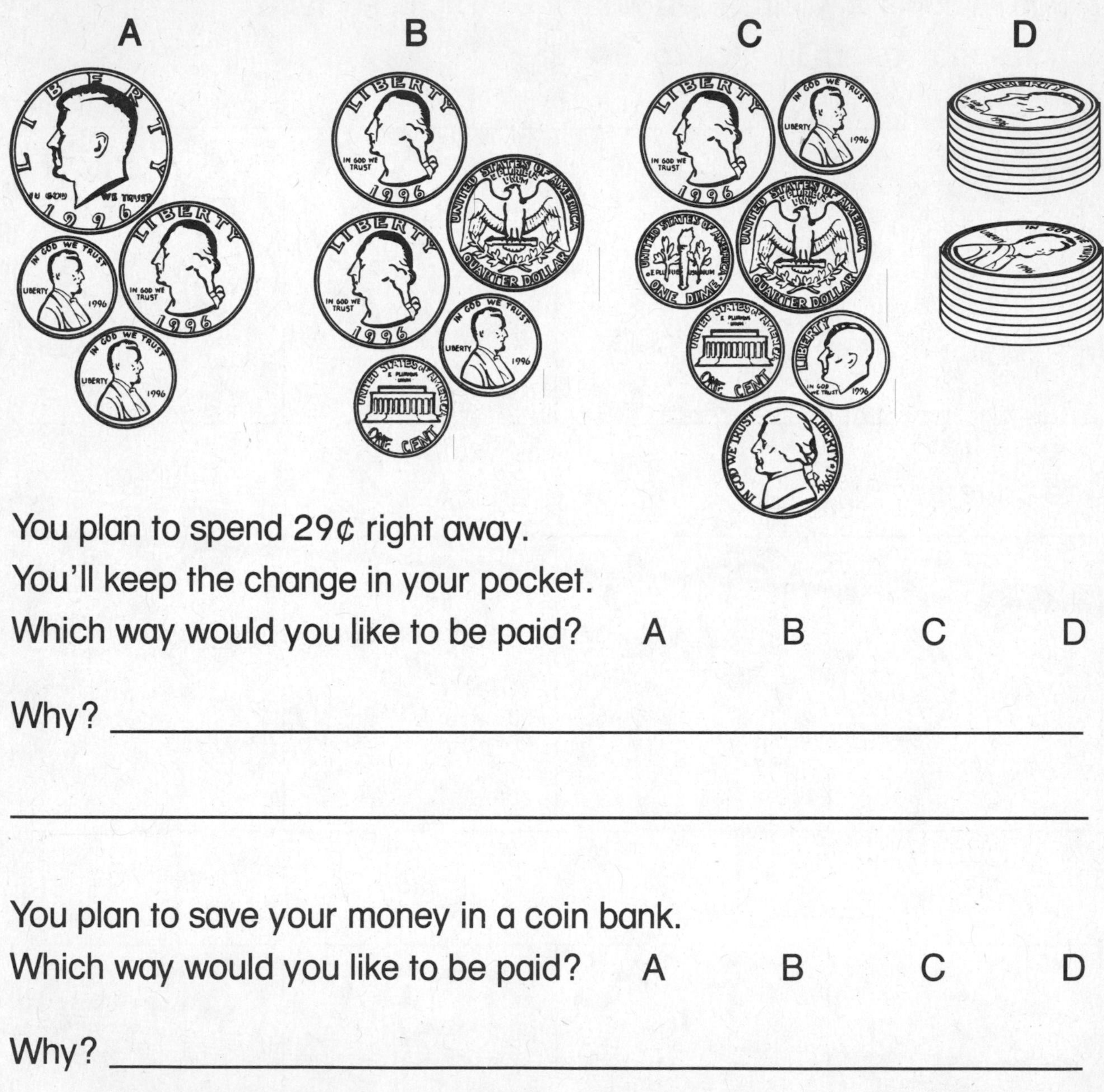

You plan to spend 29¢ right away.
You'll keep the change in your pocket.
Which way would you like to be paid? A B C D

Why? ____________________

____

You plan to save your money in a coin bank.
Which way would you like to be paid? A B C D

Why? ____________________

____

You plan to save more than you spend.
What is the most you can spend and still save more? ______

Notes for Home Your child selected different coin combinations to answer questions. *Home Activity:* Ask your child to explain his or her reasons for each choice.

Name ______________________________

Decision Making

You want to earn $5.00.

Circle the jobs you would do.

Circle what you would buy with $5.00.

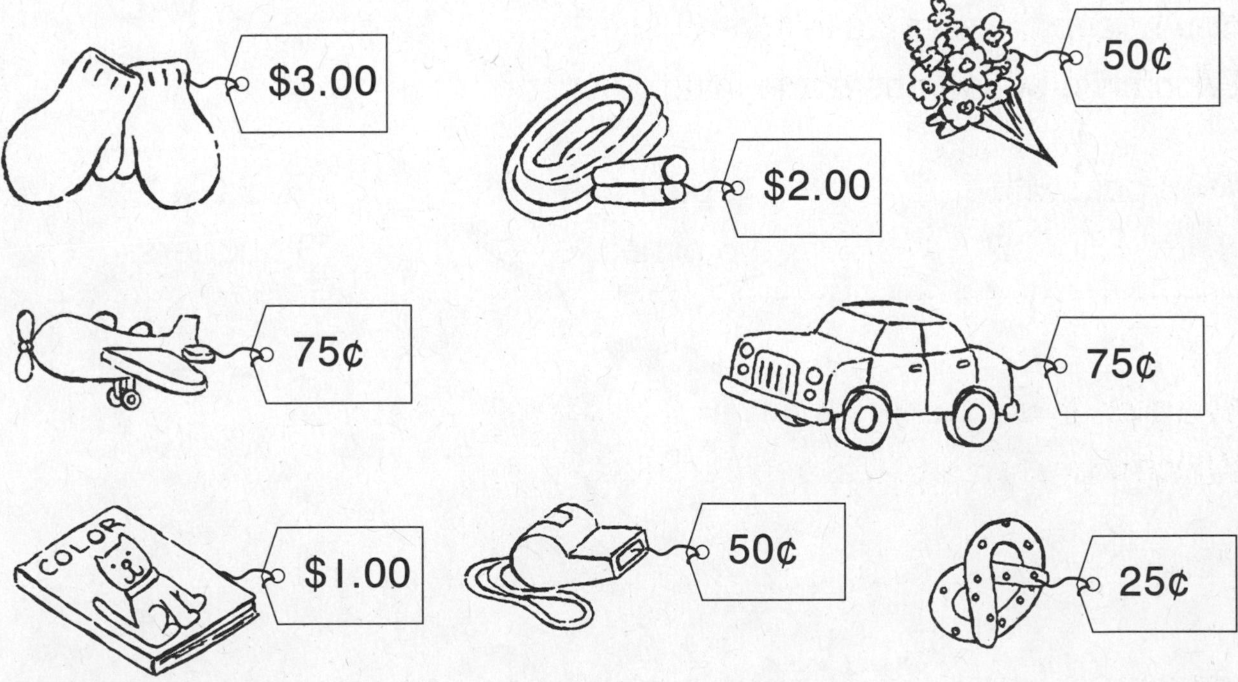

How much money is left over? ______________________________

Notes for Home Your child chose jobs to earn a total of $5.00; then chose how he or she would spend the $5.00. *Home Activity:* Ask your child to suggest a job around the house that he or she could do to earn $5.00.

Name ______________________________

Critical Thinking

Draw lines to match the children with their change.

Each child bought the same thing. It cost 39¢.

I paid with a half dollar.
I paid with 4 dimes.
I paid with a quarter and 2 dimes.

Each child bought the same thing. It cost 57¢.

I paid with a dollar bill.
I paid with 6 dimes.
I paid with 3 quarters.

Notes for Home Home Your child identified the value of each coin combination and the correct change from each. *Home Activity:* Help your child to figure out the correct change from $1.00 if it was used to buy a 39¢ item. (61¢)

Name ______________________________

Extend Your Thinking
6-7

Critical Thinking

Find out how much money each child has.

Then circle 2 price tags for items each child could pay for

and still get change.

Write the sum of the 2 price tags and the change each child would get.

Brian has 2 quarters and 2 dimes. He has _____¢.

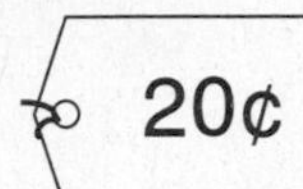

50¢ 45¢ Sum _____ Change _____

Rita has a half dollar, a quarter, and 2 dimes. She has _____¢.

25¢ 50¢ 75¢ Sum _____ Change _____

Mailee has 2 quarters and 2 nickels. She has _____¢.

15¢ 55¢ 30¢ Sum _____ Change _____

Scott has a half dollar, a quarter, a dime, and a nickel. He has _____¢.

35¢ 40¢ 90¢ Sum _____ Change _____

Notes for Home Your child solved problems by making change. *Home Activity:* Select one or two rows and ask your child to tell you how much more each child would need to spend to all of his or her money. (The answers will be the amount of change each child got.)

Name ________________________________

Visual Thinking

Play Tic-Tac-Time. Mark each picture with X or O.

X The action takes a minute or less to do.

O The action takes more than a minute to do.

Draw a line to show the winner.

Circle the winner. O X

Notes for Home Your child classified activities according to how much time they require. *Home Activity:* Ask your child to pantomime 2 activities pictured that take a minute or less to do.

Name ____________________

Extend Your Thinking
7-2

Decision Making

Read the list of things to do.
Circle the time you think you would spend doing each activity.

1. brushing your teeth

   less than 1 minute   about 1 minute   more than 1 minute

2. making a sandwich

   less than 1 minute   about 1 minute   more than 1 minute

3. eating an orange

   less than 1 minute   about 1 minute   more than 1 minute

4. waiting for a bus

   less than 1 minute   about 1 minute   more than 1 minute

5. combing your hair

   less than 1 minute   about 1 minute   more than 1 minute

6. putting on a sweater

   less than 1 minute   about 1 minute   more than 1 minute

Notes for Home Your child decided how much time he or she would spend doing a variety of activities, using a duration of less than 1 minute, about 1 minute, and more than 1 minute. *Home Activity:* Ask your child to measure the time it takes for him or her to complete everyday activities such as dressing, setting the table, etc.

Name ________________________________

Extend Your Thinking 7-3

Visual Thinking

Look at the clocks.

A letter is in the place of 12.

Decide the time each clock shows.

Find the matching clock below.

Write the letter on the line. Then find the message.

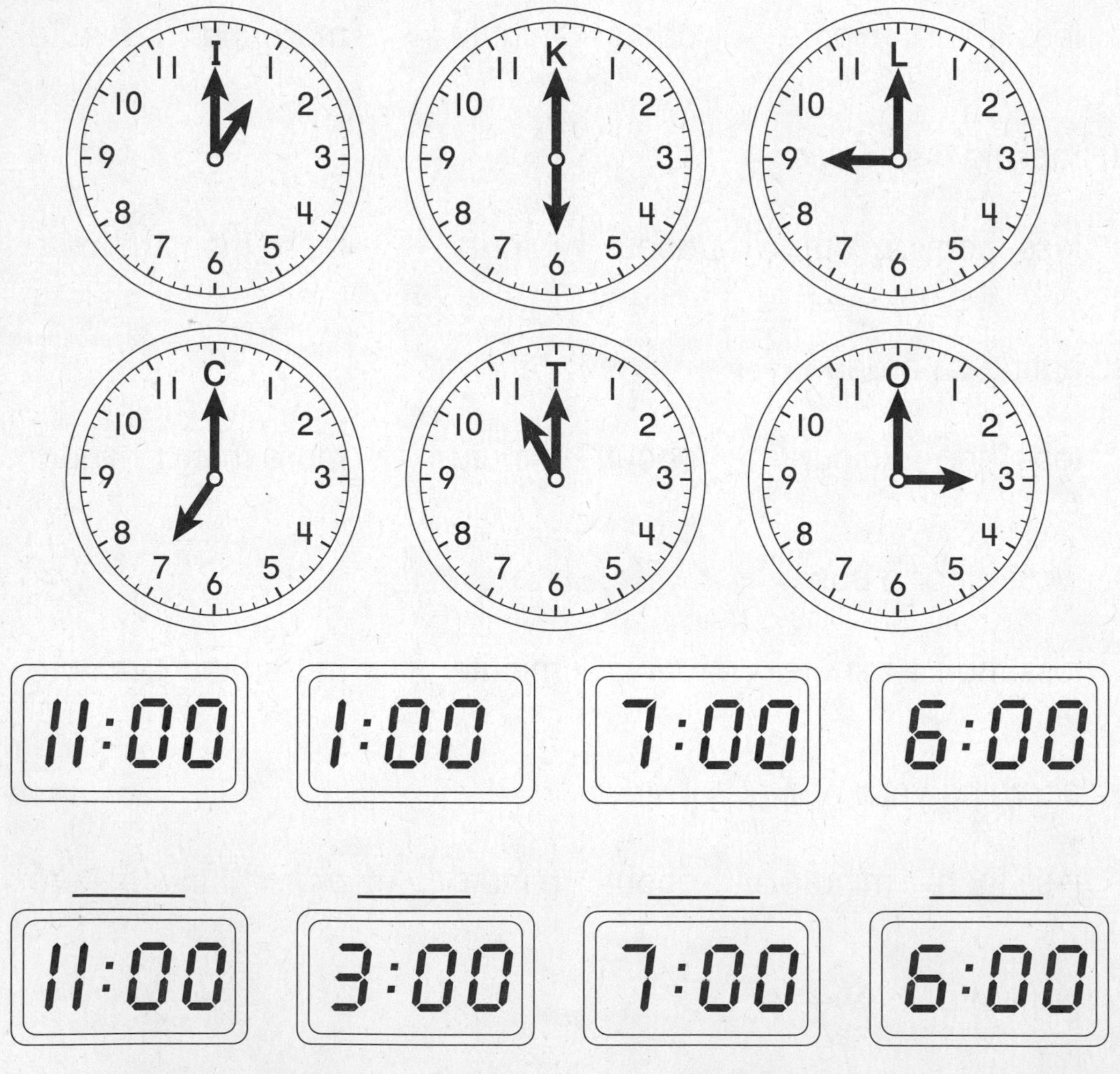

____ ____ ____ ____

____ ____ ____ ____

Notes for Home Your child told time to the hour on analog clocks and matched each clock with a digital clock showing the same time. *Home Activity:* Ask your child to read a clock on the hour in your home.

Name ___________________________

Extend Your Thinking 7-4

Critical Thinking

Match each child with what he or she spent time doing.

I did this for 2 hours.
I did this for 1 hour.
I spent 3 hours doing this.
I did this for 9 hours.
11:00
12:00
2:00
TICKETS
4:00

Notes for Home Your child matched pictured activities having specific beginning and ending times. *Home Activity:* Ask your child to record beginning and ending times to keep track of how many hours he or she spends sleeping, watching TV, and reading during a 2-day period.

Name ______________________

Extend Your Thinking 7-5

Critical Thinking

Complete the timetable.

Then answer the questions.

Schedule	
Departs Airplanes take off every half hour	**Arrival Times at Different Airports**
Airplane 1 3 : 00	4:00
Airplane 2 ____ : ____	5:00
Airplane 3 ____ : ____	6:00
Airplane 4 ____ : ____	7:00
Airplane 5 ____ : ____	8:00
Airplane 6 ____ : ____	9:00

1. How long is Airplane 4 in the air? ______________

2. How long is Airplane 5 in the air? ______________

3. Which airplane has the shortest flying time? _____

4. When would airplane 7 take off? __________

Notes for Home Your child completed a timetable using half-hour and hour times. *Home Activity:* Ask your child: *How many hours after Airplane 1 did Airplane 6 take off?* (2 1/2 hours later)

Name ______________________________

Extend Your Thinking
7-7

Patterns in Data

Two buses leave City Square at the same times.
One bus goes east to East Town Mall.
The ride to East Town Mall takes 15 minutes.
The other bus goes west to West Market.
The ride to West Market takes 5 minutes.
Fill in the missing times on these schedules.

Leave City Square	Arrive East Town Mall
9:00	9:15
9:30	9:45
10:00	
10:20	
10:40	
10:50	
11:05	
11:15	
11:30	

Leave City Square	Arrive West Market
9:00	9:05
9:30	9:35
10:00	
10:20	
10:40	
10:50	
11:05	
11:15	
11:30	

Notes for Home Your child found the arrival times in a bus schedule by adding either 5 or 15 minutes to departure times. *Home Activity:* Show your child a bus (or other) timetable and ask him or her to read a column of starting times and relate it to the first column in these tables.

Name ___________________________

Extend Your Thinking
7-6

Critical Thinking

Cross out the one in each row that does not belong.

10 o'clock

5 minutes past 8

5 minutes past 7

10 minutes past 2

Choose a time. Write it 3 different ways.

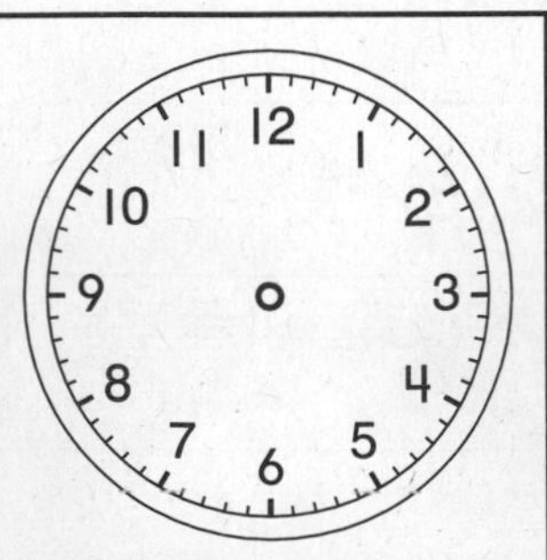

Notes for Home Your child crossed out the time in each row that did not match the time that was recorded in 3 different ways. *Home Activity:* Ask your child to write the current time to the next half hour in 3 different ways.

Name ______________________________

Patterns in Numbers

Write the time under each clock.
Find the pattern in the row.
Write and draw the next time in the pattern.

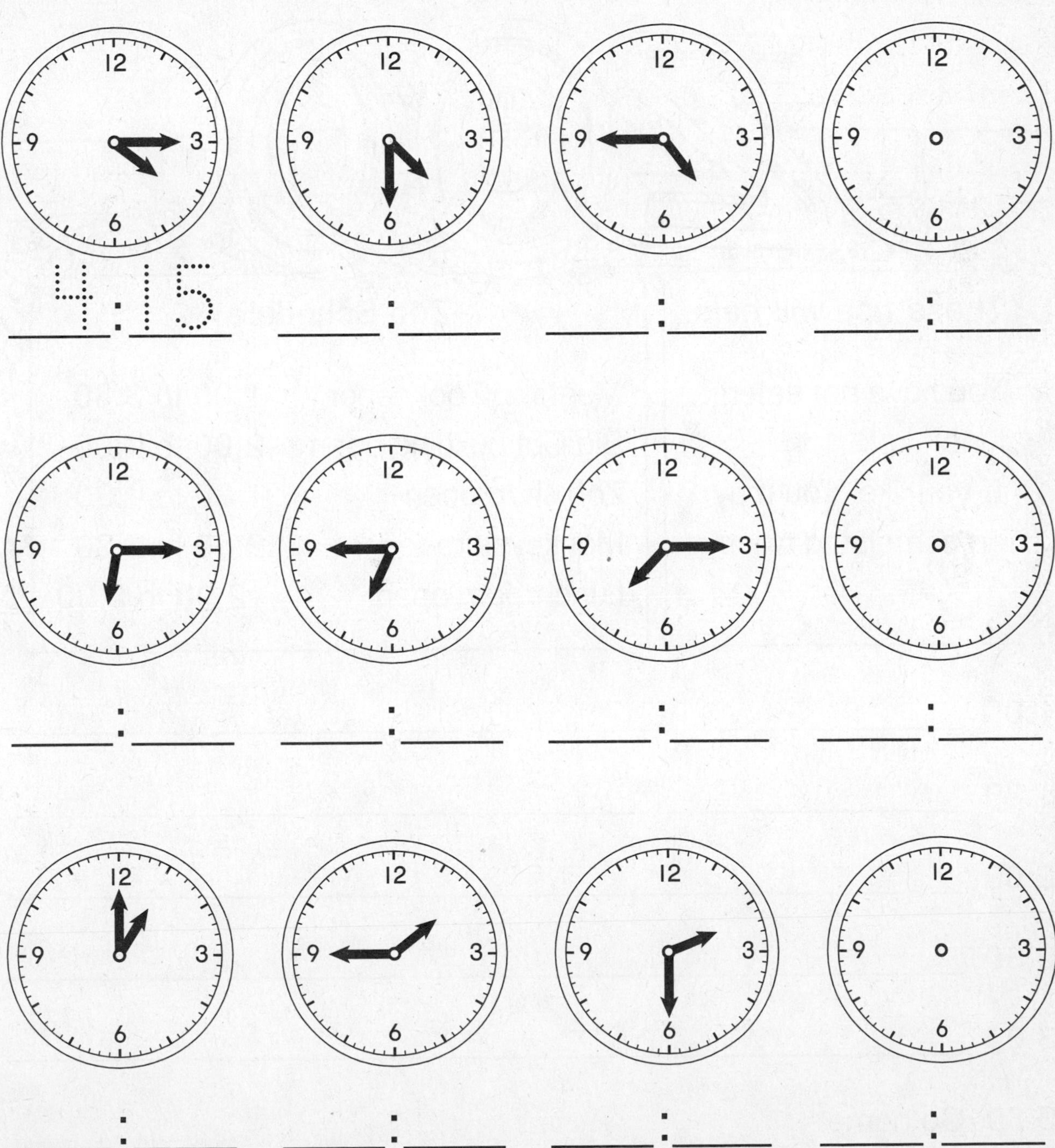

Notes for Home Your child told time in increments of 15 minutes on analog clock faces, recorded the time, identified a pattern, and drew hands on a clock face to continue the pattern. *Home Activity:* Ask your child to point out the next time an analog clock in your home shows 15 minutes before or after the hour.

Name ______________________

Decision Making

You are at the zoo.

Decide what to do there. Decide when to do it.

Write what you will do next to the time.

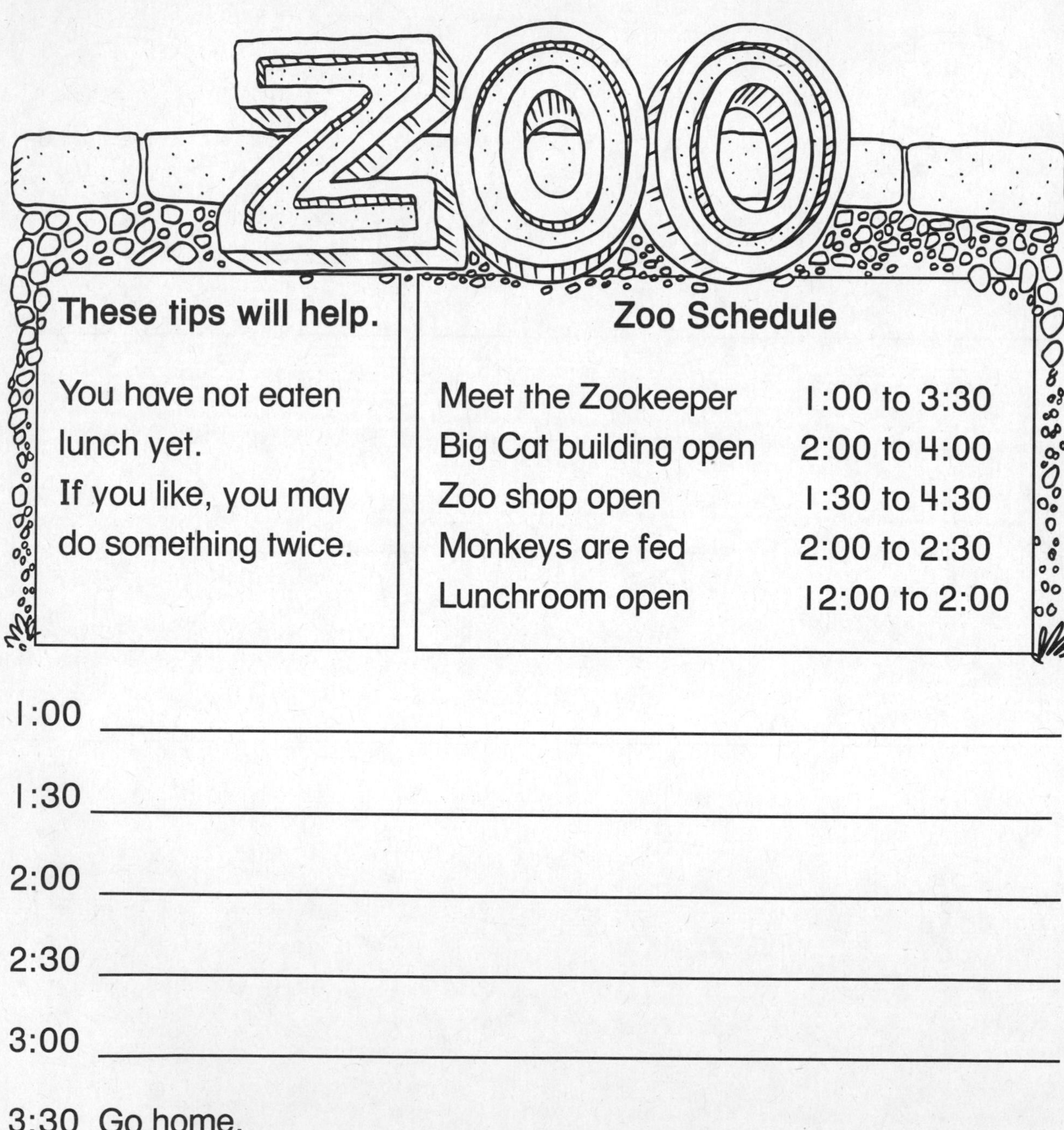

These tips will help.

You have not eaten lunch yet.
If you like, you may do something twice.

Zoo Schedule

Meet the Zookeeper	1:00 to 3:30
Big Cat building open	2:00 to 4:00
Zoo shop open	1:30 to 4:30
Monkeys are fed	2:00 to 2:30
Lunchroom open	12:00 to 2:00

1:00 ______________________

1:30 ______________________

2:00 ______________________

2:30 ______________________

3:00 ______________________

3:30 Go home.

Notes for Home Your child decided on a schedule for a zoo visit, taking into account opening and closing times and personal preferences. *Home Activity:* Ask your child to help you schedule a shopping trip or a trip to a museum, based on real-life time considerations.

 Use with pages 255–256.

Name ______________________________

Extend Your Thinking 8-1

Critical Thinking

Find the plane that each skydiver jumped from.

Draw a line from each skydiver to the plane with the correct sum.

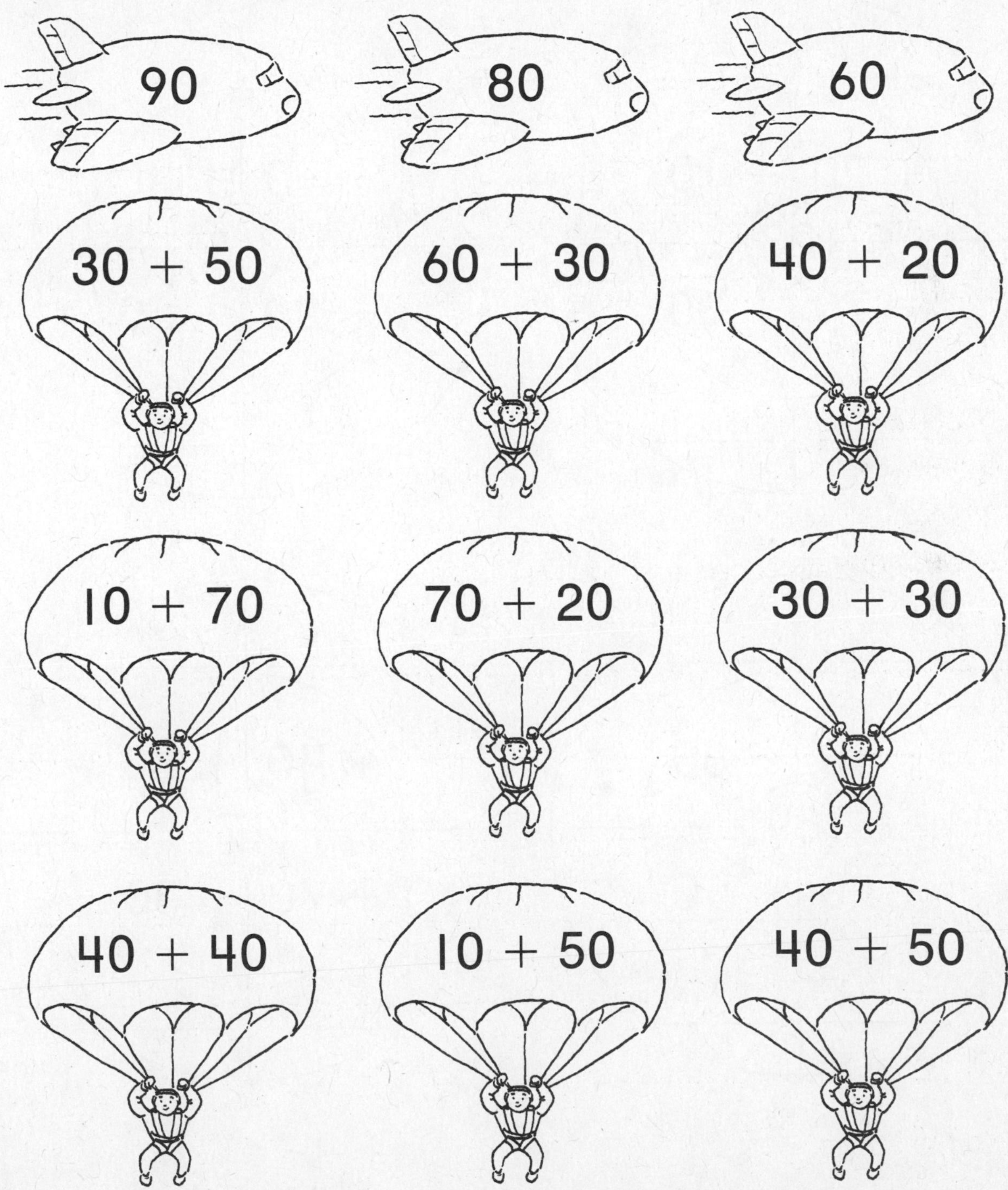

Notes for Home Your child matched addition problems involving multiples of ten with their sums. *Home Activity:* Ask your child to suggest other addition problems involving multiples of ten for the sum of 90 (80 + 10 or 20 + 70) and 80 (20 + 60 or 70 + 10).

Name ___________________________

Visual Thinking

Solve each addition problem.

Write the sum in the outer circle.

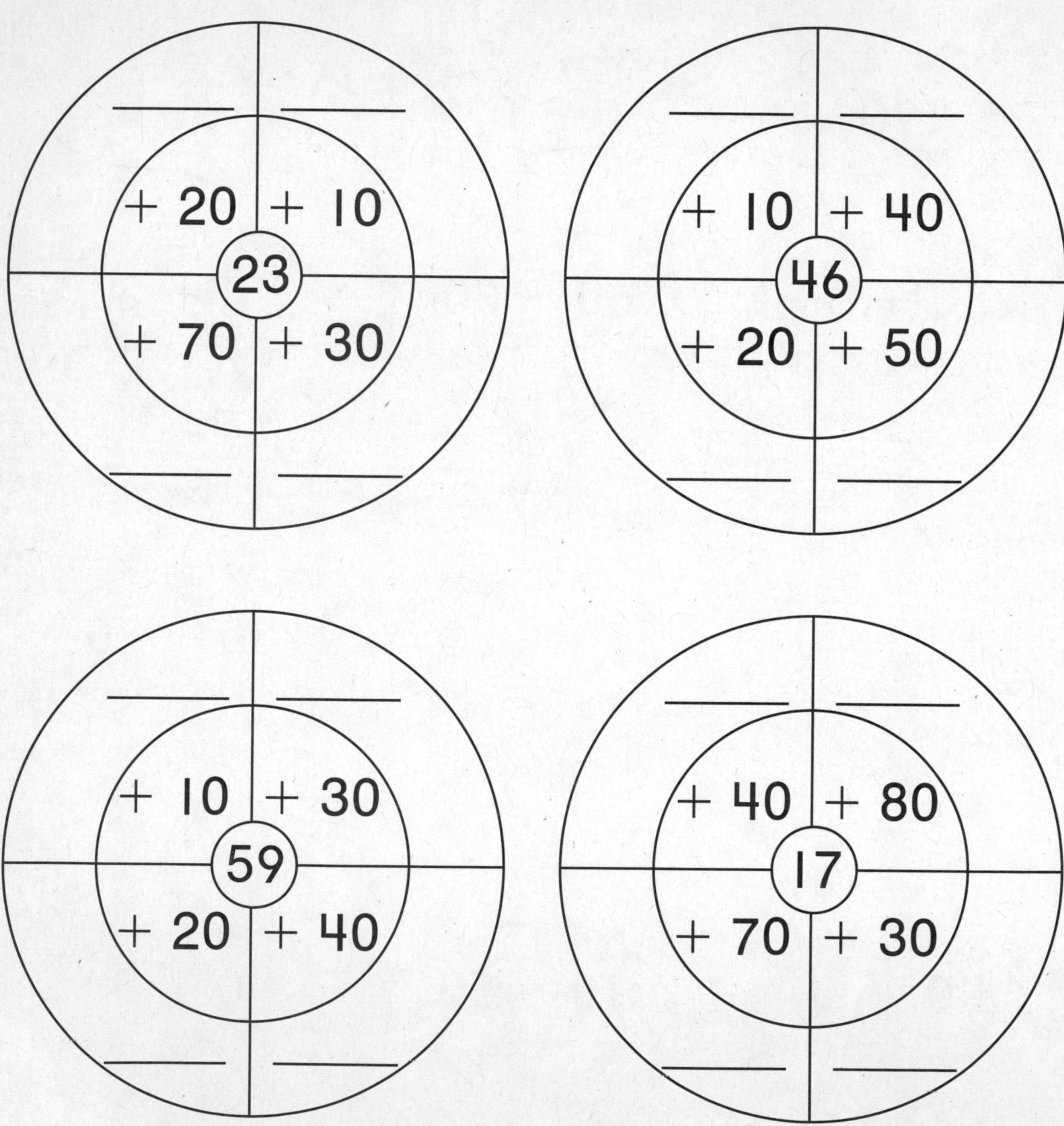

Notes for Home Your child added multiples of 10 to two-digit numbers. *Home Activity:* Ask your child to solve the following problems mentally: 36 + 50 (86); 89 + 10 (99).

Name ______________________________

Extend Your Thinking
8-3

Decision Making

Sometimes it's useful to have an **exact count** of things, such as the number of people in your family.
Sometimes it's useful to **count by 10s**, such as finding the number of children in your grade.
Other times, it's useful to **count in larger groups**, such as finding the number of window panes in your school.

Decide how to count the things below. Write **E** for exact count. Write **10** for groups of 10. Write **L** for larger groups.

1.  in a forest ______

2. in your desk ______

3. 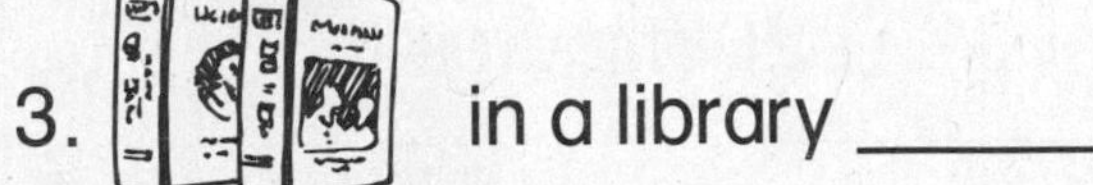 in a library ______

4.  in a restaurant ______

5. 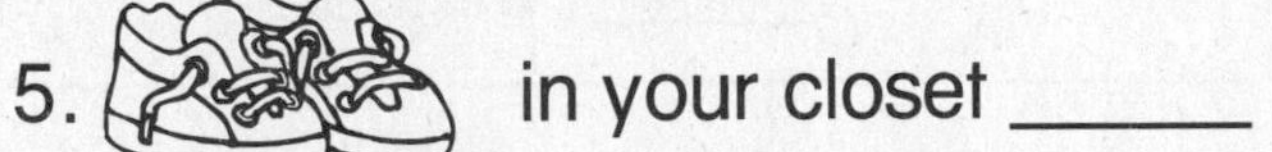 in your closet ______

6. in a post office ______

7. in a parking lot ______

8. 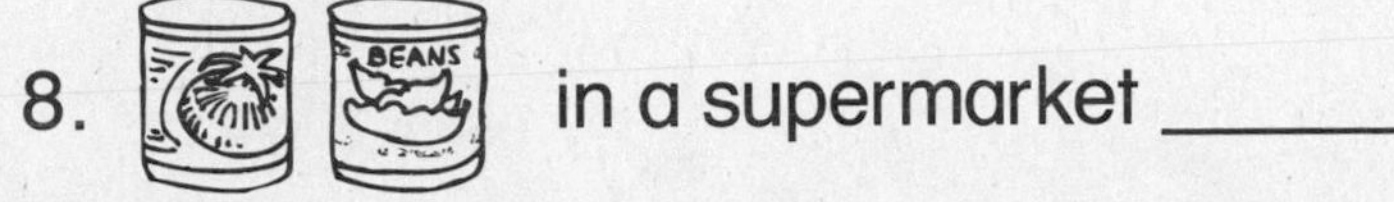

in a supermarket ______

Notes for Home Your child classified items for which it would be useful to have an exact count, a count by tens, or an even less exact count by larger groups. *Home Activity:* Ask your child to explain the reasons for several of his or her decisions.

Name ______________________________

Extend Your Thinking
8-4

Patterns in Data

Jill spends 1 hour at the gym every day.
This chart tells how Jill plans to use her time for 6 days.
Jill will keep up the pattern she began in the first 2 days.
Fill in the missing numbers.

	Running	Swimming
Monday	10 minutes	50 minutes
Tuesday	20 minutes	40 minutes
Wednesday	30 minutes	_____ minutes
Thursday	_____ minutes	20 minutes
Friday	_____ minutes	_____minutes
Saturday	_____ minutes	_____ minutes

What is Jill's pattern? ______________________________

____

On which day does Jill spend equal times running and swimming?

____

On which day does Jill not swim? ______________

Notes for Home Your child read a chart which recorded a pattern and then made a prediction about future events based on that pattern. *Home Activity:* Ask your child to explain his or her reasoning.

Name ______________________

Extend Your Thinking
8-5

Visual Thinking

This machine makes big candles from little candles.

For every 10 little candles that go in, 1 big candle comes out.

If little candles can't be used, they come back out.

Draw the candles the machine puts out.

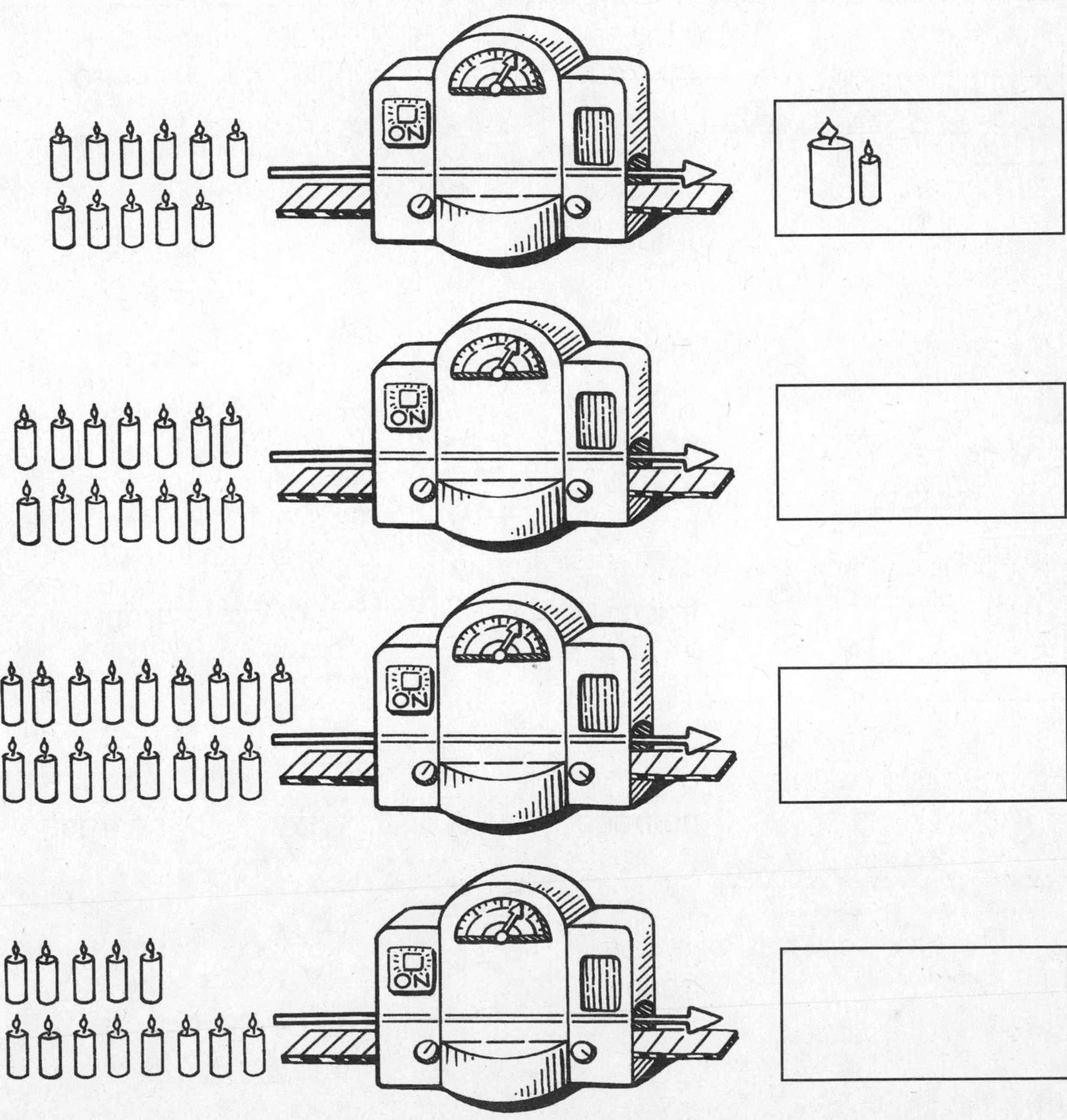

Notes for Home Your child predicted the output of a machine that exchanges 1 big candle for 10 small candles. *Home Activity:* Ask your child to draw what the machine would put out if 18 little candles were put into it. (1 big candle and 8 little candles)

Name ______________________________

Visual Thinking

Ten balls will fit into each triangle.

In each problem, look at all the balls.

Circle the loose balls that will fit into the triangles.

If the balls will fill a triangle completely, circle **trade**.

If the triangle still has space, circle **no trade**.

15
+ 7
?

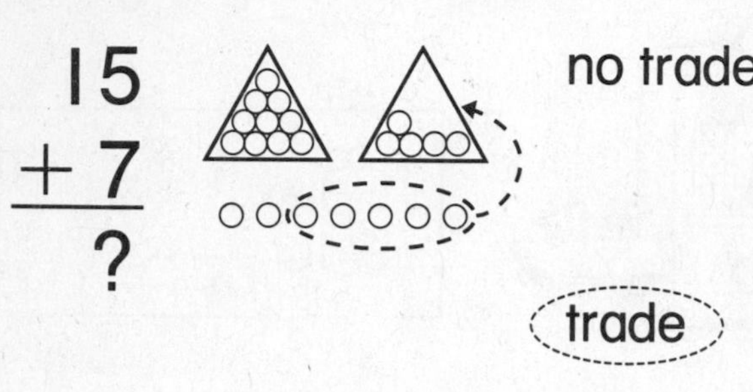

no trade

trade

24
+ 6
?

no trade

trade

46
+ 3
?

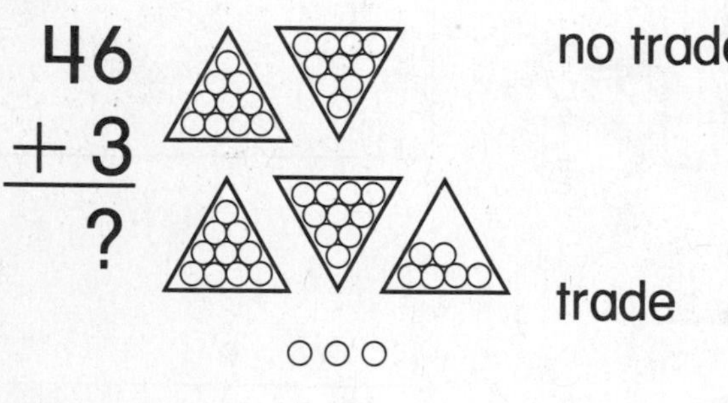

no trade

trade

32
+ 9
?

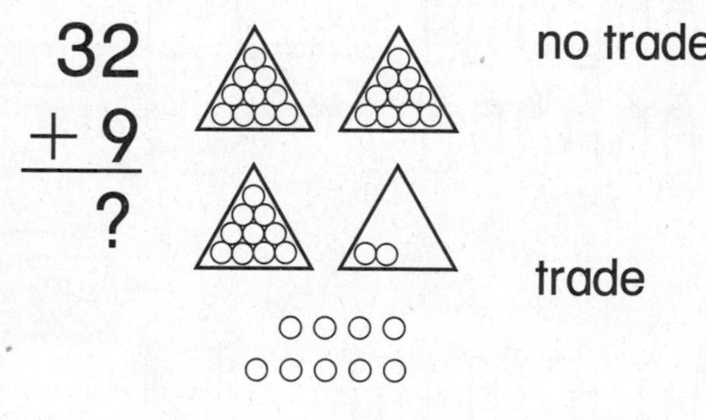

no trade

trade

57
+ 5
?

no trade

trade

69
+ 4
?

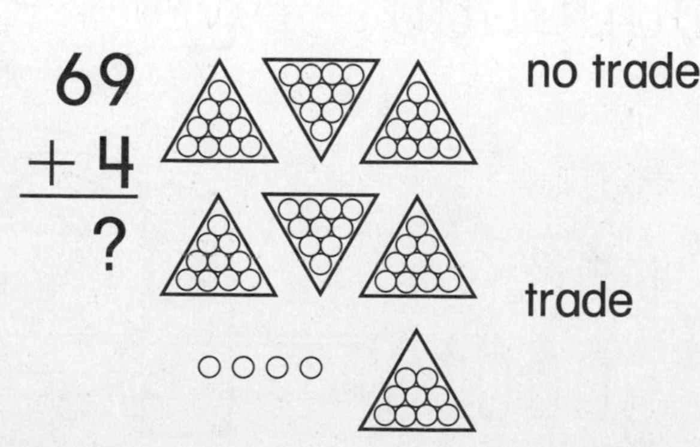

no trade

trade

Notes for Home Your child determined when a trade of 10 ones for one ten was necessary in given addition problems. *Home Activity:* Have your child explain his or her answers.

Name ______________________________

Extend Your Thinking
8-7

Critical Thinking

Each row has four problems.
In three problems, you need to trade 10 ones for 1 ten.
Cross out the problem that does NOT have 10 ones to be traded for a ten.

16 + 7 = ??	16 + 5 = ??	16 + 2 = ??	16 + 8 = ??

25 + 6 = ??	25 + 8 = ??	37 + 4 = ??	37 + 1 = ??

63 + 8 = ??	92 + 7 = ??	48 + 7 = ??	71 + 9 = ??

Notes for Home Your child identified problems that involve trading 10 ones for a ten by crossing off the one out of four that did not involve a trade. *Home Activity:* Ask your child to tell you the answers for one row of problems.

Name ______________________________

Extend Your Thinking
8-8

Decision Making

Make your own problems.
Circle the sentence that tells what happens next.
Find the answers to your problems.

1. Last night, 13 inches of snow fell.

Today 9 more inches fell.	Today 3 more inches fell.
$\begin{array}{r} 13 \\ +9 \\ \hline \end{array}$	$\begin{array}{r} 13 \\ +3 \\ \hline \end{array}$

How many inches of snow fell in all? _____

2. There were 38 children waiting to sled down the hill.

Then 5 more came.	Then 1 more came.
$\begin{array}{r} 38 \\ +5 \\ \hline \end{array}$	$\begin{array}{r} 38 \\ +3 \\ \hline \end{array}$

How many children were on the hill then? _____

3. John and Kate made 24 snowballs.

Then John made 7 more.	Then Kate made 2 more.
$\begin{array}{r} 24 \\ +7 \\ \hline \end{array}$	$\begin{array}{r} 24 \\ +2 \\ \hline \end{array}$

How many snowballs are there in all? _____

Notes for Home Your child chose situations for word problems and then solved the problems he or she made. *Home Activity:* Ask your child to solve the problems again, this time using the remaining situation.

Name ______________________________

Extend Your Thinking
8-9

Patterns in Numbers

Which rule do the numbers in the row follow?

Circle the correct rule.

Write the next number in the pattern.

Rule: +25 +35

18	43	68	93

Rule: +17 +7

13	20	27	

Rule: +14 +24

9	33	57	

Rule: +16 +26

15	31	47	

Rule: +9 +19

21	40	59	

Work Area

Notes for Home Your child identified the rule applied to each step in a pattern and provided the next step in each pattern. *Home Activity:* Ask your child to explain how he or she determined the rule for one of the rows.

Name ___________________________

Extend Your Thinking 8-10

Visual Thinking

Look at each group of coins and answer the questions.

dimes **pennies**

Do you have 10 pennies to trade for a dime? Yes No

What are the coins worth altogether? ______ ¢

Do you have 10 pennies to trade for a dime? Yes No

What are the coins worth altogether? ______ ¢

Do you have 10 pennies to trade for a dime? Yes No

What are the coins worth altogether? ______ ¢

Do you have 10 pennies to trade for a dime? Yes No

What are the coins worth altogether? ______ ¢

Notes for Home Your child added the values of groups of coins and decided whether it was possible to trade in 10 pennies for 1 dime. *Home Activity:* Ask your child to set up a similar problem, using real dimes and pennies, for you to solve.

Name ______________________

Extend Your Thinking 8-11

Critical Thinking

Match the 4 players to their scores.

Do your adding next to each board.

Sumi's score is 45. Which board is hers?

Paco's score is 47. Which board is his?

Willy's score is 43. Which board is his?

What is Juanita's score? ______

Addends in the following calculations may be arranged in any order.

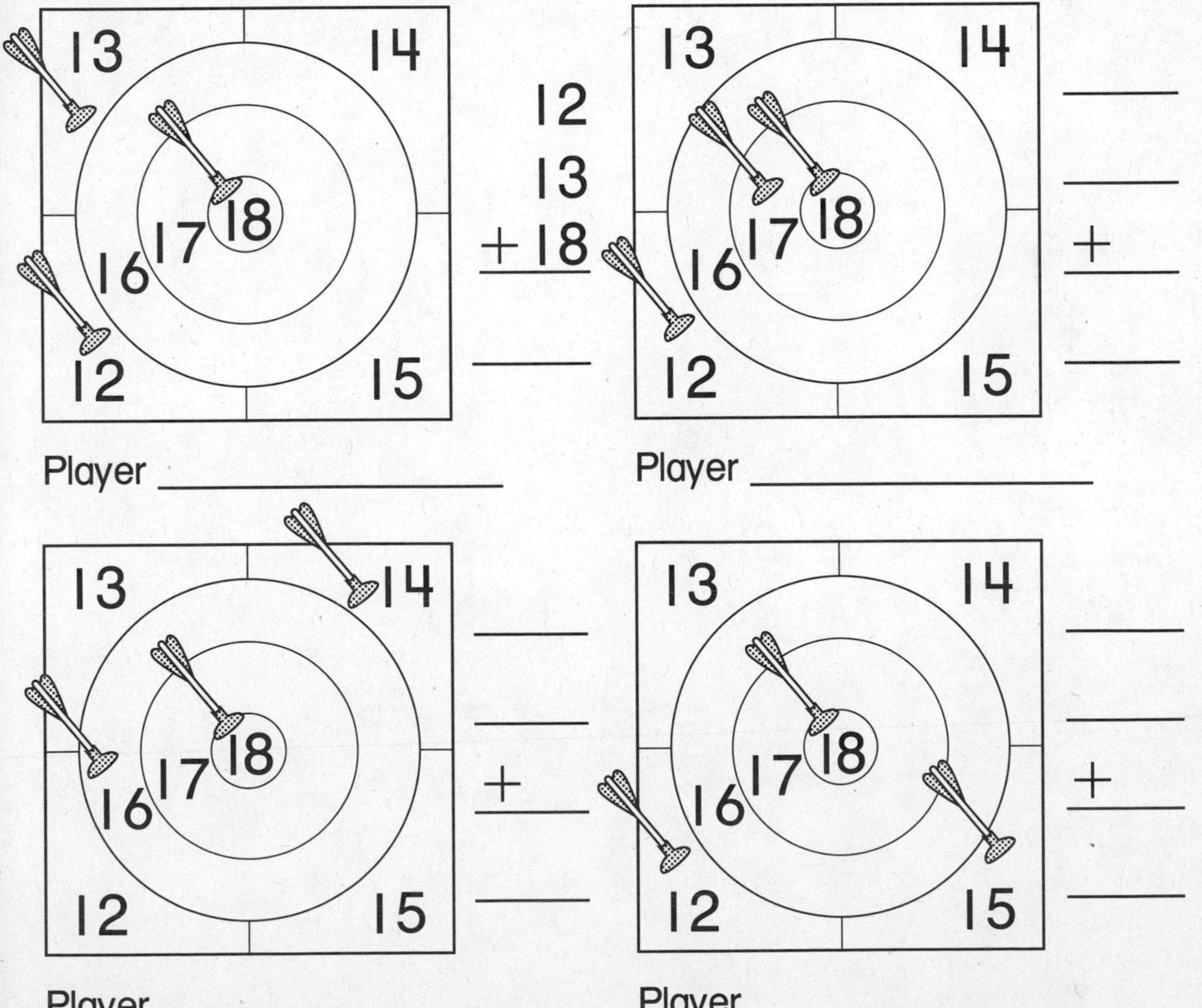

Player ______________________ Player ______________________

Player ______________________ Player ______________________

Notes for Home Your child added to match total scores with addends. *Home Activity:* Discuss with your child whether changing the order of the dart board scores in the calculation makes the addition easier.

Name ______________________________

Extend Your Thinking
8-12

Decision Making

Some problems are easier for you than other problems.
Find problems below that you can do in your head very easily.
If you have to think about a problem, skip it.
Write 5 or more answers.

5 5 + 7	15 5 + 7	6 9 + 4	40 10 + 20
32 + 14	64 + 20	11 + 49	41 + 9
50 + 27	33 + 33	46 + 24	27 + 37

Notes for Home Your child chose and worked 5 or more problems that he or she can do by mental math.
Home Activity: Help your child solve the problems he or she found to be too difficult.

Name ____________________

Extend Your Thinking
8-13

Patterns in Geometry

What comes next in each pattern? Draw it.

Notes for Home Your child identified the pattern in each row of geometric shapes and drew the next shape.
Home Activity: Ask your child to explain one of the patterns to you.

Name ______________________________

Extend Your Thinking
9-1

Visual Thinking

A treasure is hidden under one of these numbers.
Follow the clues to find the treasure. Draw your path.

Start at 91.

Subtract 20.

Add 8.

Subtract 30.

Subtract 1.

Subtract 10.

Subtract 2.

Add 20.

Subtract 2.

Subtract 10.

1	2	3	4	5	6	7	8	9	10
11	12	13	14	15	16	17	18	19	20
21	22	23	24	25	26	27	28	29	30
31	32	33	34	35	36	37	38	39	40
41	42	43	44	45	46	47	48	49	50
51	52	53	54	55	56	57	58	59	60
61	62	63	64	65	66	67	68	69	70
71	72	73	74	75	76	77	78	79	80
81	82	83	84	85	86	87	88	89	90
91	92	93	94	95	96	97	98	99	100

The treasure is under the number _____.

Notes for Home Your child added and subtracted numbers that include multiples of 10 to two-digit numbers to find a hidden treasure. *Home Activity*: Ask your child to find the number on the chart that is the answer to 67 – 30. (37)

Name ________________________________

Extend Your Thinking
9-2

Decision Making

Circle at least 3 things you would like to do in 60 minutes.

Decide how many minutes you want to spend doing each activity. Write 10, 20, or 30 minutes.

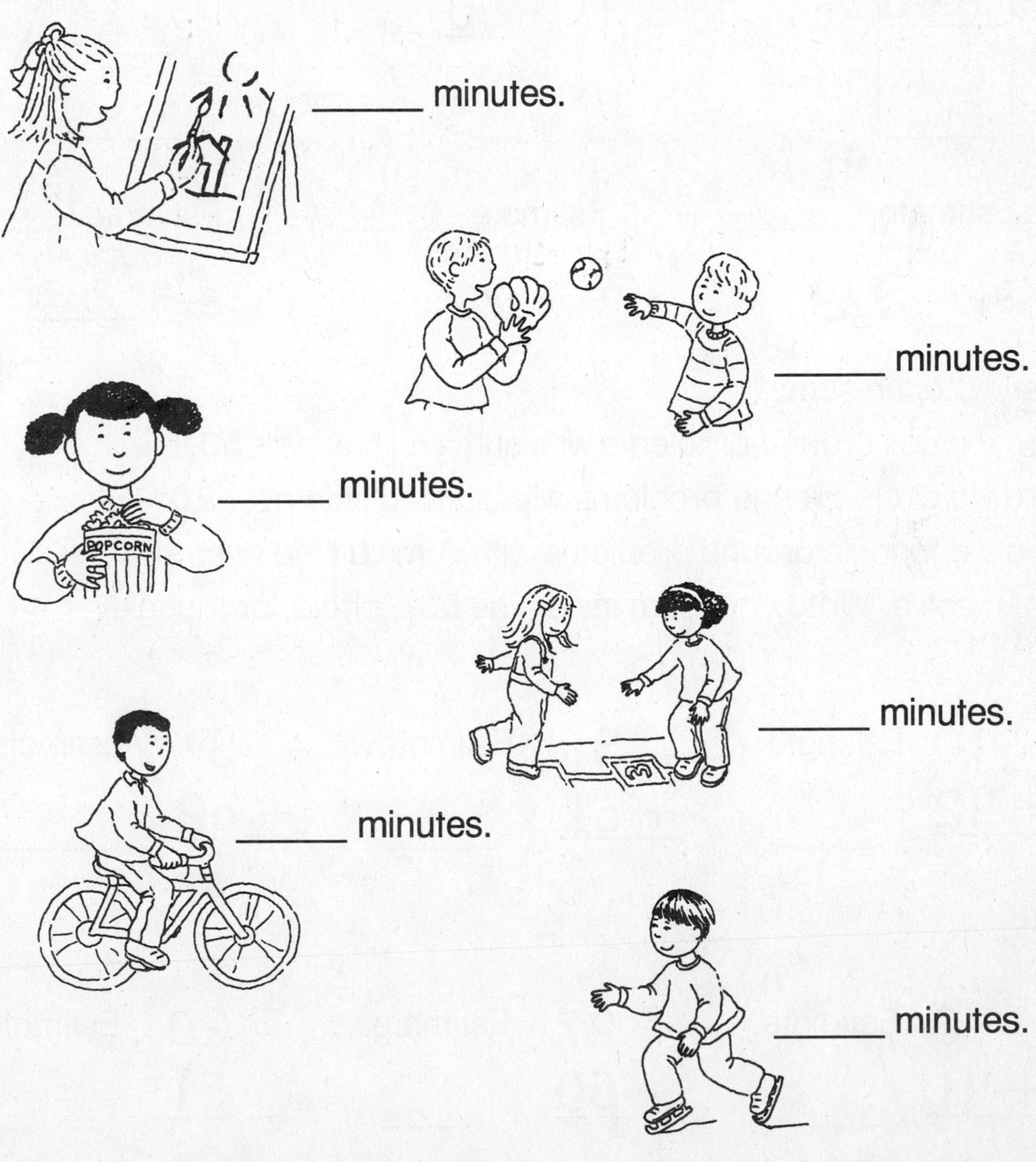

Notes for Home Your child chose at least 3 activities to do during a 60-minute period and specified the length of time he or she wished to spend doing each activity. *Home Activity*: Ask your child how many minutes he or she would spend in each activity if 90 minutes were available.

Name ________________________________

Extend Your Thinking 9-3

Critical Thinking

You can estimate sums by adding only the digits in the tens place. Study these examples.

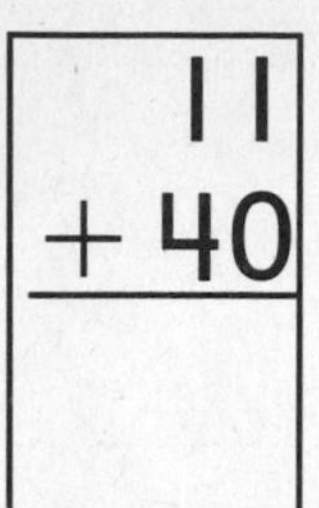

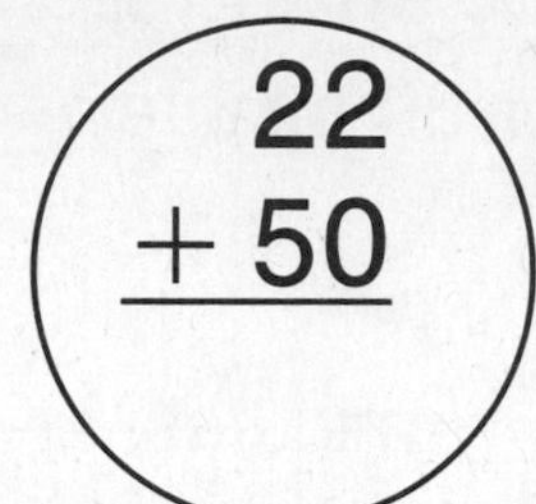

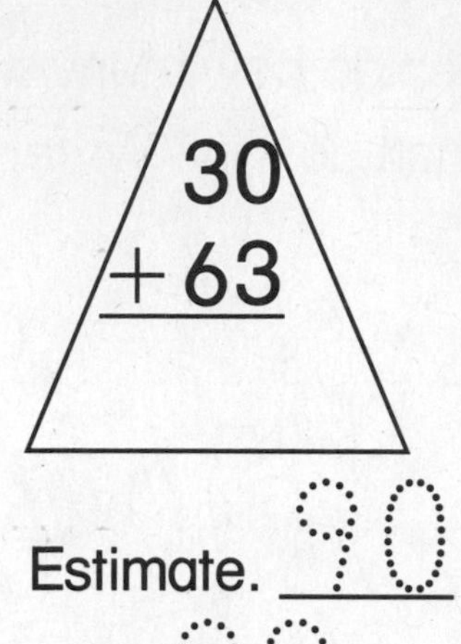

Estimate. 50 Sum 51

Estimate. 70 Sum 72

Estimate. 90 Sum 93

Estimate the sums.

Draw a box around problems with sums a little over 50.

Draw a circle around problems with sums a little over 70.

Draw a triangle around problems with sums a little over 90.

Then solve. Write your sum inside the box, circle, or triangle.

$$\begin{array}{r} 10 \\ +\ 42 \\ \hline \end{array}$$ Estimate. ____

$$\begin{array}{r} 31 \\ +\ 61 \\ \hline \end{array}$$ Estimate. ____

$$\begin{array}{r} 31 \\ +\ 62 \\ \hline \end{array}$$ Estimate. ____

$$\begin{array}{r} 13 \\ +\ 41 \\ \hline \end{array}$$ Estimate. ____

$$\begin{array}{r} 27 \\ +\ 50 \\ \hline \end{array}$$ Estimate. ____

$$\begin{array}{r} 20 \\ +\ 51 \\ \hline \end{array}$$ Estimate. ____

Notes for Home Your child used his or her understanding of estimation to find the sums of problems.
Home Activity: Ask your child to estimate the answer to these problems: 42 + 31 and 73 + 21. (70 and 90)

Name ______________________________

Critical Thinking

Find the one that does not belong.
Cross it out.

3 tens 5 ones	35	2 tens 15 ones	twenty-five

54	5 tens 4 ones	4 tens 14 ones	4 tens 15 ones

1 ten 16 ones	sixteen	2 tens 6 ones	26

7 tens 18 ones	seventy-eight	78	7 tens 8 ones

forty-nine	4 tens 19 ones	49	4 tens 9 ones

Notes for Home Your child recognized different ways of naming the same number and crossed out the name that did not belong in each row. *Home Activity*: Ask your child to write the number 53 in 3 different ways. (fifty-three, 53, five tens and 3 ones, or 4 tens and 13 ones)

Name ______________________

Extend Your Thinking
9-5

Critical Thinking

Decide if you need to trade.
Look at the ones in each problem.
Draw a box around the larger number.

If the box is here, a trade is needed. ➔

$$\begin{array}{r} \overset{6}{\cancel{7}}\overset{13}{\cancel{3}} \\ -\ 2\boxed{8} \\ \hline 45 \end{array}$$

If the box is here, a trade is not needed. ➔

$$\begin{array}{r} 6\boxed{7} \\ -\ 24 \\ \hline 43 \end{array}$$

Circle **Trade** or **No Trade**. Solve!

1. $\begin{array}{r} 63 \\ -\ 57 \\ \hline \end{array}$ Trade No Trade

2. $\begin{array}{r} 45 \\ -\ 14 \\ \hline \end{array}$ Trade No Trade

3. $\begin{array}{r} 92 \\ -\ 36 \\ \hline \end{array}$ Trade No Trade

4. $\begin{array}{r} 88 \\ -\ 57 \\ \hline \end{array}$ Trade No Trade

5. $\begin{array}{r} 45 \\ -\ 29 \\ \hline \end{array}$ Trade No Trade

6. $\begin{array}{r} 51 \\ -\ 24 \\ \hline \end{array}$ Trade No Trade

7. $\begin{array}{r} 99 \\ -\ 72 \\ \hline \end{array}$ Trade No Trade

8. $\begin{array}{r} 40 \\ -\ 21 \\ \hline \end{array}$ Trade No Trade

Notes for Home Your child identified and compared the numbers in the ones place of subtraction problems, and marked when regrouping (or a trade) is needed. *Home Activity*: Ask your child to explain why a trade is needed when the second amount of ones is larger than the first amount of ones.

Name ______________________

Extend Your Thinking
9-6

Patterns in Numbers

Each row follows a rule.

Use the rule to find the next 3 numbers.

Rule −6 94 88 82 76 70 64

$$\begin{array}{r}94\\-6\\\hline 88\end{array}\quad\begin{array}{r}88\\-6\\\hline 82\end{array}\quad\begin{array}{r}82\\-6\\\hline 76\end{array}\quad\begin{array}{r}76\\-6\\\hline 70\end{array}\quad\begin{array}{r}70\\-6\\\hline 64\end{array}$$

Rule −7 86 79 72 ____ ____ ____

$$\begin{array}{r}86\\-7\\\hline 79\end{array}\quad\begin{array}{r}79\\-7\\\hline 72\end{array}\quad\begin{array}{r}72\\-7\\\hline \end{array}\quad\begin{array}{r}\square\\-7\\\hline \end{array}\quad\begin{array}{r}\square\\-7\\\hline \end{array}$$

Rule −9 99 90 81 ____ ____ ____

$$\begin{array}{r}99\\-9\\\hline 90\end{array}\quad\begin{array}{r}90\\-9\\\hline 81\end{array}\quad\begin{array}{r}81\\-9\\\hline \end{array}\quad\begin{array}{r}\square\\-9\\\hline \end{array}\quad\begin{array}{r}\square\\-9\\\hline \end{array}$$

Notes for Home Your child applied a rule in each row, subtracting a one-digit number from a two-digit number to find the next 3 numbers in the pattern. *Home Activity*: Ask your child to explain when he or she should make a trade of one ten for 10 ones. (when the number being subtracted has a greater ones digit than the other number)

Name ______________________________

Decision Making

Extend Your Thinking 9-7

Suppose you are in art class and you are asked to design a class flag.
You only can put between 15 and 25 items on your flag.
You can take no more than 9 items from any pack.
Write how many things are left in each pack.

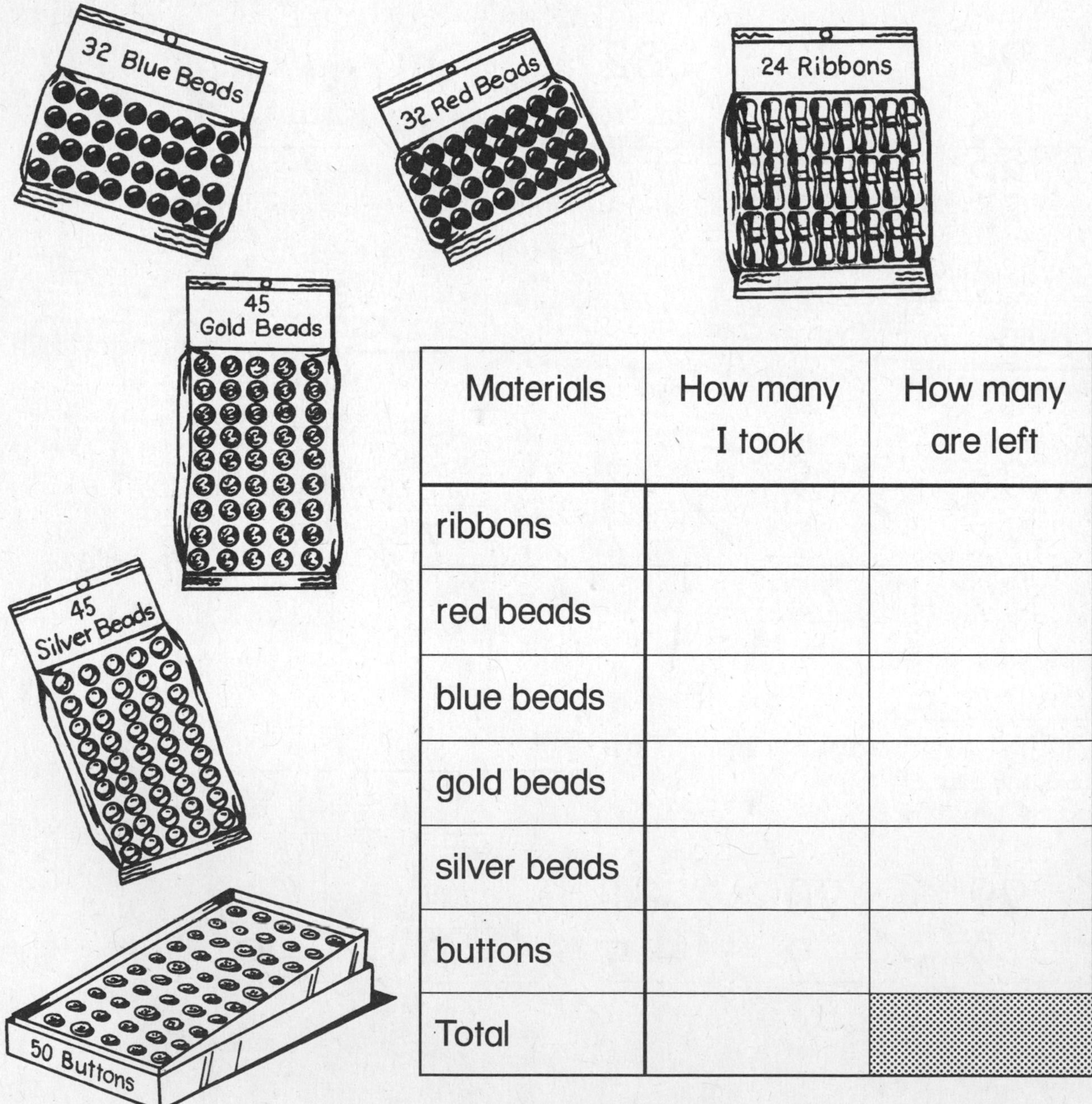

Materials	How many I took	How many are left
ribbons		
red beads		
blue beads		
gold beads		
silver beads		
buttons		
Total		

Notes for Home Your child selected materials and did subtraction involving trades of tens for ten ones to find how many materials were left. *Home Activity*: Using buttons or other small objects, ask your child to take a handful, count them aloud, take out 7, subtract to find how many are left, and then recount to check.

Name ______________________________

Extend Your Thinking
9-8

Critical Thinking

How many letters are in the alphabet?

To answer this riddle, first subtract. Then use the code below.

74	50	44	72	72
− 39	− 20	− 8	− 63	− 29
35				

61	91	89	95
− 46	− 17	− 77	− 56

Code:	1 A	3 E	5 L	7 P	9 T
	2 B	4 H	6 N	8 S	0 V

Copy your answers in order in the top boxes. Write the letters below.

3	5							
						—	-	-

-	-	-	-	-	-	-	

Notes for Home Your child solved subtraction problems involving trading tens for ones to find the coded answer to a riddle. *Home Activity*: Ask your child to identify the problems that involve trades. (74 – 39, 44 – 8, 72 – 63, 72 – 29, 61 – 46, 91 – 17, 95 – 56)

Name ____________________

Extend Your Thinking 9-9

Patterns in Numbers

Which rule do the numbers on the trucks follow?

Draw a box around the rule.

Write the next number in the pattern.

Work Area

Rule: −14 −16 −18

Rule: −23 −25 −27

Rule: −15 −19 −28

Rule: −17 −23 −27

Rule: −9 −16 −21

Notes for Home Your child identified the rule applied to each step in a pattern and provided the next step in each subtraction pattern. *Home Activity*: Ask your child to explain one of the patterns to you.

 Use with pages 335–336.

Name ____________________

Extend Your Thinking
9-10

Visual Thinking

If you need to trade 1 ten for 10 ones, color the square red.

If you don't need to trade, do not color the square.

The colored squares will answer the riddle.

Which 2 letters scare teeth the most? __________

50 − 9	42 − 3	29 − 20	62 − 21	30 − 7	77 − 30	69 − 20	23 − 5
60 − 3	41 − 30	50 − 4	34 − 10	20 − 19	82 − 41	74 − 58	94 − 50
45 − 26	67 − 30	70 − 35	93 − 40	63 − 27	90 − 38	68 − 40	45 − 20
30 − 14	58 − 20	80 − 38	63 − 12	40 − 14	29 − 10	85 − 47	79 − 53
96 − 69	30 − 17	36 − 20	75 − 30	60 − 39	96 − 24	41 − 10	80 − 54

Notes for Home Your child decided when it was necessary to trade 10 ones for 1 ten to solve subtraction problems, especially those involving zero. *Home Activity*: Ask your child which is easier to solve and why: 47 − 20 or 40 − 27.

Name ________________________________

Extend Your Thinking 9-11

Critical Thinking

Which addition problem helps you check your subtraction?

Solve the subtraction problems.

Solve the addition problems.

Then match each subtraction problem with an addition problem.

36 − 17	66 − 29	71 − 37	65 − 48	93 − 64

34 + 37	29 + 64	17 + 48	19 + 17	37 + 29

Write a subtraction problem of your own. Then write the addition problem you used to check the subtraction problem.

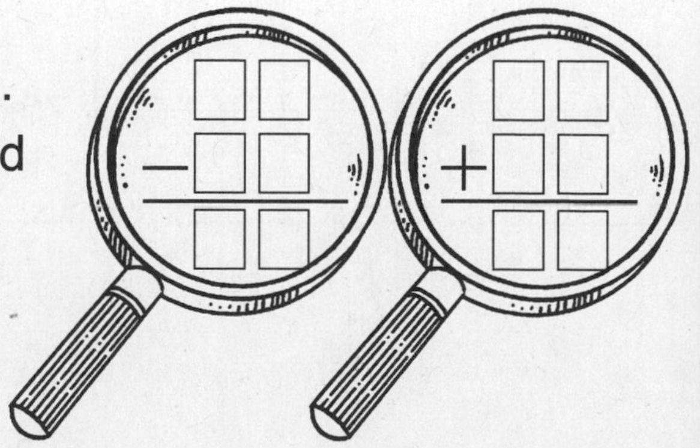

Notes for Home Your child subtracted 2 two-digit numbers and then identified the addition problem that could be used to check the subtraction. *Home Activity*: Show your child how you use addition to check subtraction in everyday life, such as when you check your subtraction in a checkbook.

Name ______________________________

Extend Your Thinking 9-12

Critical Thinking

Sometimes you have to add and subtract to find the answer to a problem. Circle the steps you need to find each answer. Then find the answer.

1. Martin has a quarter and 2 dimes. He buys a pen for 39¢.

   How much change does he get? ______

   $\begin{array}{r} 25¢ \\ +\ 39¢ \\ \hline 64¢ \end{array}$ $\begin{array}{r} 25¢ \\ +\ 20¢ \\ \hline 45¢ \end{array}$ $\begin{array}{r} 39¢ \\ -\ 25¢ \\ \hline 14¢ \end{array}$ $\begin{array}{r} 45¢ \\ -\ 39¢ \\ \hline 6¢ \end{array}$

2. Pencils cost 10¢ each or 3 for a quarter. If you have 40¢,

   how many pencils can you buy? ______

   $\begin{array}{r} 10¢ \\ +\ 40¢ \\ \hline 50¢ \end{array}$ $\begin{array}{r} 40¢ \\ -\ 25¢ \\ \hline 15¢ \end{array}$ $\begin{array}{r} 40¢ \\ -\ 38¢ \\ \hline 2¢ \end{array}$ $\begin{array}{r} 15¢ \\ -\ 10¢ \\ \hline 5¢ \end{array}$ $\begin{array}{r} 3 \\ +\ 1 \\ \hline 4 \end{array}$

3. A small notepad is 43¢. A large one is 75¢. Which costs more,

   2 small pads or 1 large pad? By how much? ______________

   $\begin{array}{r} 43¢ \\ +\ 2¢ \\ \hline 45¢ \end{array}$ $\begin{array}{r} 43¢ \\ +\ 43¢ \\ \hline 86¢ \end{array}$ $\begin{array}{r} 75¢ \\ -\ 45¢ \\ \hline 30¢ \end{array}$ $\begin{array}{r} 86¢ \\ -\ 75¢ \\ \hline 11¢ \end{array}$ $\begin{array}{r} 43¢ \\ -\ 1¢ \\ \hline 42¢ \end{array}$

Notes for Home Your child identified addition and subtraction problems that are part of multi-step story problems, and answered the problems. *Home Activity*: Ask your child to explain his or her reasoning.

Name ______________________________

Visual Thinking

Circle the facts that you use.

Cross off the facts you do not use.

Solve the problems about some of the items in this grocery ad.

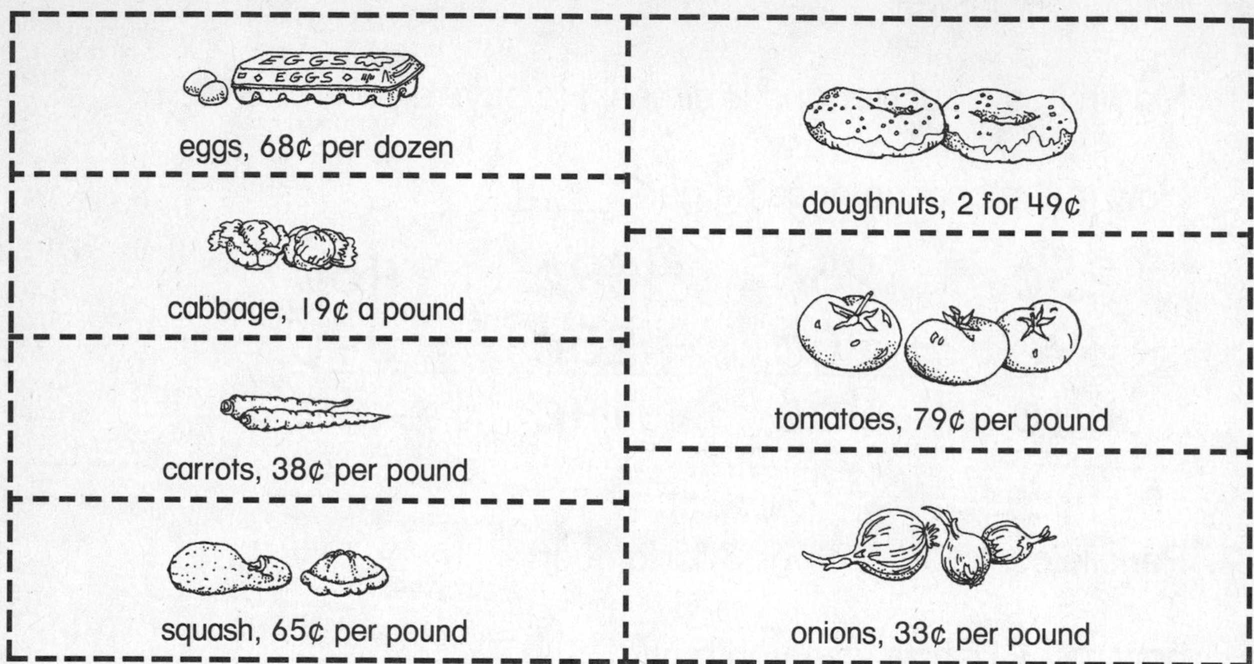

1. Katie has 3 quarters. She buys a dozen eggs. How much change does she get? ______
2. Steve has 90¢. Can he buy 4 doughnuts? ______
3. How much more does one pound of squash cost than one pound of carrots? ______
4. Anna has 95¢. She buys a pound each of carrots and onions. How much change does she get? ______

Notes for Home Your child identified details given in an ad that were relevant to story problems and crossed off unneeded information. *Home Activity*: Ask your child to find and compare the number of calories listed on two different cereal boxes.

Name ___________________________

Extend Your Thinking 10-1

Visual Thinking

Count the items in each set.

Circle each group of 100. Cross out extra items.

If a set has less than 100, draw enough to fill it with 100.

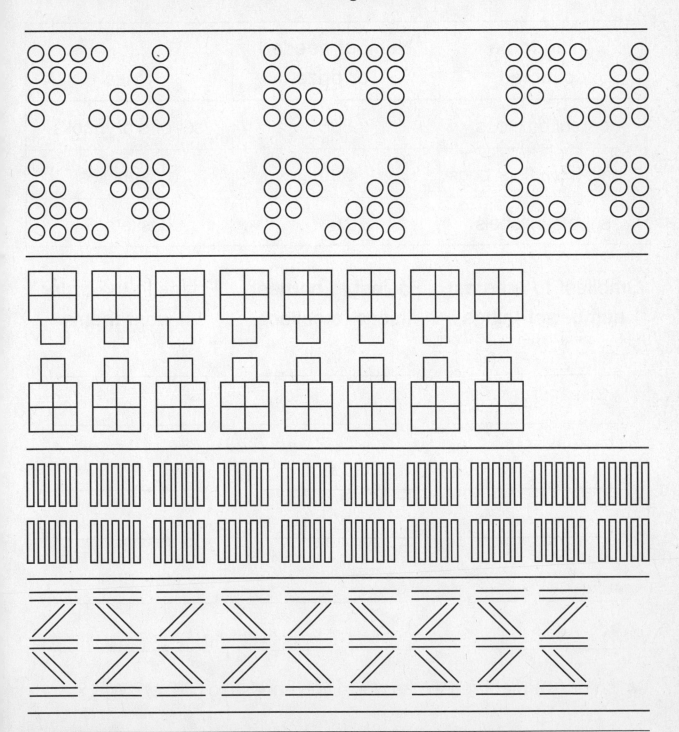

Notes for Home Your child identified or completed pictures of groups of 100. *Home Activity:* Ask your child to name items in your home which may number 100, such as pins, paper clips, rubber bands.

Name ______________________________

Decision Making

Suppose you can get prizes for your school by collecting these things. Fill in the lists and answer the question below.

Thing to be collected	Number needed for prize	Prize
cereal box tops	800	set of storybooks
labels from flour bags	500	art supplies
soup can labels	700	basketball

Smallest to greatest number of things	Easiest to hardest things to collect	Prizes in the order I want them
flour bag labels	______	______
______	______	______
______	______	______
______	______	______

Which one of the three things would you choose to collect? Why?

Notes for Home Your child listed 3 items in 3 different orders: from smallest to greatest quantities, from most available to least available, and from most desired personally to least desired. *Home Activity:* Ask your child to explain his or her reasons for the order in column 2 and in column 3.

Name ______________________________

Extend Your Thinking
10-3

Visual Thinking

Help Kate get to Grandma's house.

Draw a line to show her the way.

Count how many hundreds, tens, and ones she passed.

______ hundreds ______ tens ______ ones

Now write the number that says the same amount. ____________

Notes for Home Your child drew a path through a maze and counted hundred, tens, and ones that were passed. *Home Activity:* Ask your child to open a book with more than one hundred pages at random, read the page number, and then tell how many hundreds, tens, and ones that number represents.

Name ______________________________

Critical Thinking

Five pets came with their owners to a hotel.
Use the clues to match the animals with their room numbers.
Draw a line from each door to the correct animal.

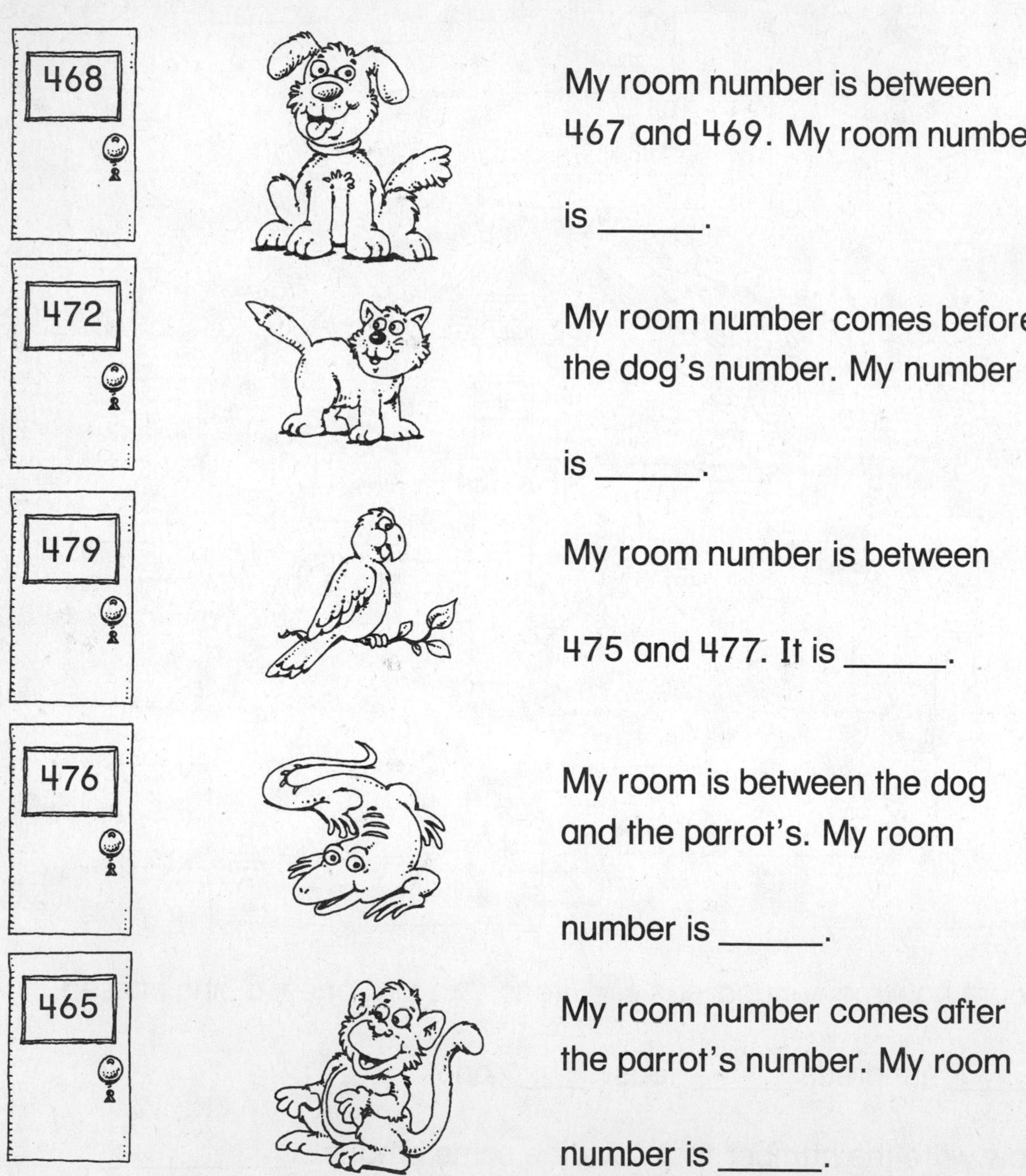

My room number is between 467 and 469. My room number is ______.

My room number comes before the dog's number. My number is ______.

My room number is between 475 and 477. It is ______.

My room is between the dog and the parrot's. My room number is ______.

My room number comes after the parrot's number. My room number is ______.

Notes for Home Your child used logical thinking to identify 3-digit numbers *before*, *after*, and *between* other 3-digit numbers. *Home Activity:* Ask your child to identify the number that comes just before 465 (464), the number that comes just after 479 (480), and the even number that comes between 476 and 479 (478).

Name ______________________________

Extend Your Thinking
10-5

Critical Thinking

These charts show how much skating 3 children did in 2 months.
Each skate stands for skating around the rink 20 times.

Skater	Times around the rink in January
Lois	
Max	
Anna	

Skater	Times around the rink in February
Lois	
Max	
Anna	

How many times did each skater go around the rink in January?

Lois ____________ Max ____________ Anna____________

How many times did each skater go around in February?

Lois ____________ Max ____________ Anna____________

How many times did each skater go around in both months?

Lois ____________ Max ____________ Anna____________

Notes for Home Your child used symbols on a chart to identify how many times each child skated around the rink each month. *Home Activity:* Ask your child to find which skater had the best and worst record in each month. (January: Best-Anna, Worst-Lois; February; Best-Max, Worst-Lois)

Name ______________________________

Extend Your Thinking
10-6

Visual Thinking

Find the answer to this riddle.

Count by 100s to complete the dot-to-dot puzzle.

Riddle:

I am full when I am away, and I am empty when I am home.

What am I?

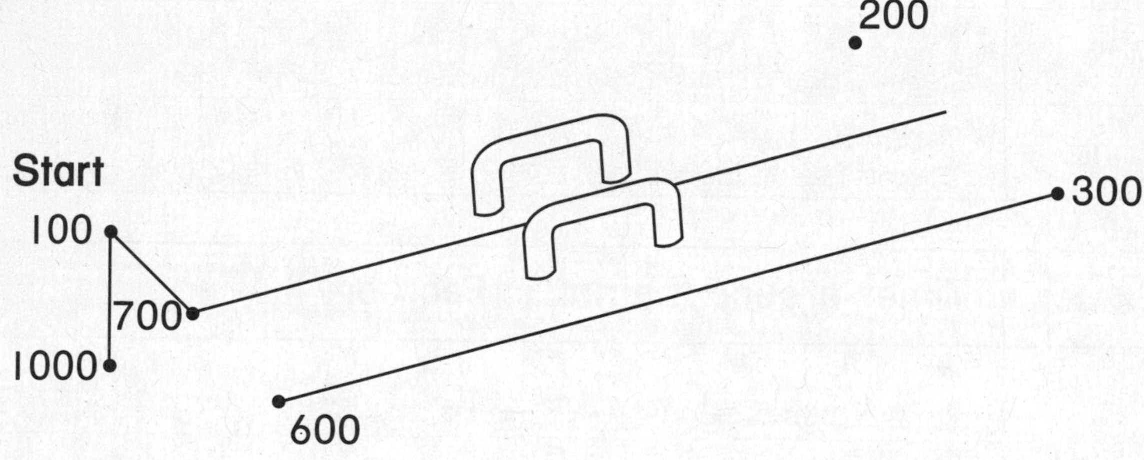

400

900

800

500

I am ______________________________

Notes for Home Your child answered a riddle by completing a dot-to-dot puzzle with 3-digit numbers.
Home Activity: Ask your child to count by 100s from 200 to 700. (200, 300, 400, 500, 600, 700)

Name ______________________________

Critical Thinking

In each row, cross out any number that does NOT belong in the box at the left.

☐ > 145	322	158	147	139
☐ < 577	575	579	534	641
☐ > 399	400	407	388	436
426 > ☐	423	462	421	384
912 < ☐	914	917	911	918

Notes for Home Your child used the symbols for greater than (>) and less than (<) to compare 3-digit numbers. *Home Activity:* Ask your child to write the symbol that shows the relationship between each of these pairs of numbers: 522 and 499 (>); 345 and 782 (<).

Name ________________________________

Patterns in Numbers

Each pattern is missing a number.
Find the number in the box.
Write it in the pattern.
Then cross out the number out in the box.

531	601	341	542	259

301 401 501 ________ 701

522 532 ________ 552 562

253 256 ________ 262 265

941 741 541 ________ 141

631 ________ 431 331 231

Notes for Home Your child recognized patterns involving 3-digit numbers and chose numbers to complete the patterns. *Home Activity:* Ask your child to choose a pattern and extend it with 2 more numbers.

Name ______________________________

Extend Your Thinking
10-9

Decision Making

Each time you visit King Park, you stop at only 2 places.
Where would you go on your first 2 visits?
Draw 2 paths from the gate. Each path may go to 2 places.

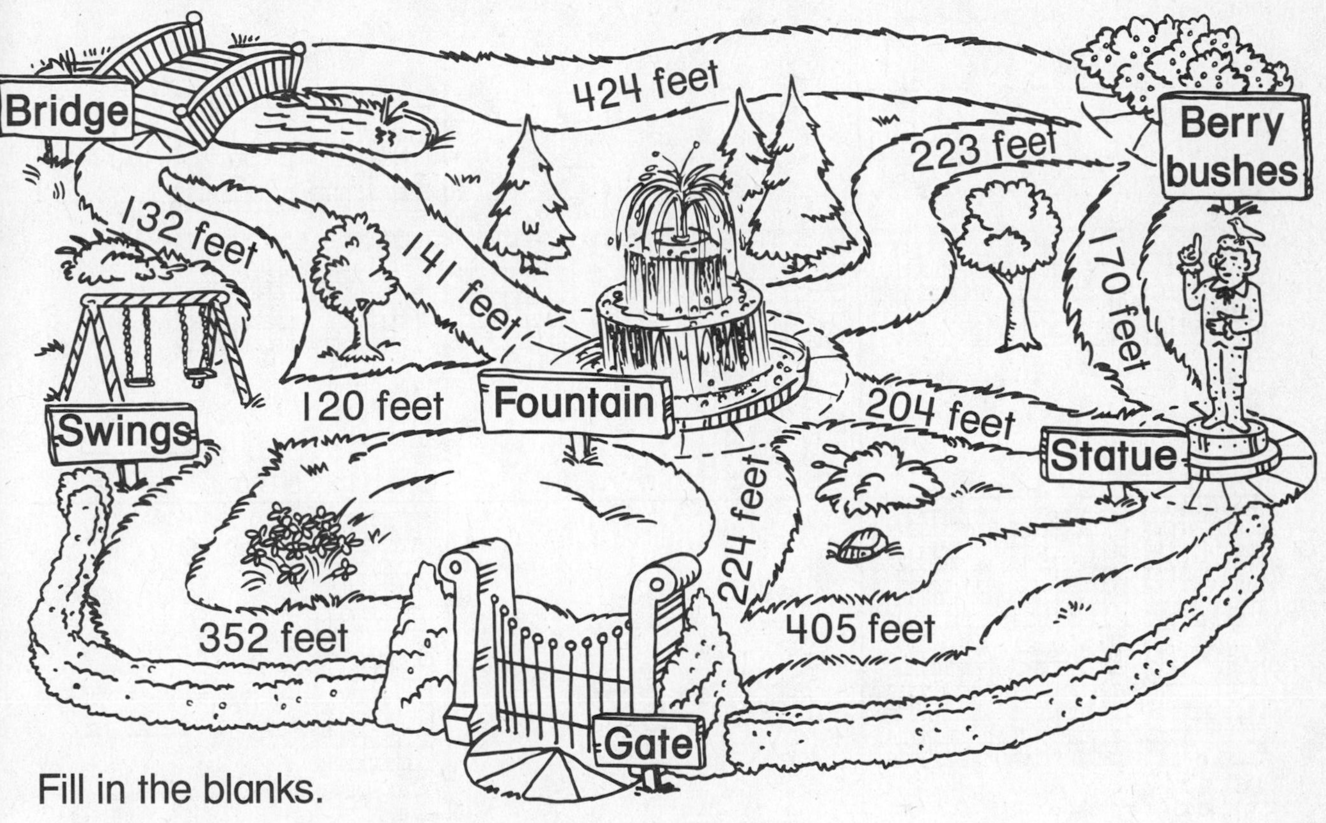

Fill in the blanks.

1. I went from the gate to the __________ (_____ feet)

   and from there to the __________ (_____ feet)

   for a total distance of _____ feet.

2. I went from the gate to the __________ (_____ feet)

   and from there to the __________ (_____ feet)

   for a total distance of _____ feet.

Notes for Home Your child chose two places to visit in the park and figured the total distances between the gate and both places. *Home Activity:* Ask your child to choose a third place to visit and draw a path.

Name ______________________________

Visual Thinking

Play Tic-Tac-Add. First, write the numbers.
Then draw a line to connect the two numbers that show the sum given in the center.

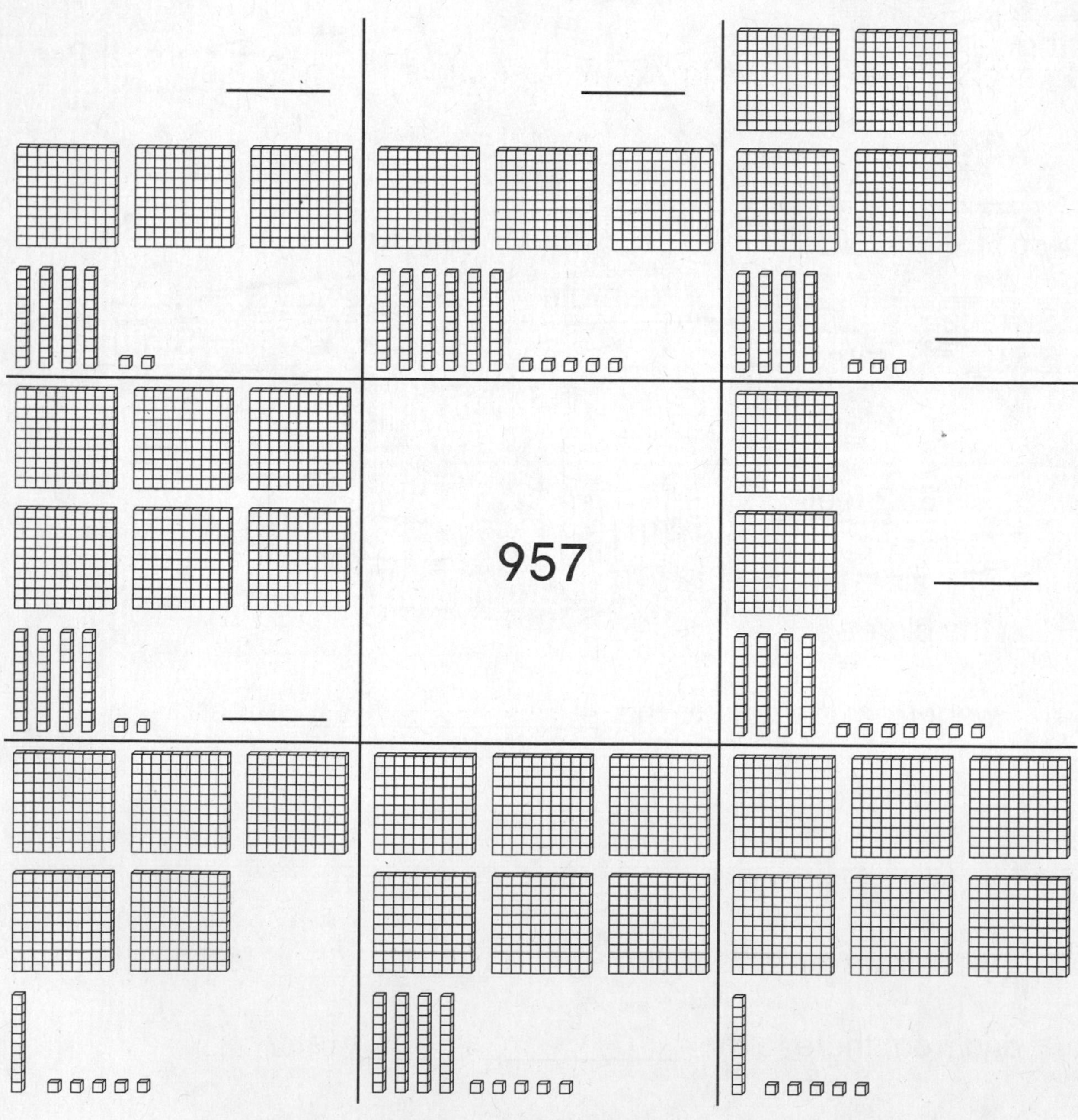

Notes for Home Your child identified pictures that represent the given amounts being added by drawing lines between the pictures. *Home Activity:* Ask your child to select two other pictures on this game and write the addition problem that results from adding those amounts.

Name ______________________________

Extend Your Thinking
10-11

Decision Making

A mosaic is made of small stones or tiles pasted in a pattern.
On the grid, show a mosaic you would make with these tiles.

 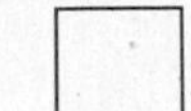  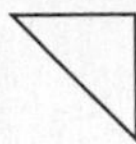

In each space, use tiles in any of these ways:

 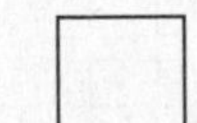    

1 square—black or white OR 2 triangles—black and white

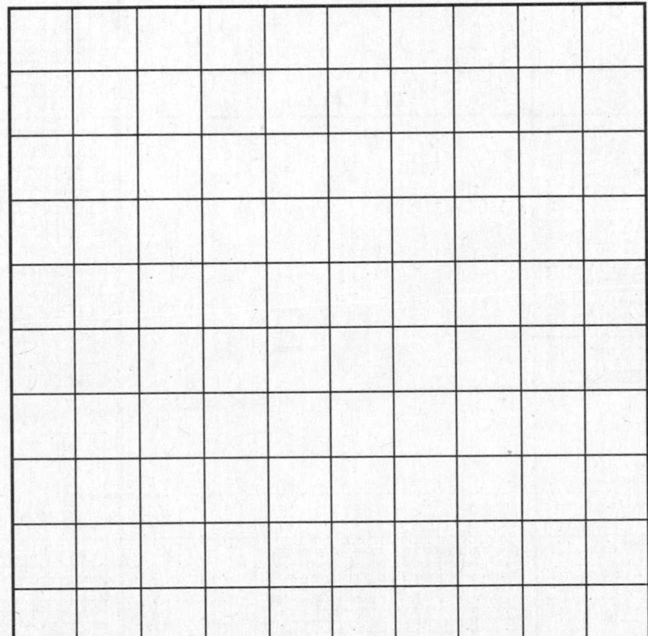

How many tiles does your pattern use?

black squares ______ black triangles ______

white squares ______ white triangles ______

Notes for Home Your child created a pattern using square and triangular tiles and counted the number of tiles needed for making a mosaic in the pattern. *Home Activity:* Help your child to count the total number of tiles needed for his or her design.

Name ______________________________

Visual Thinking

Extend Your Thinking 10-12

Play Tic-Tac- Subtract. First, write each number. Then draw a line to connect the two numbers that have their difference given in the center.

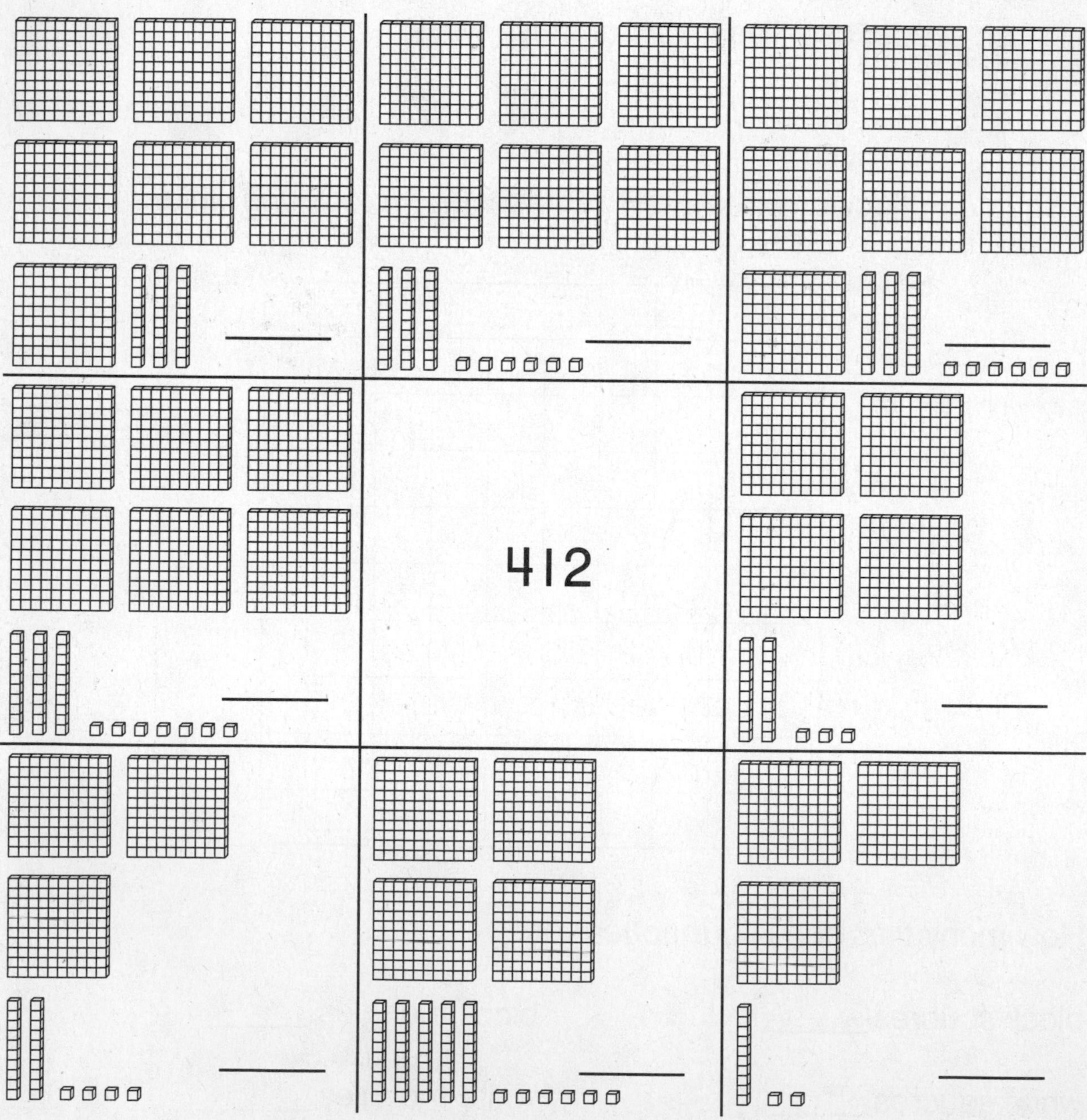

Notes for Home Your child identified pictures that represent the amounts being subtracted and the remainders by drawing lines between the pictures. *Home Activity:* Ask your child to select two other pictures on this game and change the center subtraction problem to show those amounts.

Name ______________________________

Extend Your Thinking
10-13

Critical Thinking

Kevin has 564 trading cards about sports.

Find the way to answer each problem about Kevin's cards.

Draw a line. Then answer the problem.

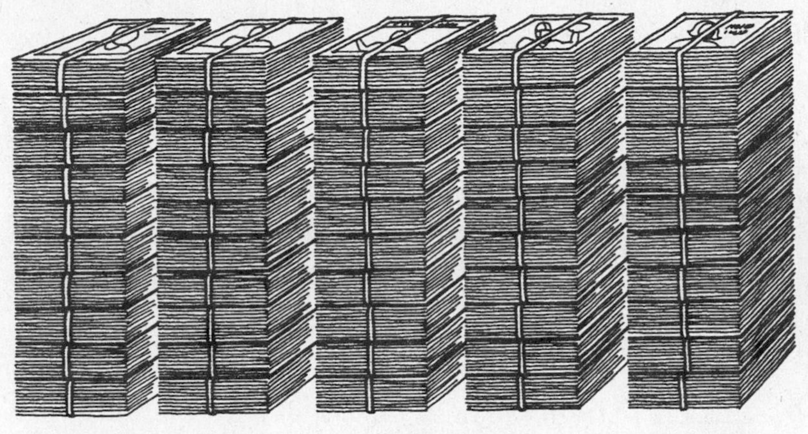
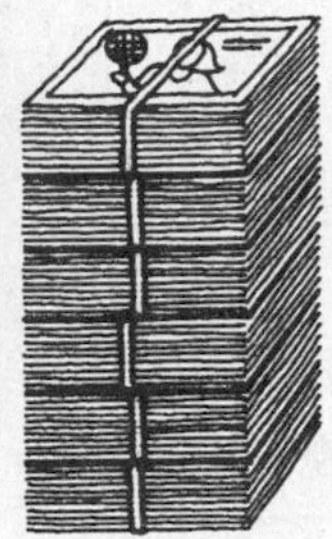

1. Kevin forgot 113 cards at his friend's house. How many did he remember to take home? __________ cards	564 − 450
2. Kevin would like to trade 232 of the cards. How many cards does he want to keep? __________ cards	564 − 113
3. Only 450 cards will fit in Kevin's box. How many will not fit in the box? __________ cards	564 − 232

Notes for Home Your child solved story problems requiring subtraction of two 3-digit numbers. *Home Activity:* Ask your child to make up a story problem about Kevin's trading cards and then have him or her show you how to solve the problem.

Name ______________________________

Visual Thinking

Use a pencil as a unit of measuring.
Call the measure a **pud**. The pencil is 1 pud long.

Look at your desk. Look at this paper.
Look at your arm, leg, and shoe.
How many times will your pud fit end-to-end along each length?

Measure

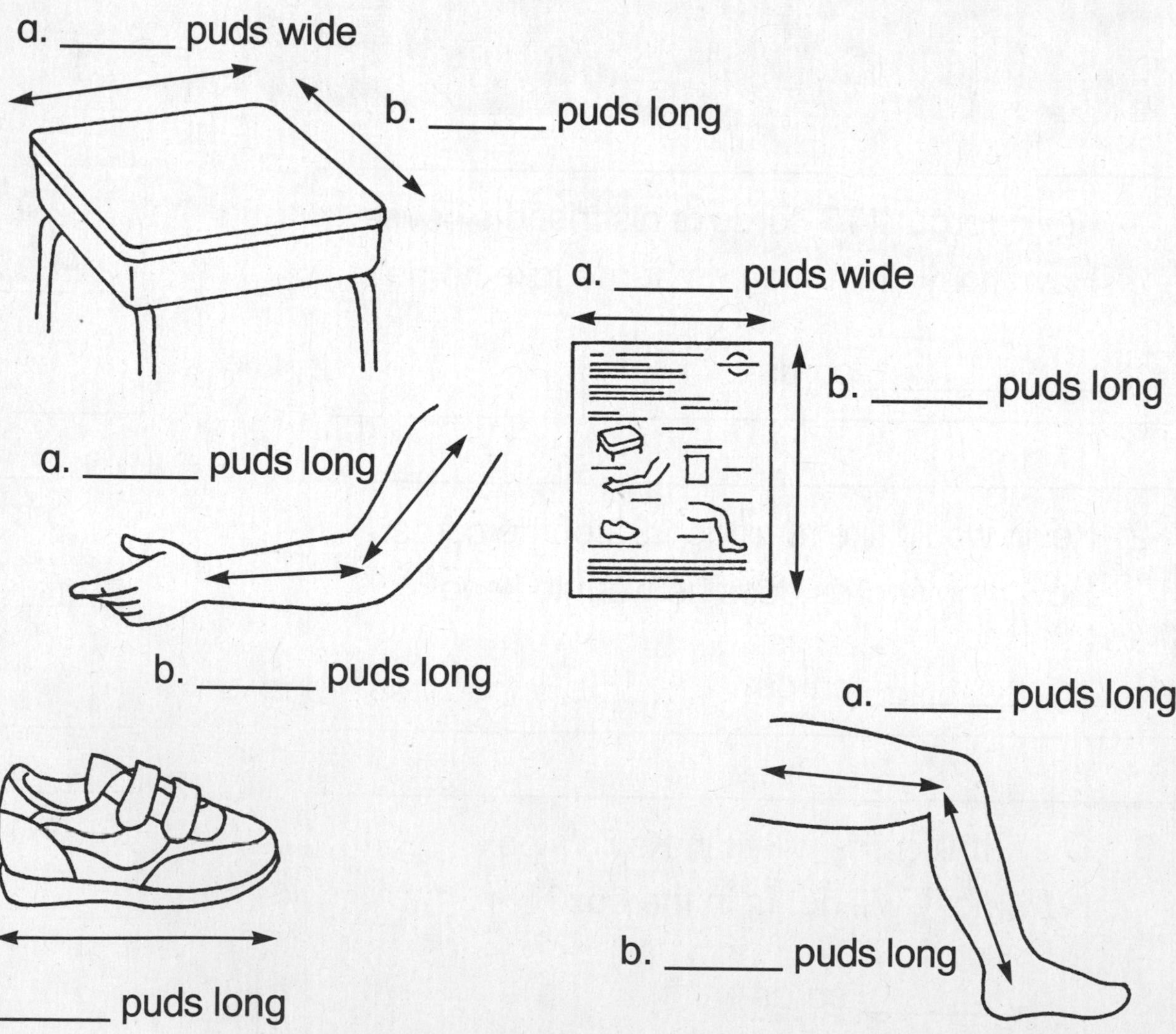

Notes for Home Your child used a pencil as a nonstandard unit of measurement to measure things. *Home Activity:* Ask your child to remeasure his or her arm, leg, and shoe with a different nonstandard unit of measure, such as a book, and compare the results.

Name ______________________________

Visual Thinking

How long is the path out of this maze? Guess.

_____ inches

Now draw the path. Use straight lines so you can measure.

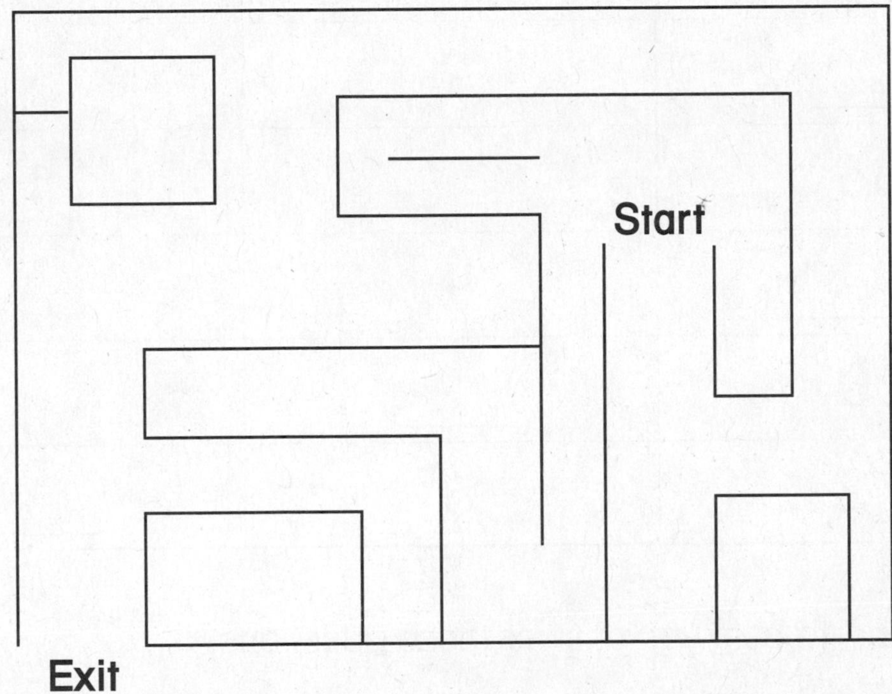

Then use a ruler to measure each part of the path.
Add the lengths together.
How long is the path? Put an X before the closest answer.

_____ 9 inches _____ 10 inches _____ 11 inches _____ 12 inches

How close to the answer was your guess? _____ inches
Try to draw a shorter path. Hint: Draw along inner walls and use diagonals. About how long is this path? _____ inches

Notes for Home Your child estimated the length of a path out of a maze, solved the maze, and used a ruler to determine the path's approximate length. *Home Activity:* Ask your child to use a ruler to measure the width and length of the maze to the nearest inch. (about 5 inches wide and about 3 inches tall)

Name ______________________________

Patterns in Data

Fill in the missing numbers in this chart.

Inches	Feet	Yards
12	1	
____	2	
36	____	1
____	4	
60	____	
72	6	____

Use the chart to help you answer these questions.

1. If a rug is 6 feet long, how many yards long is it? ______ yards
2. If a ribbon is 48 inches long, how many feet is it? ______ feet
3. If you jump 6 feet, how many inches did you jump? ______ inches
4. If a row of flowers is 60 inches long, how many feet is it? ______ feet
5. If a hole is 2 yards deep, how deep is it in inches? ______ inches
6. If a blanket is 84 inches long, how many feet is it? ______ feet

Notes for Home Your child figured out the pattern in a chart converting inches to feet and yards. *Home Activity:* Ask your child which is longer: 72 inches or 3 yards; 4 feet or 2 yards; 6 feet or 60 inches. (3 yards; 2 yards; 6 feet)

Name ______________________________

Critical Thinking

Andy has a string that is 15 centimeters long.

Circle the shapes that Andy can make with his string.

1 cm 2 cm 3 cm 4 cm 5 cm 6 cm 7 cm 8 cm 9 cm 10 cm 11 cm 12 cm 13 cm 14 cm

Notes for Home Your child identified shapes that could be created with a string that is 15 centimeters long. *Home Activity:* Ask your child to identify household items that are about 15 centimeters long.

Name ______________________________

Critical Thinking

Study the large figure.

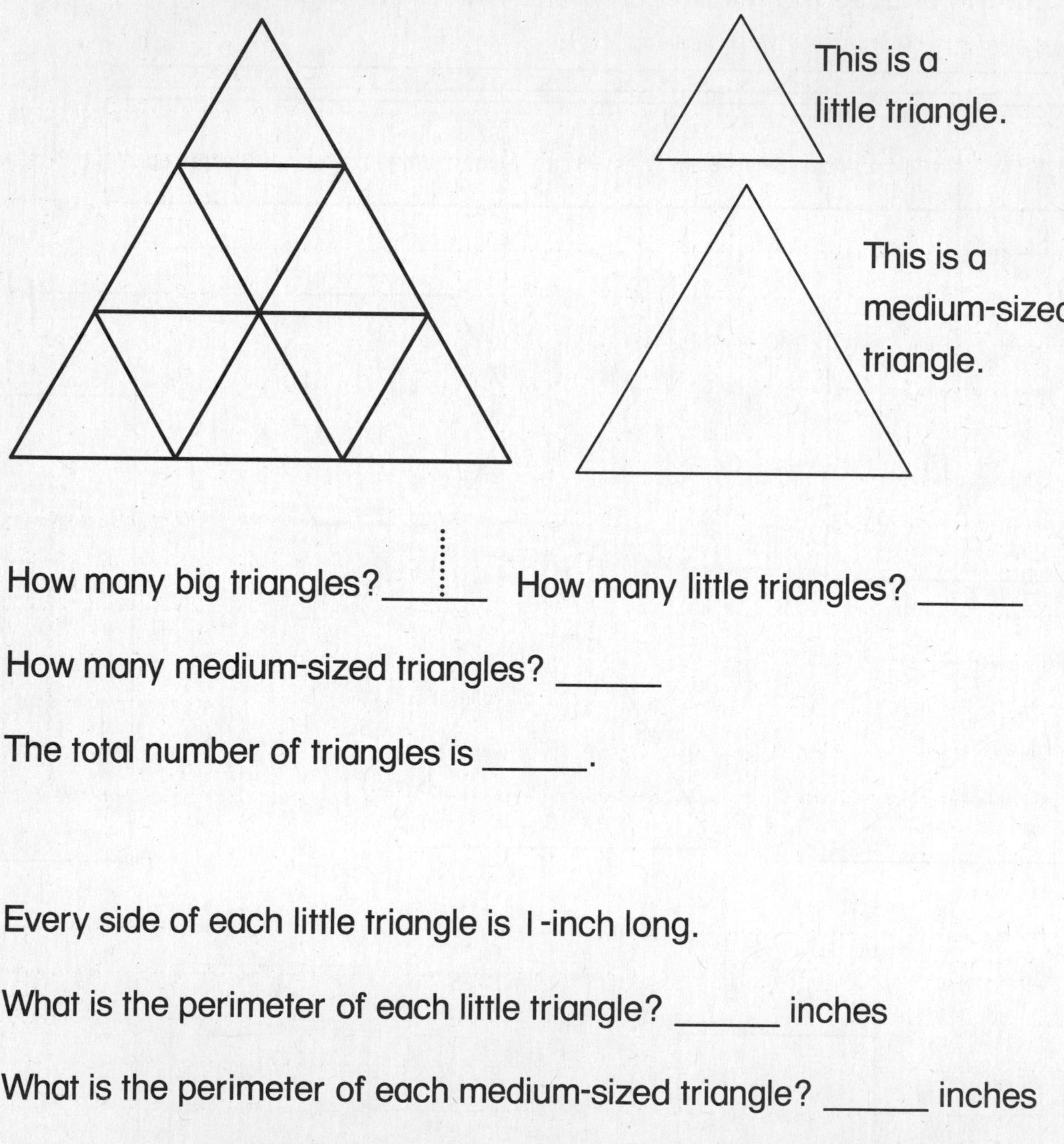
This is a
little triangle.
This is a
medium-sized
triangle.

How many big triangles? ______ How many little triangles? ______

How many medium-sized triangles? ______

The total number of triangles is ______.

Every side of each little triangle is 1-inch long.

What is the perimeter of each little triangle? ______ inches

What is the perimeter of each medium-sized triangle? ______ inches

What is the perimeter of the big triangle? ______ inches

Notes for Home Your child counted the number of triangles in a large triangle and, given the length of one side of a small triangle, found different perimeters. *Home Activity:* Ask your child to find the perimeter of a four-sided shape in the large triangle.

Name ______________________________

Extend Your Thinking 11-6

Visual Thinking

In each row, count the squares inside each shape.

Write **L** on the shape with the largest area.

Write **S** on the one with the smallest area.

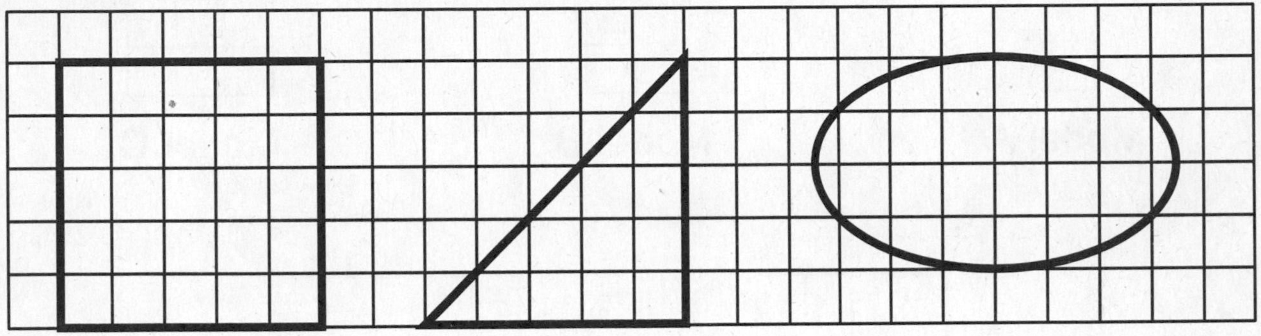

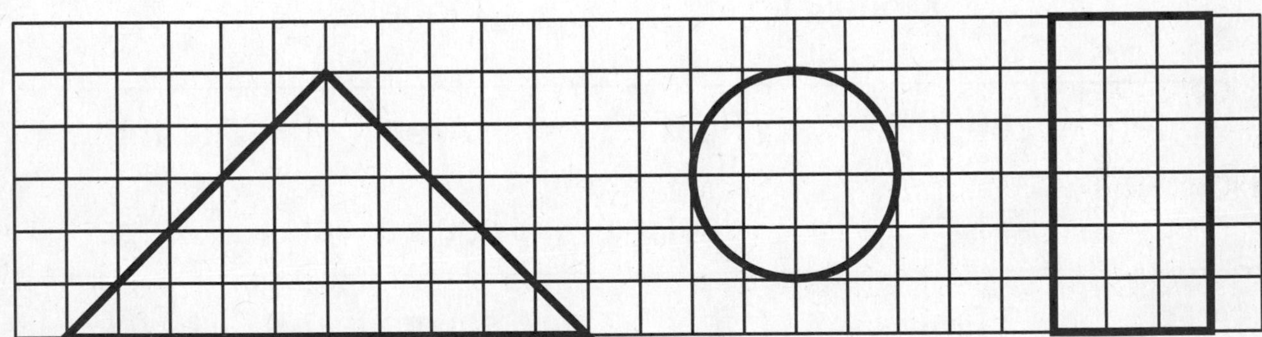

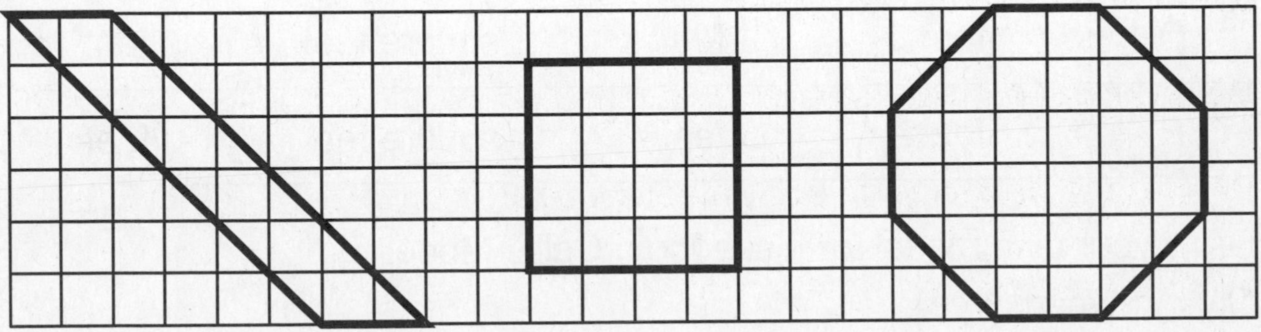

Notes for Home Your child counted square units within figures to compare their areas. *Home Activity:* Ask your child to draw a figure with an area of about 10 square units on one of the grids.

Name ______________________________

Patterns in Data

A company makes sandboxes.

Fill in the chart below to tell about some of this year's models.

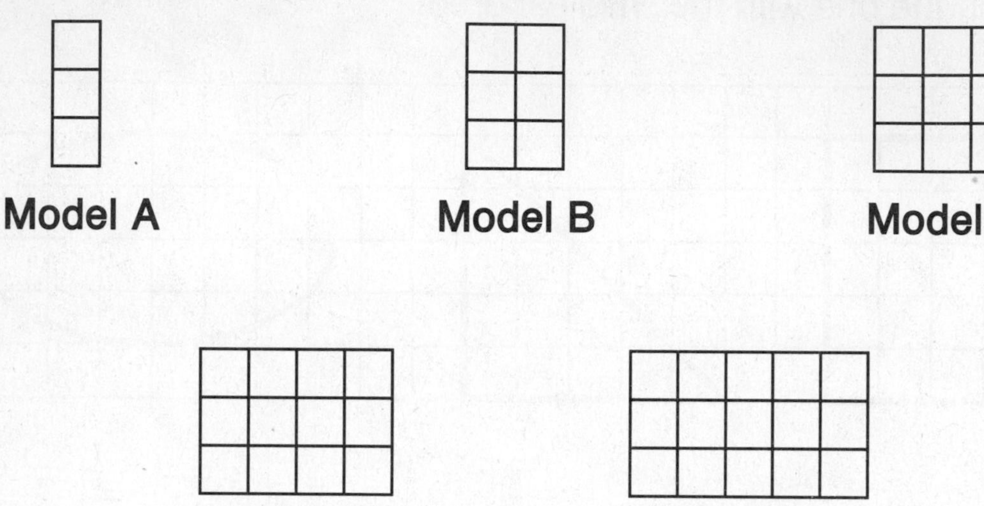

Model	Length	Width	Area	Perimeter
A	3 feet	1 feet	3 square feet	8 feet
B	3 feet	2 feet	6 square feet	10 feet
C	feet	3 feet	square feet	feet
D	feet	4 feet	square feet	feet
E	feet	5 feet	square feet	feet

Draw your own model for a sandbox. Call it Model F.

Give the measures.

Length ______ Width ______ Area ______ Perimeter ______

Notes for Home Your child completed a chart listing measurement data about a series of boxes, using diagrams as a guide. *Home Activity:* Ask your child to predict the dimensions of the next model in the series of boxes. (3 feet long, 6 feet wide, 18 square feet, 18 feet)

Name ______________________________

Extend Your Thinking
11-8

Visual Thinking

Each pair will get on the seesaw.

Who will be up?

Circle the animal or the person.

Notes for Home Your child estimated the weight of people and animals, and circled the one in each pair who weighs less. *Home Activity*: Ask your child to explain why the circled person or animal would rise to the top on the seesaw.

Name ______________________________

Extend Your Thinking
11-9

Critical Thinking

Draw lines to match each animal to its weight class.

K-O Caterpillar

Gray Squirrel

Featherweight—
less than 1 kilogram

Rocky Crocodile

Sam (a Ham) Pig

Kilo-weight—
about 1 kilogram

Junior Rabbit

Ice-C Canary

Heavyweight—
much more than 1
kilogram

Maxine Mouse

Babyface Kitten

Notes for Home Your child drew lines to match each pictured animal with its approximate weight—greater than, less than, or equal to 1 kilogram. *Home Activity:* Ask your child to identify an object that weighs about 1 kilogram. (1 kilogram equals about 2.2 pounds.)

Name ______________________________

Decision Making

For each punch recipe, write what you need for 2 batches of that punch. Use the chart at the right to help you.

Cups	Pints	Quarts
2	1	
4	2	1

Strawberry Spree

One batch — Amount needed for 2 batches

1 pint frozen strawberry yogurt — _____ pints or _____ quarts

2 cups milk — _____ cups or _____ pints or _____ quarts

1 cup whole strawberries — _____ cups or _____ pints

Mix in sliced strawberries. Blend yogurt and milk.

Double Raspberry Drink

One batch — Amount needed for 2 batches

1 cup of raspberries — _____ cups or _____ pints

1 quart lemonade — _____ cups or _____ pints or _____ quarts

3 cups raspberry juice — _____ cups or _____ pints

Blend raspberries, lemonade, and juice together.
Add ice cubes. Which punch would you make for a party? Why?

Notes for Home Your child doubled amounts in a recipe and chose containers holding those quantities.
Home Activity: Help your child make a drink from a mix or concentrate requiring cups or pints of water.

Name ___________________________

Extend Your Thinking 11-11

Visual Thinking

Find the 8 hidden objects.

Color the objects that can hold more than 1 liter red.

Color the objects that can only hold less than 1 liter green.

Hidden Objects			
cup	barrel	thimble	kitchen sink
glass	bucket	eye dropper	bathtub

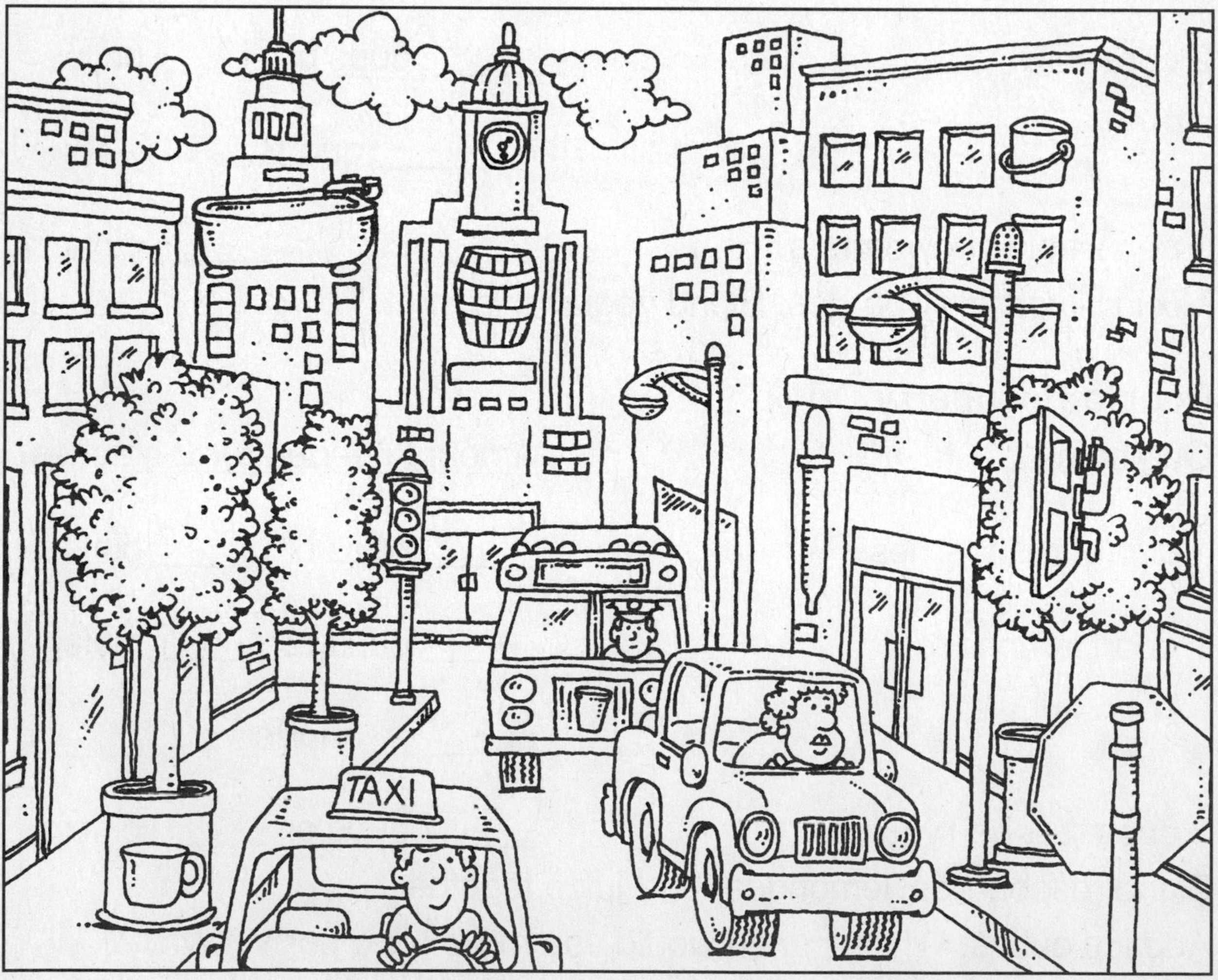

Notes for Home Your child found 8 objects hidden in a picture and estimated the capacity of those objects in comparison to 1 liter. *Home Activity:* Ask your child to look in your refrigerator and find one container that holds less than 1 liter and one that holds more than 1 liter.

Name ________________________________

Decision Making

Extend Your Thinking
11-12

You are making a box of gifts to send to a friend.

You want to send 5 gifts that weigh less than 1 pound each.

Cross out the ones that are too heavy.

Circle the 5 you would send.

Notes for Home Your child decided whether objects weighed more or less than 1 pound and chose 5 objects each weighing less than 1 pound to send to a friend. *Home Activity:* Ask your child to think of one more object weighing less than 1 pound that he or she would send to a friend.

Name ______________________________

Extend Your Thinking
11-13

Decision Making

Circle 2 things you would do at this temperature.

Draw a box around 2 things you would do at this temperature.

Notes for Home Your child read thermometers showing temperatures in Fahrenheit and Celsius scales and chose activities he or she would enjoy at each given temperature. *Home Activity:* Ask your child to watch a weather forecast on the television and decide whether the temperatures are given in degrees Fahrenheit or degrees Celsius.

 Use with pages 431–432.

Name ___________________________________

Extend Your Thinking
12-1

Visual Thinking

Follow the path through Solids Land.

Count the solids you pick up as you go.

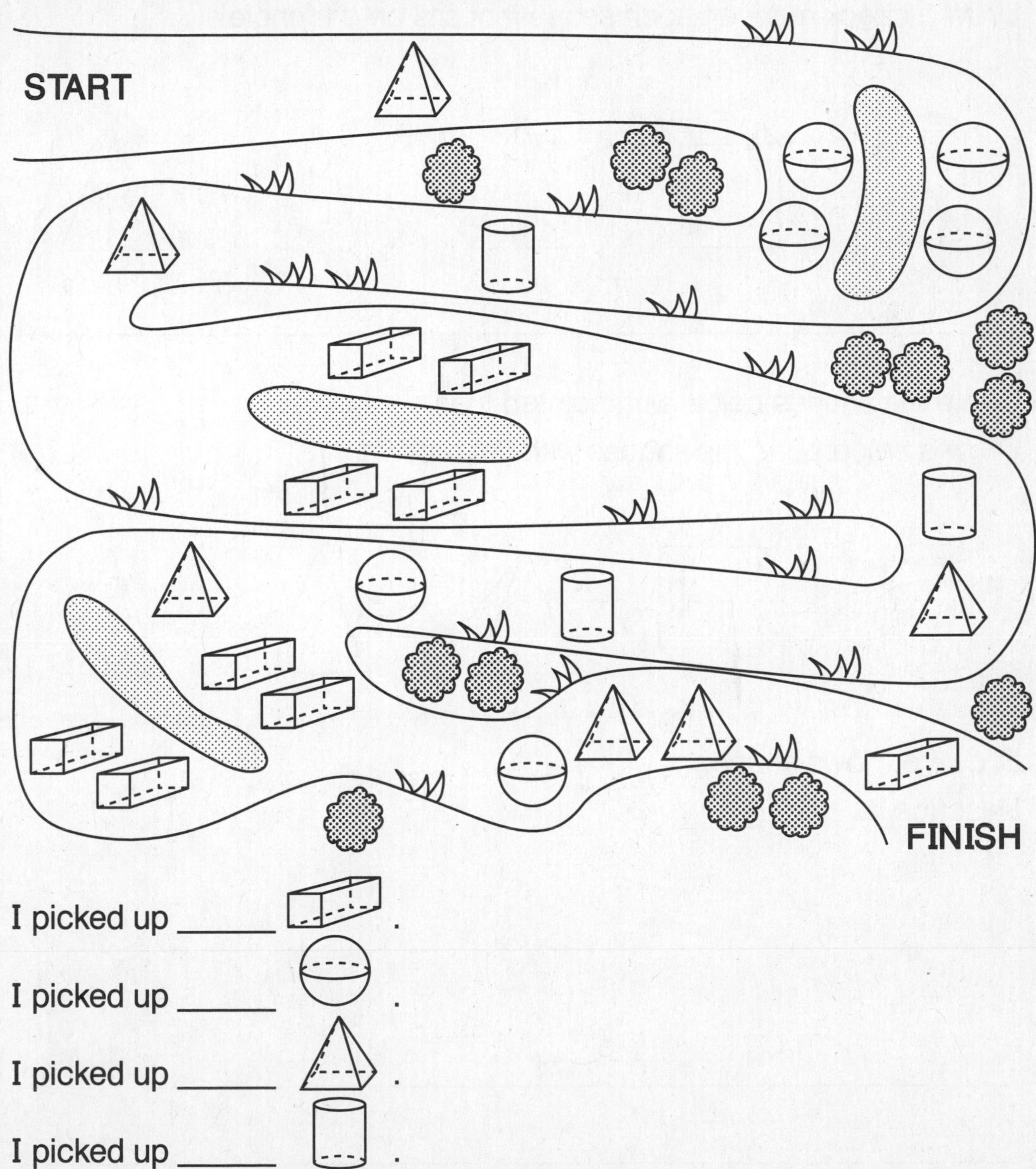

I picked up ______ [rectangular prism].

I picked up ______ [sphere].

I picked up ______ [pyramid].

I picked up ______ [cylinder].

Notes for Home Your child grouped the solid figures he or she encountered along the puzzle path and wrote the total number for each. *Home Activity:* Ask your child to name at least one food or object that is shaped like each solid, such as an ice cube, peas, ice cream cone, and a can.

Name ______________________________

Extend Your Thinking
12-2

Critical Thinking

Circle each shape that sits on a round base.

Draw a box around each shape with a 4-sided base.

Draw a check mark on each shape that sits on a triangle.

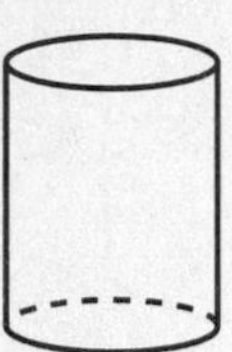 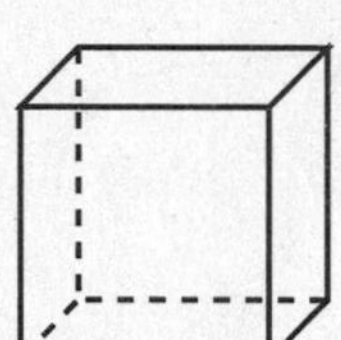 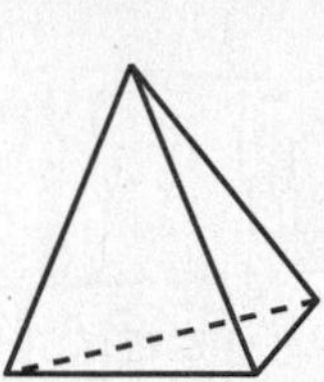 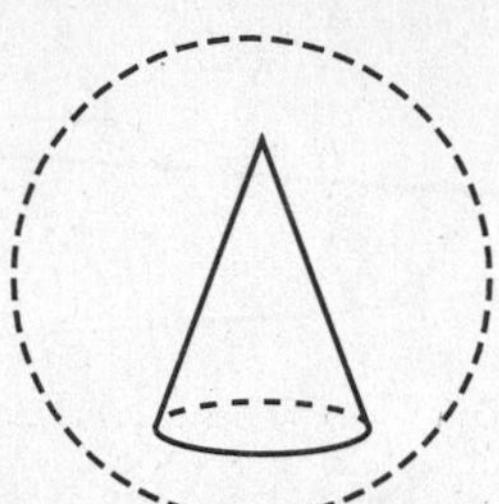 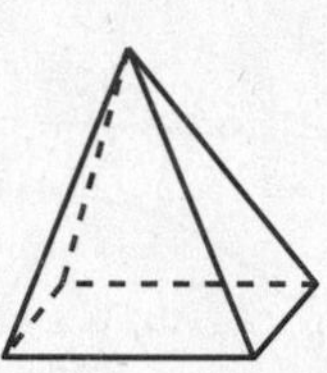

Circle the shapes below with pointed tops.

Draw a box around the shapes with flat tops.

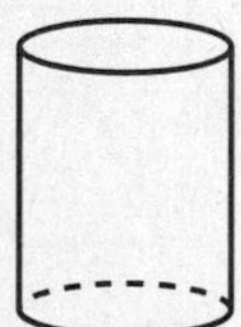 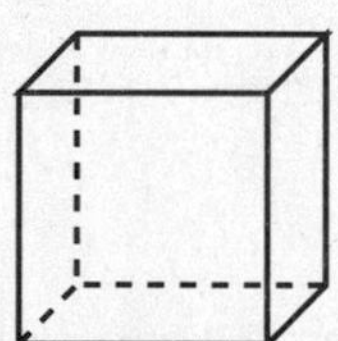 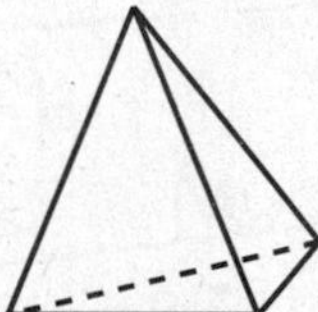  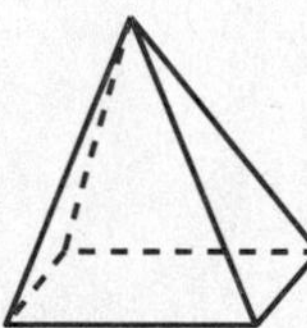

Draw your own shape.

Describe it.

____

____

Notes for Home Your child placed solid shapes in categories according to characteristics of their bases and tops. *Home Activity:* Ask your child to find household objects that have the same shapes as those pictured on this page.

Name ______________________________

Extend Your Thinking
12-3

Visual Thinking

What kind of key will never fit into a lock?

Color in every shape with 3 sides to find the answer.

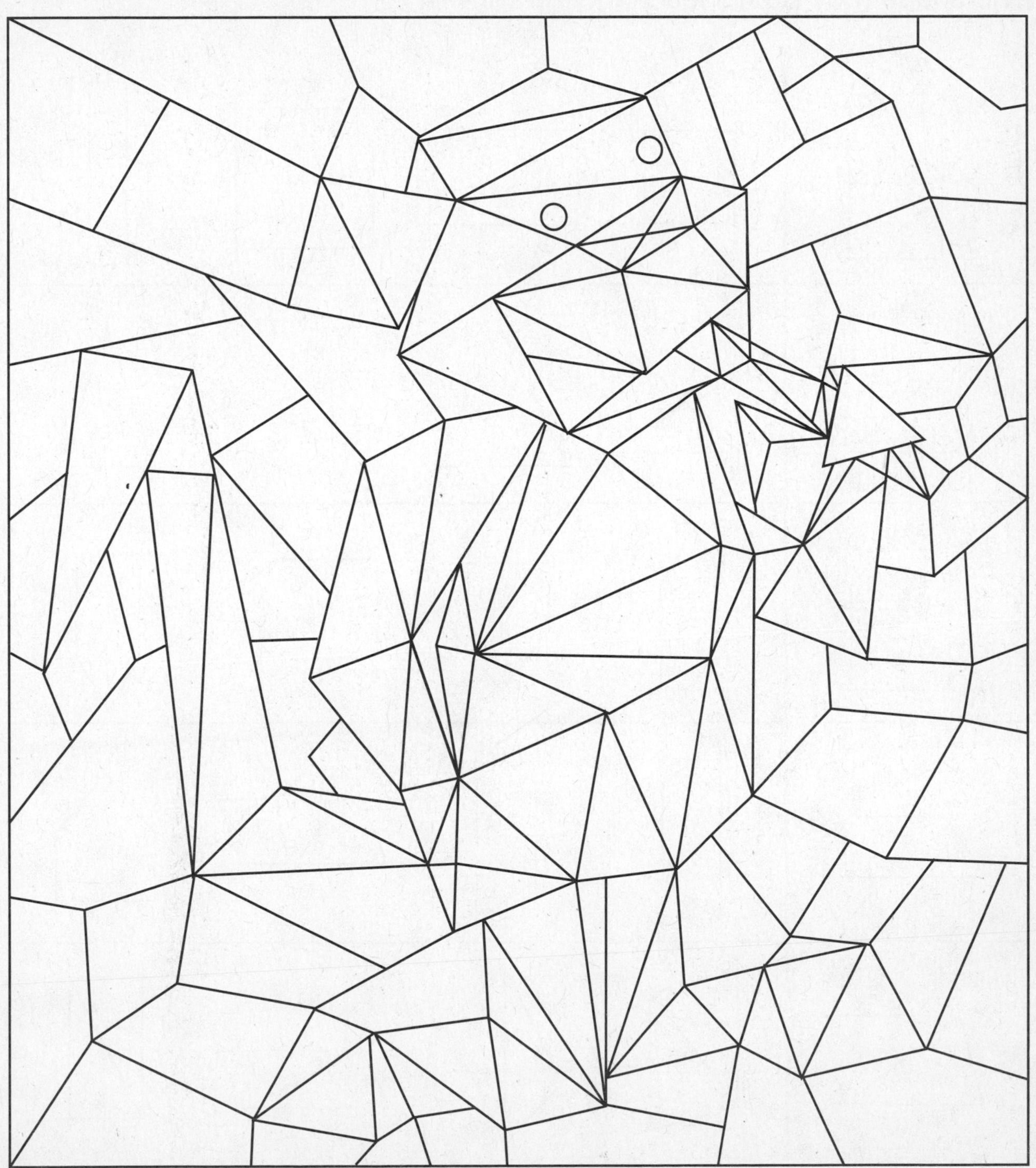

Notes for Home Your child found and colored in shapes with 3 sides to complete a picture and find the answer to a riddle. *Home Activity*: Ask your child to draw no more than 16 triangles to create a picture of a house with a chimney.

Name ______________________________

Critical Thinking

Look at the shape in each box at the left.
In each row, circle the shape that is the same.
The shape may be turned in a different way.

1.

2.

3.

4.

5.

Notes for Home Your child found the congruent shape (exactly the same shape) to match the first shape in each row. *Home Activity*: Ask your child to explain how he or she found the answers.

Name ___________________________________

Decision Making

Design your own writing paper.

Begin with your initials.

Example Jane Fargo ___J___ ___F___ Your initials ______ ______

1. Flip your initials from top to bottom.

Example J F Yours

2. Flip your initials from side to side.

Example J F Yours

3. Turn your initials different ways.

Example Yours

Now make a design that uses your initials several times.

Turn or flip your initials any way you choose.

Example J F Your design

J F

Notes for Home Your child drew his or her initials as they would look after four separate moves, to create a design. *Home Activity*: Ask your child to use his or her initials to create a different design on a separate sheet of paper.

Name ______________________________

Patterns in Geometry

Here is half of the border for a party invitation.

Complete the border.

Make the right half look like the mirror image of the left half.

*Then write the invitation: where? when? who? Be creativ

Notes for Home Your child created a symmetrical pattern by drawing the missing shapes on the right-hand side of an invitation. *Home Activity*: Ask your child to add a shape on the left and draw its matching shape on the right.

Name ______________________________

Extend Your Thinking
12-7

Critical Thinking

How did Shape A change to make Shape B?
Shape C changes in the same way to make Shape D.
Circle the shape that should be Shape D.

A **B** **C** **D**

1. 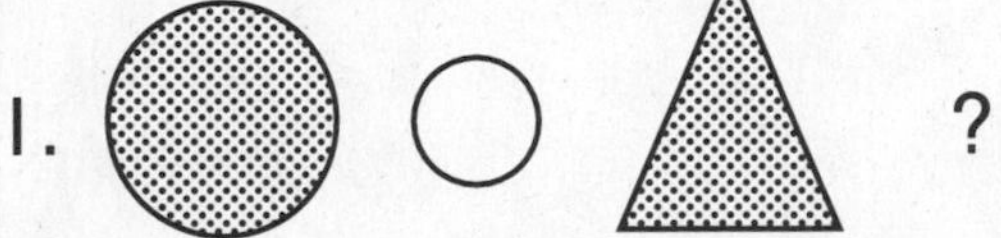 ? 

2. 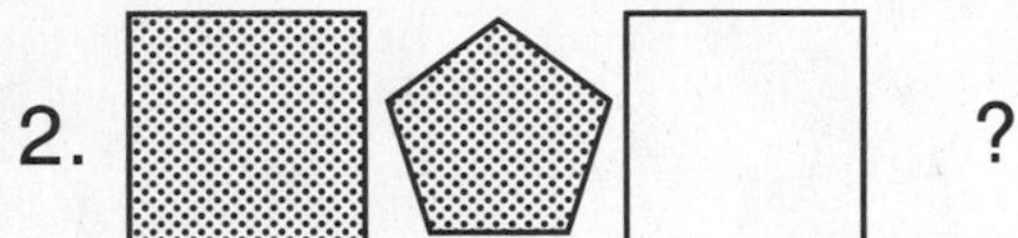 ? 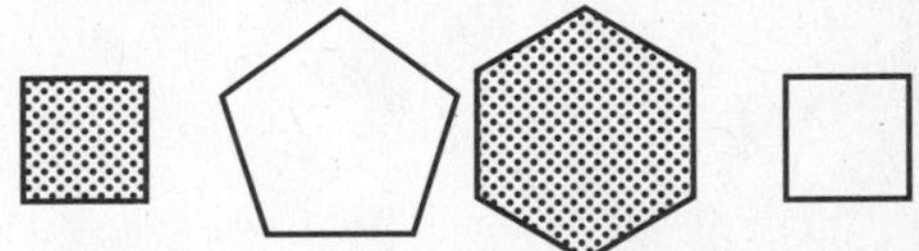

3. ? 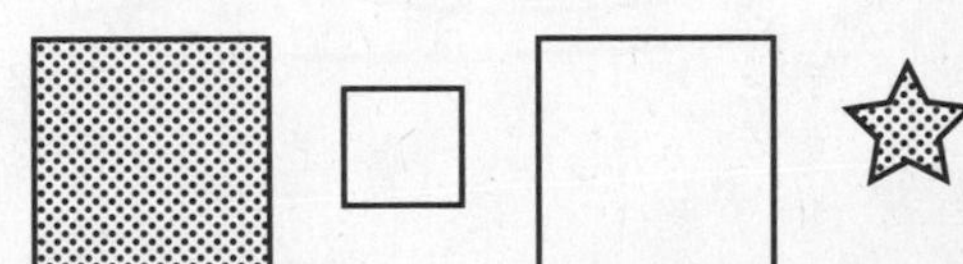

4. ?

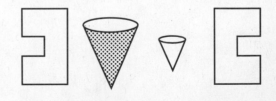

5. ?

Notes for Home Your child decided how shapes relate to each other. *Home Activity*: Ask your child to explain his or her reasoning in identifying the correct Shape D for each row.

Name ______________________________

Extend Your Thinking 12-8

Critical Thinking

Draw lines to show a way to cut each sandwich so 4 people get equal pieces.
Each sandwich should be cut in a different way.

Notes for Home Your child found 3 different ways to divide sandwiches into 4 equal pieces. *Home Activity*: Ask your child to draw 2 squares and challenge him or her to find 2 different ways for the squares to be cut into 2 equal pieces. (One square can be cut vertically or horizontally, and the other square can be cut diagonally.)

Name ______________________________

Decision Making

You get four coupons for free food items.

Draw lines to match each coupon with the food you choose.

On the food, color in the part you get for free.

Example:

$\frac{1}{6}$ of one food item free!

$\frac{1}{2}$ of one food item free!

$\frac{1}{4}$ of one food item free!

$\frac{1}{3}$ of one food item free

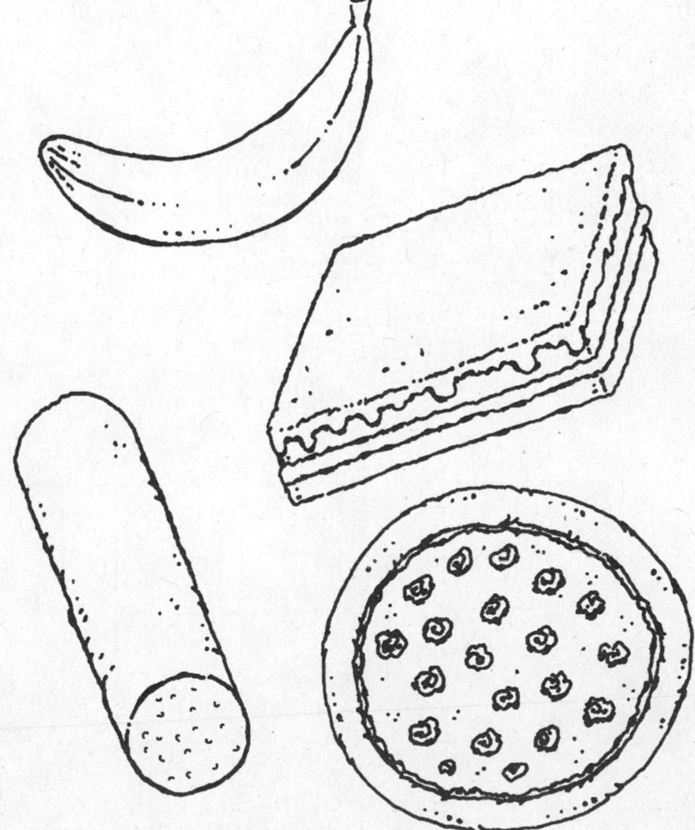

Notes for Home Your child identified fractional amounts of various food items and matched fractions in symbolic form with the pictured amounts. *Home Activity*: When you are cooking, ask your child to measure something simple that involves a fraction, such as a half teaspoon of salt.

Name ______________________________

Extend Your Thinking 12-10

Patterns in Fractions

Color the number of parts to finish each pattern and write the fraction.

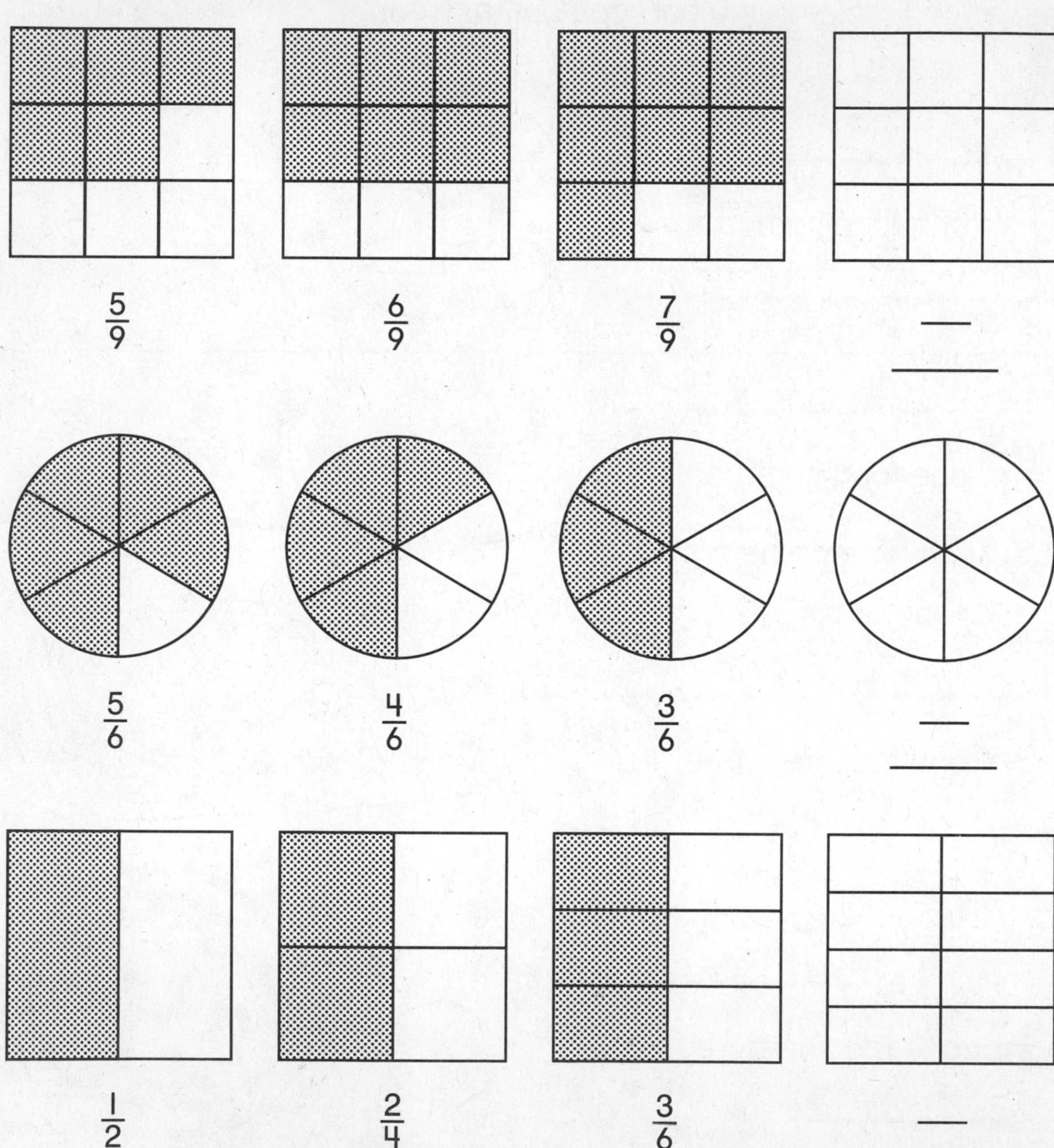

Notes for Home Your child identified patterns in fractions and completed the patterns both by coloring fractional parts in drawings and by writing fractions. *Home Activity*: Ask your child to read the fractions aloud and explain what each numeral in a fraction represents.

Name ______________________________

Extend Your Thinking
12-11

Visual Thinking

Lila puts 16 mushroom slices on each of her pizzas.
These pizzas will be cut into equal pieces.
Draw the cuts that make the number of pieces.
Then draw 16 circles on each pizza for the 16 mushroom slices.
Make the number of mushroom slices per piece equal.

1. Make 2 equal pieces.
   How many slices are on each piece? _____

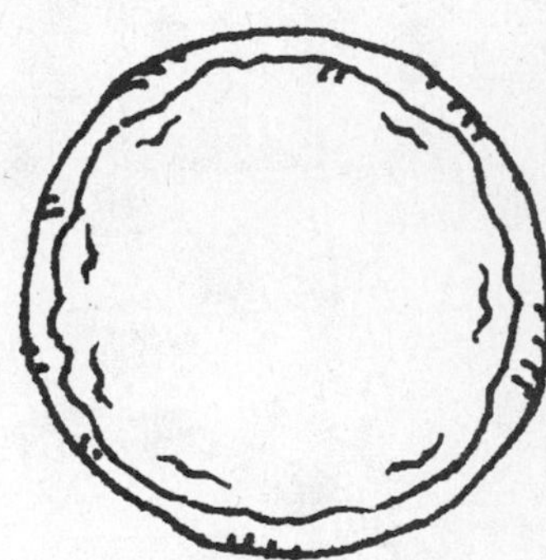

2. Make 4 equal pieces.
   How many slices are on each piece? _____

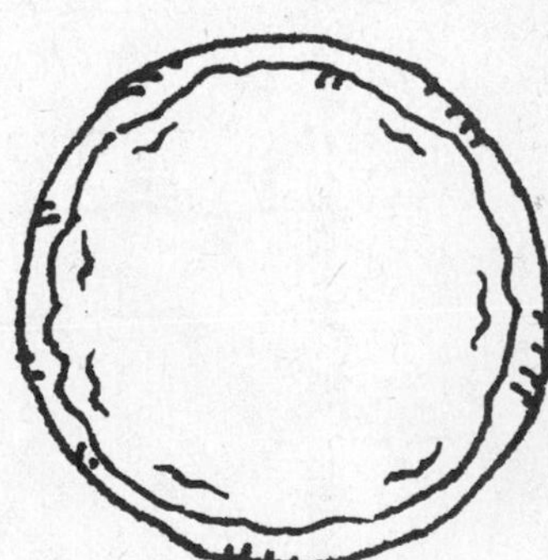

3. Make 8 equal pieces.
   How many slices are on each piece? _____

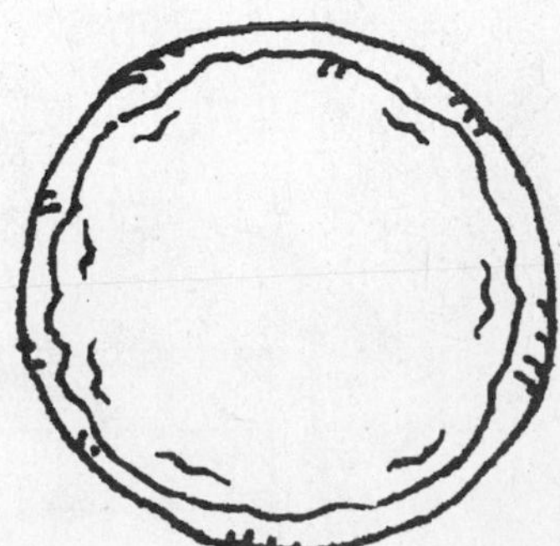

Notes for Home Your child divided sets of 16 three different ways—into halves, fourths, and eighths.
Home Activity: Ask your child to repeat item 1 (2 pieces) with 8 mushroom slices, and item 2 (4 pieces) with 12 mushrooms slices.

Name ______________________________

Extend Your Thinking 12-12

Critical Thinking

Draw a line to match the front of each T-shirt with its back.

Hint: Look for the piece that completes each shape.

Notes for Home Your child matched a shape with a missing fractional part that completes the shape. *Home Activity*: Ask your child to identify the fractions shown on each T-shirt. (Column 1: 3/4, 1/2, 2/3, 5/6. Column 2: 1/6, 1/4, 1/2, 1/3.)

Name ______________________________

Extend Your Thinking
12-13

Critical Thinking

Look at these fractions.

$\frac{1}{10}$

$\frac{1}{20}$

$\frac{1}{4}$

Write the fraction for the part of a dollar the coins show.

1. 

______

2. 

______

3.

______

4. 

______

5. 

______

6.  

______

Notes for Home Your child wrote the fraction of a dollar that the coins show. *Home Activity*: Have your child tell you the fraction for 8 nickels. (8/20)

Name ______________________

Visual Thinking

Is it more likely or less likely that the item will be picked?

Circle **more likely** or **less likely**.

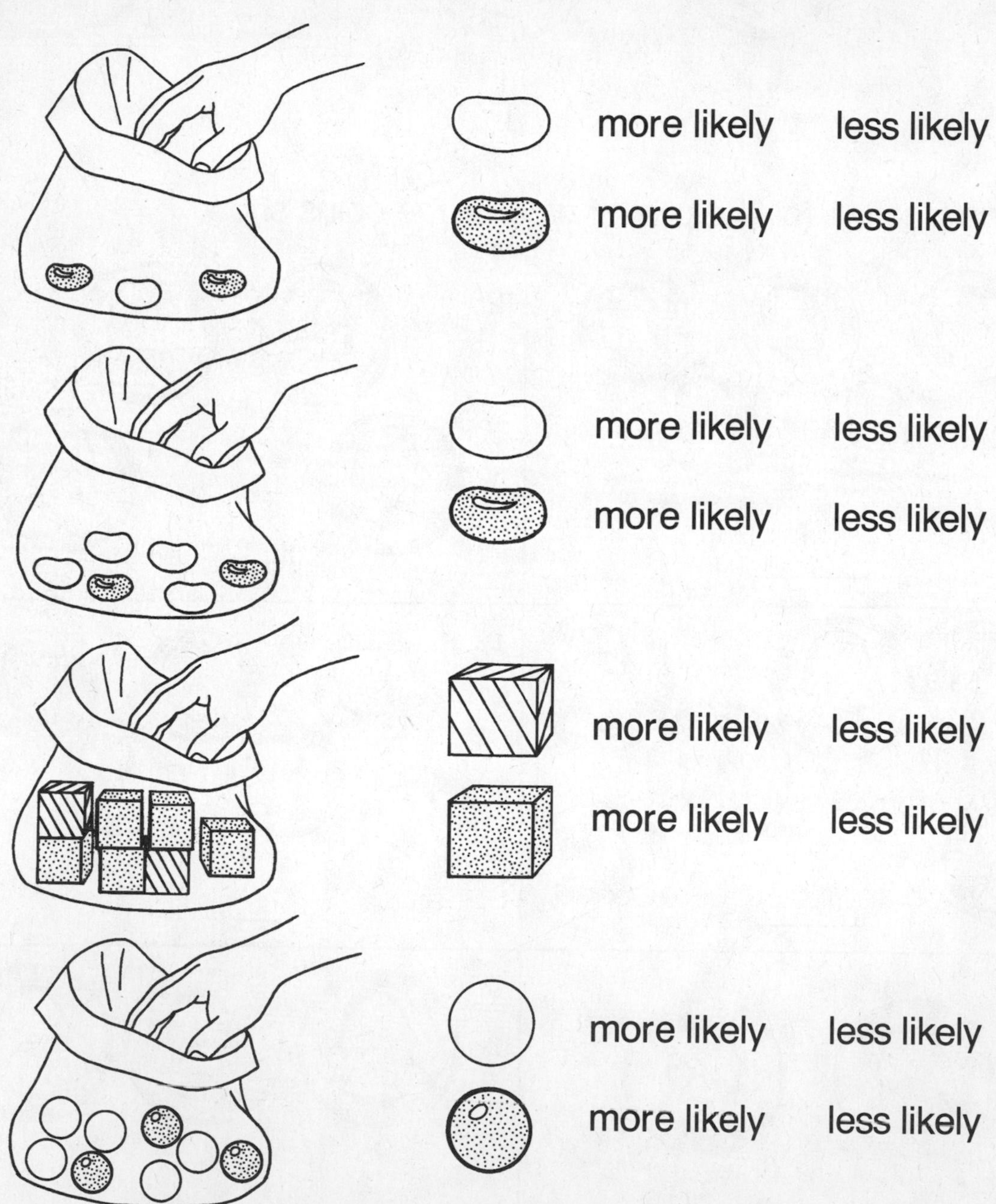

Notes for Home Your child predicted the probability of choosing a particular item from a bag, given the number of each kind of item in the bag. *Home Activity*: Ask your child to reenact one of the situations above ten times and help him or her record the outcome of each selection.

Name ______________________________

Extend Your Thinking 12-15

Decision Making

Show how you would share.

1. How many friends can you invite to share the pizza with you? _____

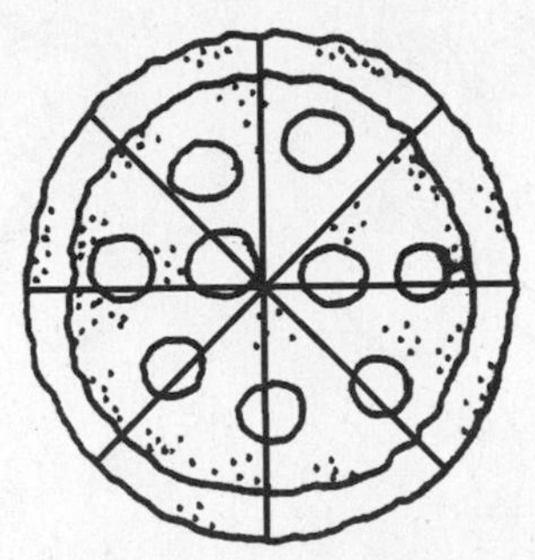

2. How many friends can you invite to share the sandwich? _____

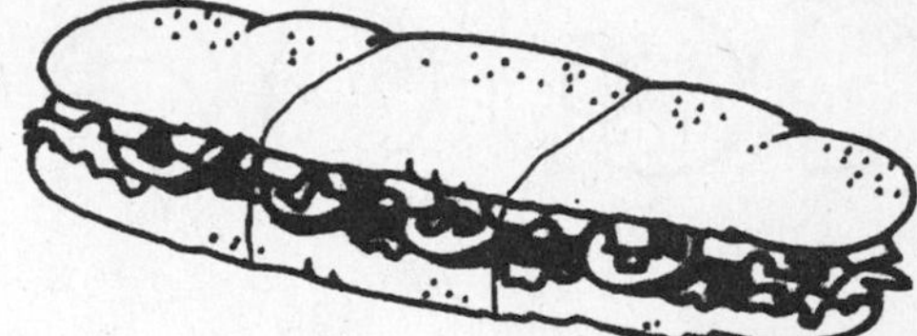

3. How many friends can you invite to share the banana bread? _____

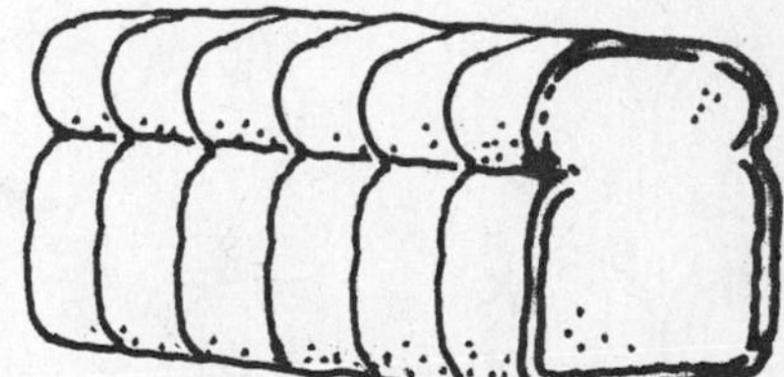

4. How many friends can you invite to share a slice of cheese? _____

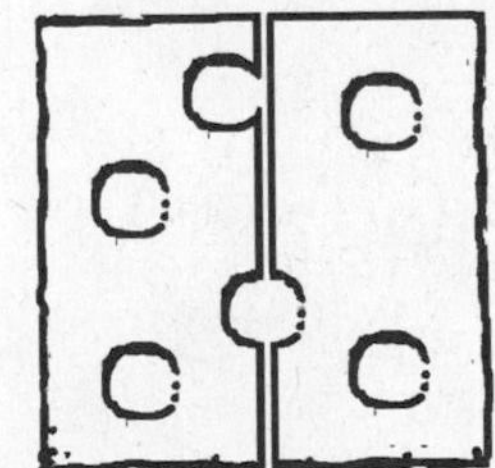

5. How many friends can you invite to share the milk? _____

Notes for Home Your child decided how to share a food by using word and picture clues. *Home Activity*: Ask your child: *How many friends can you invite to share 8 glasses of milk?* (7)

Name ______________________________

Critical Thinking

Draw a line to match the fruit with the right basket.

\+ \+ 8

\+ \+ \+

\+ \+ \+

\+ \+

\+ \+

Notes for Home Your child matched pictures showing repeated addition with the correct sum. *Home Activity:* Ask your child to draw a picture of apples that shows adding 2 apples 5 times. Have him or her tell how many apples were added altogether.

Name ____________________

Extend Your Thinking
13-2

Visual Thinking

Draw lines to match each picture with 2 problems.

3 + 3 + 3

2 × 5

6 + 6 + 6

3 × 4

5 + 5

3 × 6

4 + 4 + 4

3 × 3

6 + 6

2 × 6

Notes for Home Your child matched pictures with repeated addition problems and with multiplication problems. *Home Activity:* Ask your child to find a food item that is packaged in rows and have him or her make up an addition problem and a multiplication problem to match that package.

Name ______________________________

Extend Your Thinking
13-3

Patterns

Look at each array in the pattern and the multiplication fact that goes with it. Draw the next array in the pattern and write the multiplication fact that goes with it.

```
X X X      X X X      X X X
X X X      X X X      X X X
           X X X      X X X
                      X X X
```

$2 \times 3 = 6$ $3 \times 3 = 9$ $4 \times 3 = 12$ ____ $\times$ ____ $=$ ____

```
X X      X X X      X X X X
X X      X X X      X X X X
X X      X X X      X X X X
X X      X X X      X X X X
```

$4 \times 2 = 8$ $4 \times 3 = 12$ $4 \times 4 = 16$ ____ $\times$ ____ $=$ ____

```
X      X X      X X X
X      X X      X X X
```

$2 \times 1 = 2$ $2 \times 2 = 4$ $2 \times 3 = 6$ ____ $\times$ ____ $=$ ____

Notes for Home Your child identified patterns shown in arrays and in multiplication facts, and supplied the next array and fact in each row. *Home Activity:* Ask your child to make up a pattern for you to continue.

Name ______________________________

Extend Your Thinking
13-4

Decision Making

Lucky you! You are the big winner!
Circle the way you will use each prize.

You won 12 rides on a roller coaster.

2 visits to the park and 6 rides each visit

OR

6 visits to the park and 2 rides each visit

You won 8 .

2 pizzas at 4 different times

OR

4 pizzas at 2 different times

You won 6 chances to pick out toys.

1 trip to the toy store to get 6 toys

OR

6 trips to the toy store to get 1 toy each time

You won 10 rides down the water slide at the lake.

5 visits to the lake and 2 rides each visit

OR

2 visits to the lake and 5 rides each visit

Notes for Home Your child chose the ways in which he or she preferred to take prizes. The number of prizes remained the same, but the rate at which they were enjoyed differed. *Home Activity:* For any of the situations, ask your child whether one choice gives more prizes than the other.

Name ______________________

Extend Your Thinking 13-5

Critical Thinking

Which player can make more matches with his cards?
Write the matches you find. Circle the winner's name.

Player 1: Frank

$\begin{array}{r}3\\ \times 4\\ \hline 12\end{array}$	$\begin{array}{r}5\\ \times 2\\ \hline 10\end{array}$	$2 \times 6 = 12$
$5 \times 2 = 10$	$\begin{array}{r}2\\ \times 6\\ \hline 12\end{array}$	$3 \times 4 = 12$

Player 2: Alice

$\begin{array}{r}3\\ \times 1\\ \hline 3\end{array}$	$\begin{array}{r}2\\ \times 4\\ \hline 8\end{array}$	$3 \times 1 = 3$
$5 \times 3 = 15$	$\begin{array}{r}4\\ \times 5\\ \hline 20\end{array}$	$2 \times 4 = 8$

Match 1:

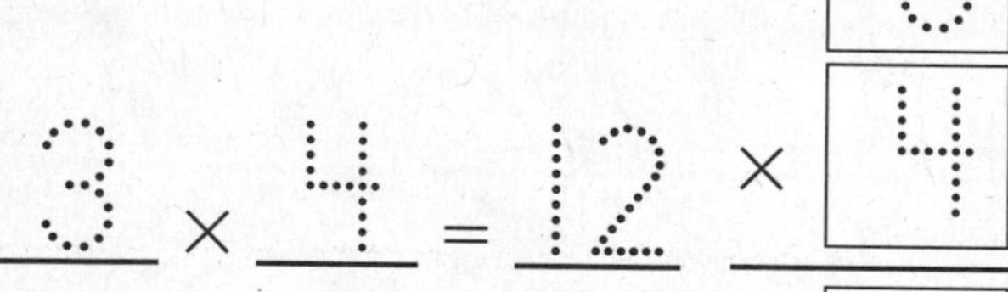

$3 \times 4 = 12$ $\begin{array}{r}3\\ \times 4\\ \hline 12\end{array}$

Match 1:

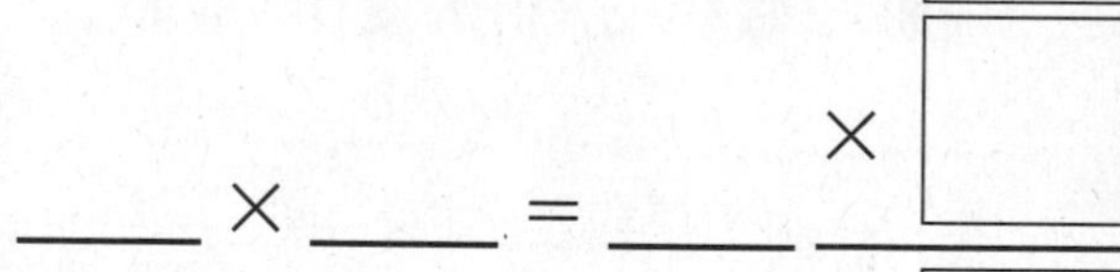

___ × ___ = ___ $\begin{array}{r}\square\\ \times \square\\ \hline \square\end{array}$

Match 2:

$\begin{array}{r}\square\\ \times \square\\ \hline \square\end{array}$ ___ × ___ = ___

Match 2:

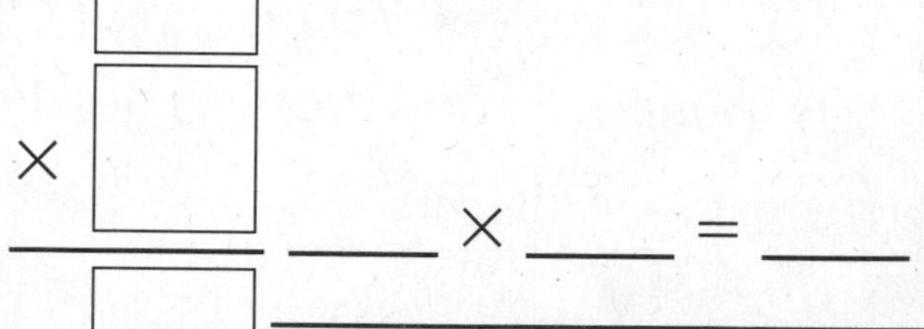

$\begin{array}{r}\square\\ \times \square\\ \hline \square\end{array}$ ___ × ___ = ___

Match 3:

___ × ___ = ___ $\begin{array}{r}\square\\ \times \square\\ \hline \square\end{array}$

Match 3:

___ × ___ = ___ $\begin{array}{r}\square\\ \times \square\\ \hline \square\end{array}$

Notes for Home Your child completed multiplication sentences in horizontal and vertical forms. *Home Activity:* Ask your child to multiply 3 x 6. (18)

Name ______________________________

Extend Your Thinking 13-6

Visual Thinking

Draw a seating plan for each class.

Draw a box for each desk.

Use the multiplication fact to draw each plan.

Room 1 5 × 4

Room 2 3 × 6

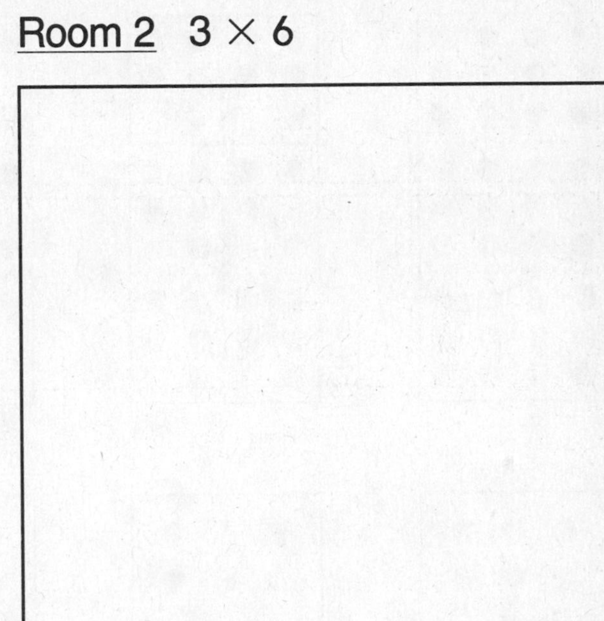

Room 3 5 × 5

Room 4 4 × 6

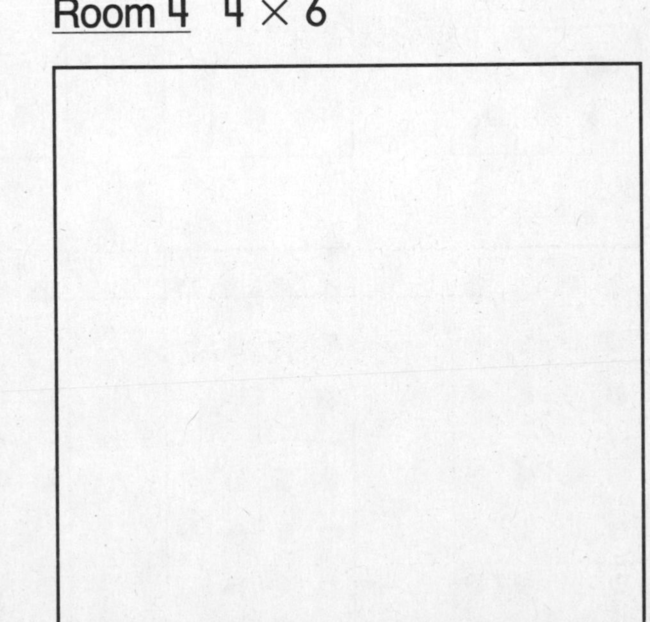

Notes for Home Your child drew pictures to match multiplication facts. *Home Activity:* Ask your child how many children could sit in each of the rooms. (Room 1: 20; Room 2: 18; Room 3: 25; Room 4: 24)

Name ______________________________

Patterns

Extend Your Thinking
13-7

Compare the boxes in each row.

Which box at the right continues the pattern?

Draw a line to the box that comes next.

Notes for Home Your child identified a pattern in each row involving both the number of groups of dots and the number of dots in each group. *Home Activity:* Ask your child to continue the pattern for row 1. (Child should show 2 dots.)

Name ______________________________

Extend Your Thinking
13-8

Decision Making

How would you pack these toys?

Write directions for the worker who will do the job.

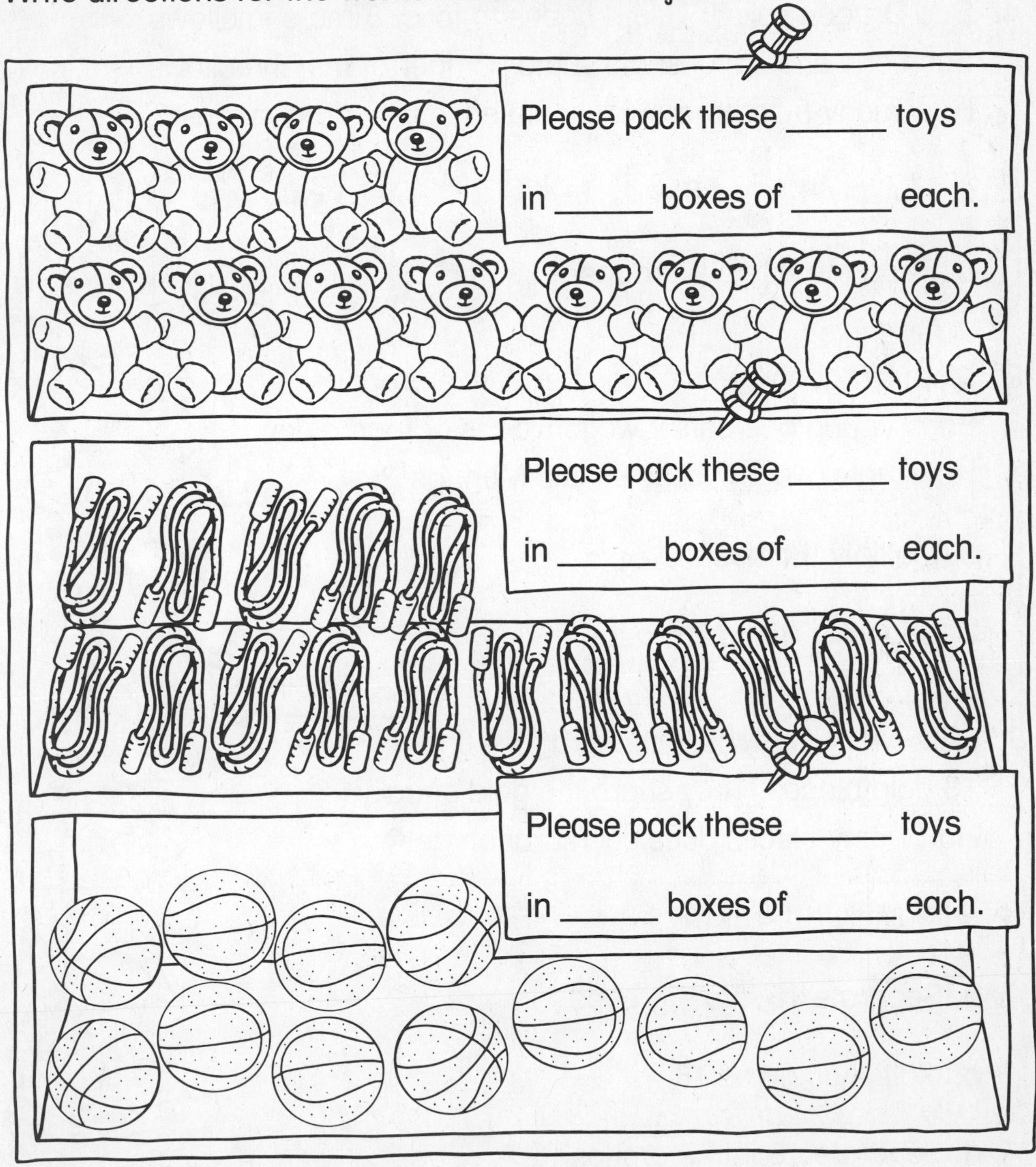

Please pack these ______ toys

in ______ boxes of ______ each.

Please pack these ______ toys

in ______ boxes of ______ each.

Please pack these ______ toys

in ______ boxes of ______ each.

Notes for Home Your child decided how to separate given numbers of toys into equal groups. *Home Activity:* Ask your child to suggest at least one alternate way of packaging each set of toys.

Name ________________________________

Critical Thinking

Circle the way to find each answer.

1. Dad Dragon asks 4 little dragons to toast 8 marshmallows. Each one should toast the same number of marshmallows. How many marshmallows should each little dragon toast?

   a. Multiply 4 times 8.

   b. Separate 8 into 4 groups.

2. Mom Dragon wants to feed her 4 little dragons. Each young one eats 2 wagon loads of food a day. How many wagon loads should Mom get?

   a. Multiply 4 times 2.

   b. Separate 4 into 2 groups.

3. Dad, Mom, and the 4 little dragons find 18 gold pieces. They share the gold equally. How many pieces does each dragon get?

   a. Multiply 4 times 18.

   b. Separate 18 into 4 groups.

   c. Multiply 6 times 18.

   d. Separate 18 into 6 groups.

Notes for Home Your child identified the correct operation to use in solving each problem. *Home Activity:* Ask your child to explain the reasoning behind each choice.

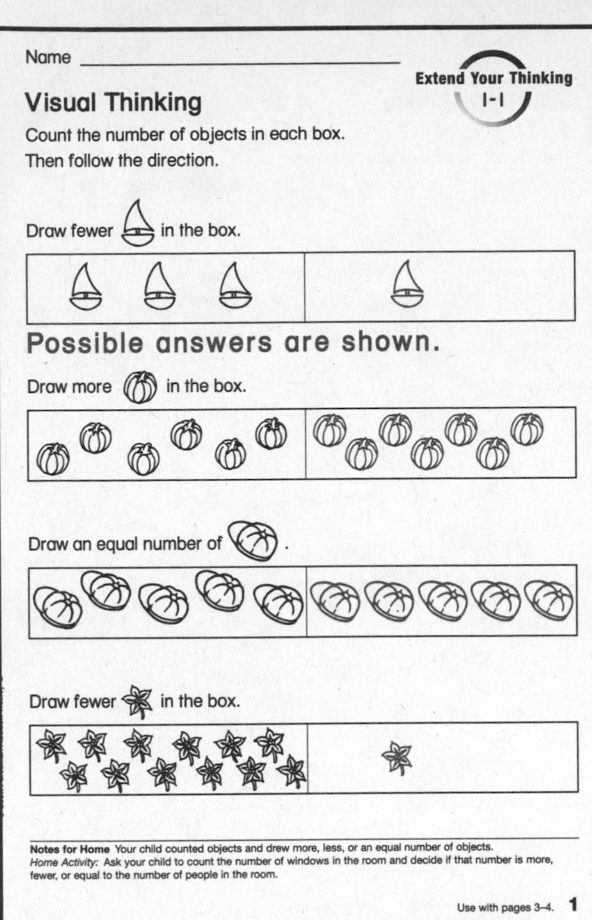

Name ______________________

Extend Your Thinking 1-1

Visual Thinking

Count the number of objects in each box.
Then follow the direction.

Draw fewer (sailboat) in the box.

Possible answers are shown.

Draw more (pumpkin) in the box.

Draw an equal number of (cap).

Draw fewer (leaf) in the box.

Notes for Home Your child counted objects and drew more, less, or an equal number of objects. *Home Activity:* Ask your child to count the number of windows in the room and decide if that number is more, fewer, or equal to the number of people in the room.

Use with pages 3–4. **1**

Name ______________________

Extend Your Thinking 1-2

Decision Making

Jamal's family is going on a camping trip.
Do they need more or less of each thing?

more	more	less
more	less	more
more	more	less

Notes for Home Your child decided whether a family preparing to go camping needed to pack more or less items for their trip. *Home Activity:* Ask your child exactly how many of each item would be needed for the trip. (4 of each)

2 Use with pages 5–6.

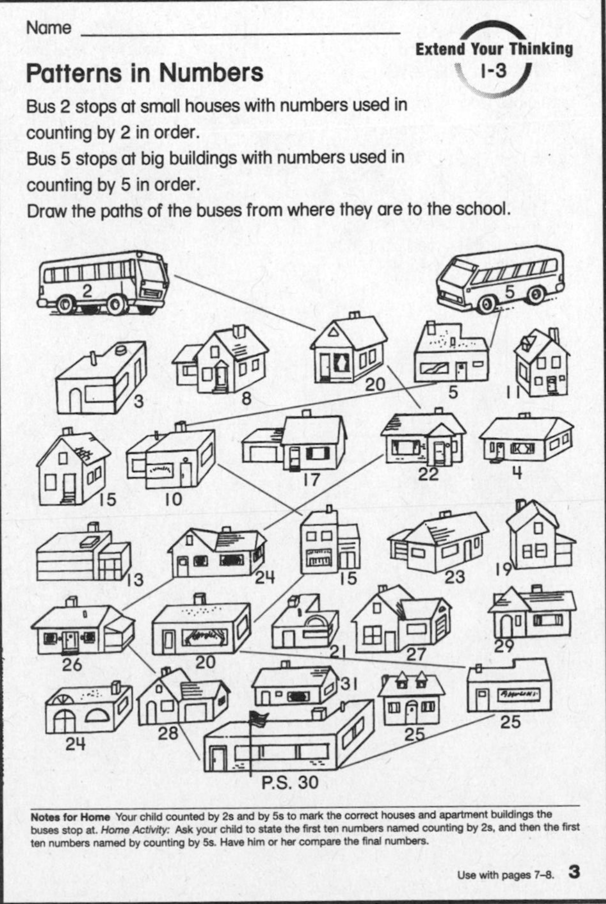

Name ______________________

Extend Your Thinking 1-3

Patterns in Numbers

Bus 2 stops at small houses with numbers used in counting by 2 in order.
Bus 5 stops at big buildings with numbers used in counting by 5 in order.
Draw the paths of the buses from where they are to the school.

Notes for Home Your child counted by 2s and by 5s to mark the correct houses and apartment buildings the buses stop at. *Home Activity:* Ask your child to state the first ten numbers named counting by 2s, and then the first ten numbers named by counting by 5s. Have him or her compare the final numbers.

Use with pages 7–8. **3**

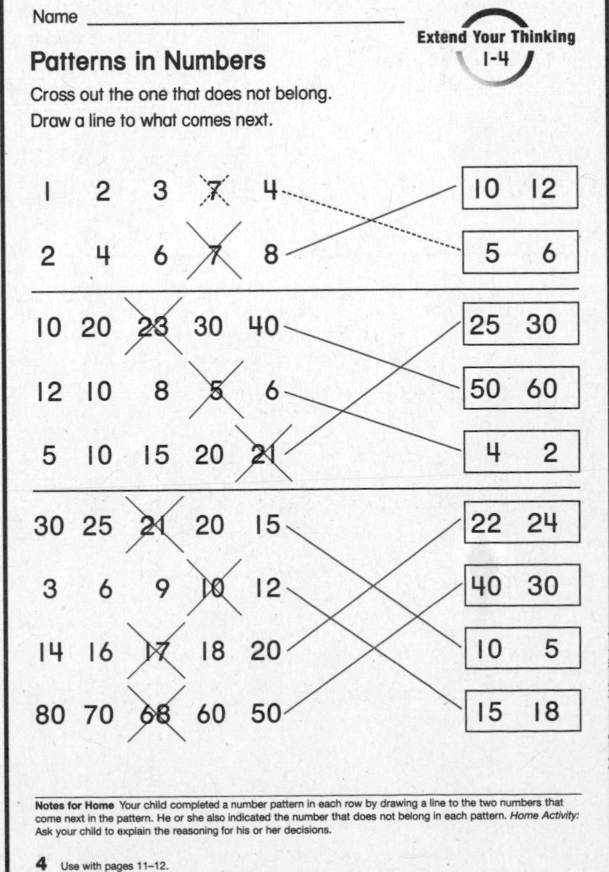

Name ______________________

Extend Your Thinking 1-4

Patterns in Numbers

Cross out the one that does not belong.
Draw a line to what comes next.

1 2 3 ~~7~~ 4	10 12
2 4 6 ~~7~~ 8	5 6
10 20 ~~23~~ 30 40	25 30
12 10 8 ~~5~~ 6	50 60
5 10 15 20 ~~21~~	4 2
30 25 ~~21~~ 20 15	22 24
3 6 9 ~~10~~ 12	40 30
14 16 ~~17~~ 18 20	10 5
80 70 ~~68~~ 60 50	15 18

Notes for Home Your child completed a number pattern in each row by drawing a line to the two numbers that come next in the pattern. He or she also indicated the number that does not belong in each pattern. *Home Activity:* Ask your child to explain the reasoning for his or her decisions.

4 Use with pages 11–12.

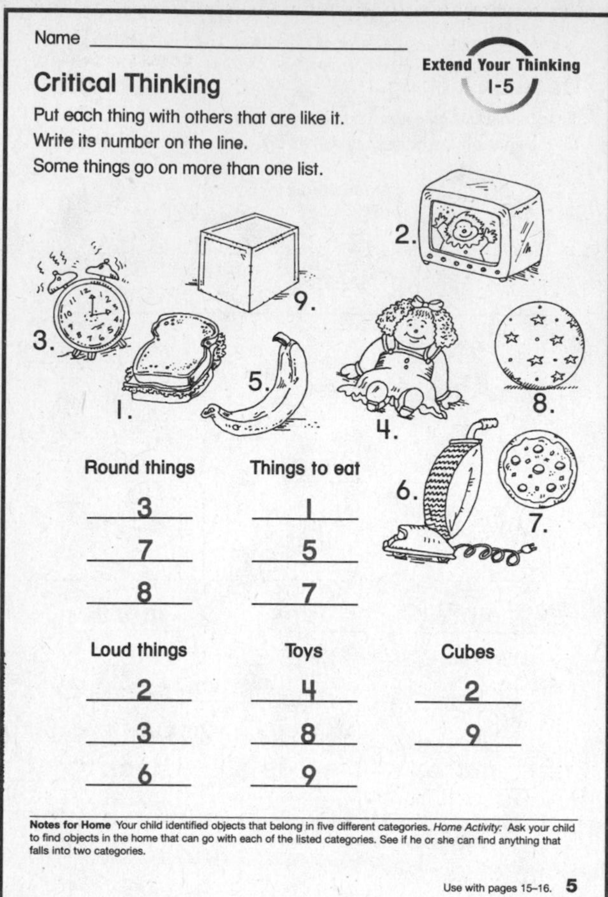

Name ______________________

Extend Your Thinking 1-5

Critical Thinking

Put each thing with others that are like it.
Write its number on the line.
Some things go on more than one list.

1. 2. 3. 4. 5. 6. 7. 8. 9.

Round things	Things to eat
3	1
7	5
8	7

Loud things	Toys	Cubes
2	4	2
3	8	9
6	9	

Notes for Home Your child identified objects that belong in five different categories. *Home Activity:* Ask your child to find objects in the home that can go with each of the listed categories. See if he or she can find anything that falls into two categories.

Use with pages 15–16. **5**

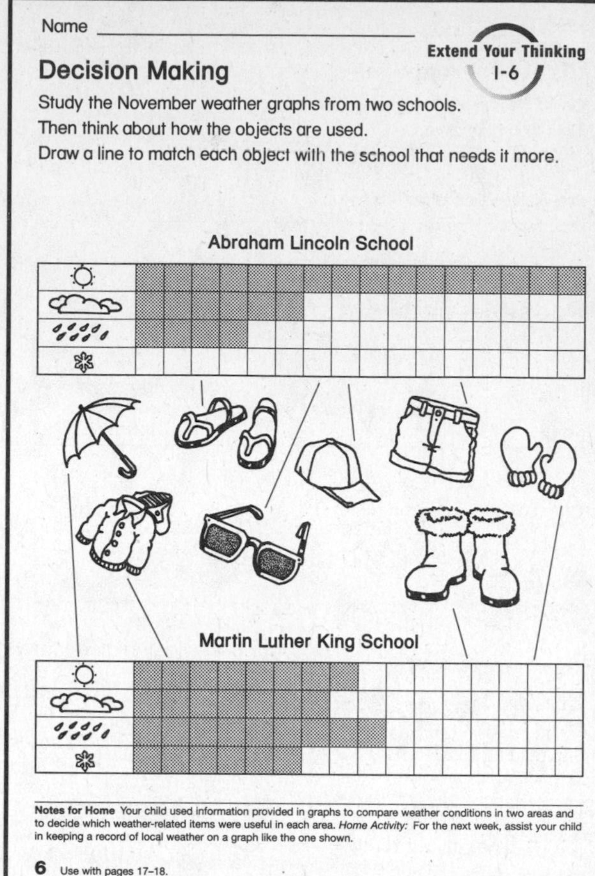

Name ______________________

Extend Your Thinking 1-6

Decision Making

Study the November weather graphs from two schools.
Then think about how the objects are used.
Draw a line to match each object with the school that needs it more.

Abraham Lincoln School

Martin Luther King School

Notes for Home Your child used information provided in graphs to compare weather conditions in two areas and to decide which weather-related items were useful in each area. *Home Activity:* For the next week, assist your child in keeping a record of local weather on a graph like the one shown.

6 Use with pages 17–18.

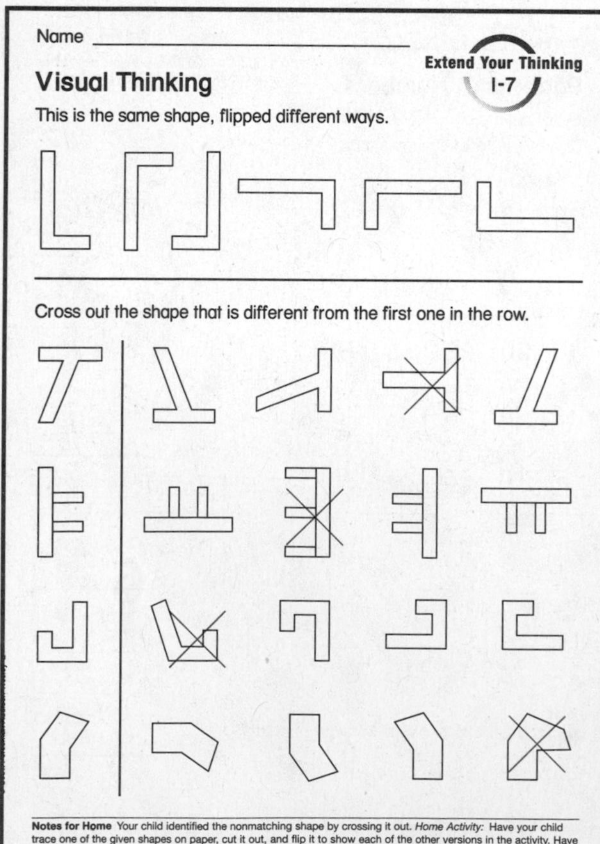

Name ______________________

Extend Your Thinking 1-7

Visual Thinking

This is the same shape, flipped different ways.

Cross out the shape that is different from the first one in the row.

Notes for Home Your child identified the nonmatching shape by crossing it out. *Home Activity:* Have your child trace one of the given shapes on paper, cut it out, and flip it to show each of the other versions in the activity. Have your child draw and cut out an original shape, and then flip it to find some of its variations.

Use with pages 19–20. **7**

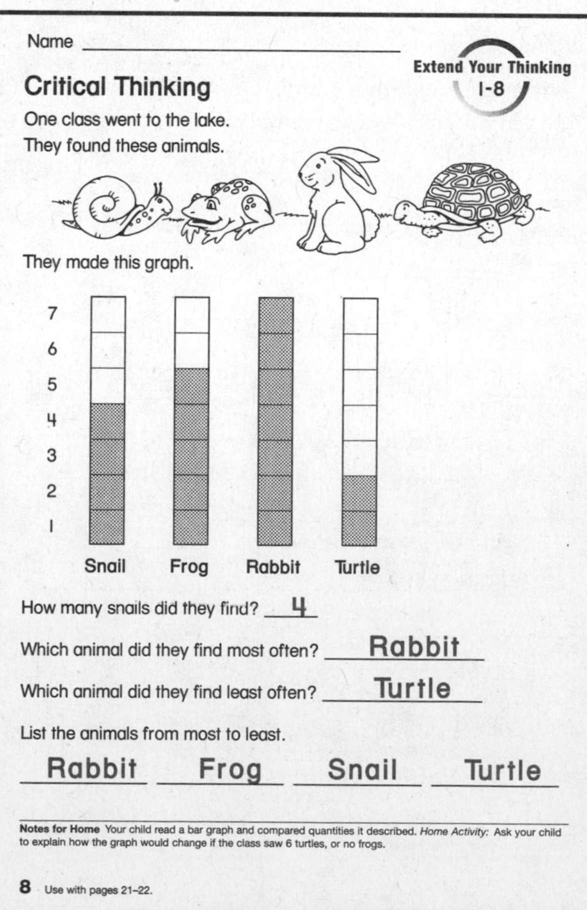

Name ______________________

Extend Your Thinking 1-8

Critical Thinking

One class went to the lake.
They found these animals.

They made this graph.

How many snails did they find? 4

Which animal did they find most often? Rabbit

Which animal did they find least often? Turtle

List the animals from most to least.

Rabbit Frog Snail Turtle

Notes for Home Your child read a bar graph and compared quantities it described. *Home Activity:* Ask your child to explain how the graph would change if the class saw 6 turtles, or no frogs.

8 Use with pages 21–22.

Name ______________________

Extend Your Thinking 1-9

Patterns in Numbers

A zookeeper bought food for four kinds of zoo animals on May 1.
At the end of each week, she weighs the food that is left.
This chart shows what she found at the end of three weeks.
How much will be left at the end of the fourth week?
Write the amounts you think will be left.

Animal	Pounds of Food Left at the End of			
	Week 1	Week 2	Week 3	Week 4
monkeys	30	20	10	0
lions	200	150	100	50
elephants	400	300	200	100
birds	16	12	8	4

How much food did the zookeeper have at the beginning of Week 1?

She had __40__ pounds for the monkeys.

She had __250__ pounds for the lions.

She had __500__ pounds for the elephants.

She had __20__ pounds for the birds.

Notes for Home Your child found number patterns and used them to identify the numbers missing from the chart. Then he or she used the numbers to complete the statements. *Home Activity:* Ask your child to explain each of the number patterns to you.

Name ______________________

Extend Your Thinking 2-1

Patterns in Geometry

Which shape comes next for each pattern? Circle it.

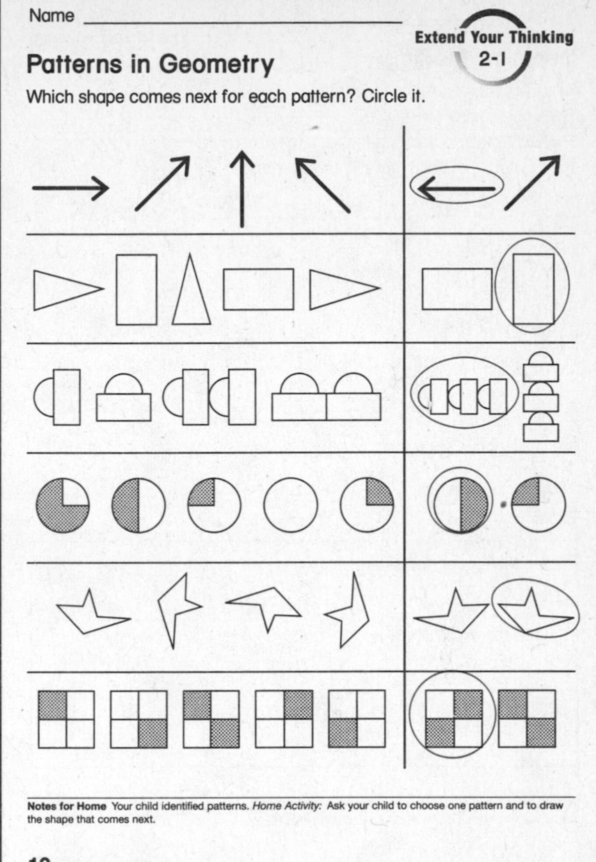

Notes for Home Your child identified patterns. *Home Activity:* Ask your child to choose one pattern and to draw the shape that comes next.

Name ______________________

Extend Your Thinking 2-2

Critical Thinking

Four classes voted for an animal for the school flag.
Circle the winning votes in each class.

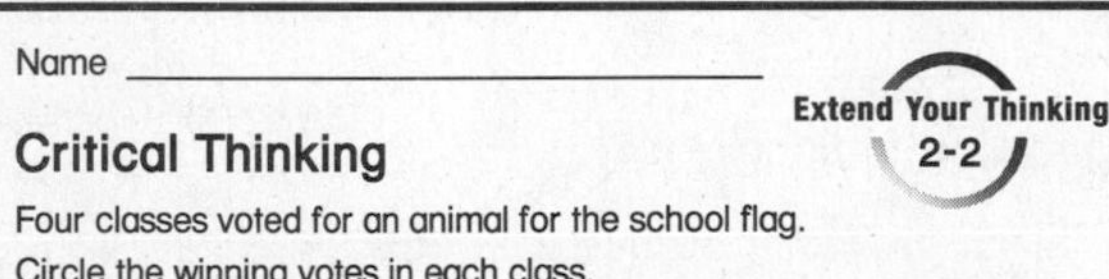

Class 1	(||||)	|||	||
Class 2	|||	(||||)	|
Class 3	||	||	(||||)
Class 4	|||	(||||)	|||

Color a box on this graph for every class each animal won in.

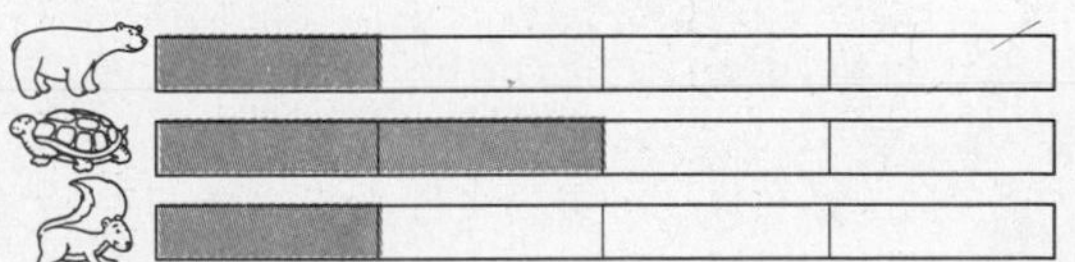

In how many classes did [bear] win? __1__

In how many classes did [turtle] win? __2__

In how many classes did [skunk] win? __1__

The animal on the school flag is [bear] (turtle) [skunk]

Notes for Home Your child created and interpreted a bar graph. *Home Activity:* Ask your child to decide if looking at the chart of tally marks or at the bar graph makes it easier to know which animal won.

Name ______________________

Extend Your Thinking 2-3

Visual Thinking

Use this calendar to make plans for Tim.
Tim's birthday is November 4. Circle that date.

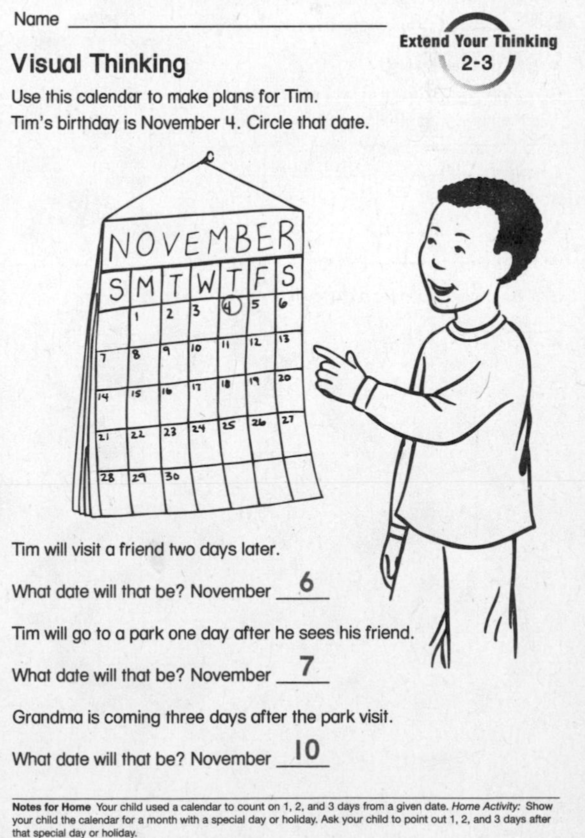

Tim will visit a friend two days later.

What date will that be? November __6__

Tim will go to a park one day after he sees his friend.

What date will that be? November __7__

Grandma is coming three days after the park visit.

What date will that be? November __10__

Notes for Home Your child used a calendar to count on 1, 2, and 3 days from a given date. *Home Activity:* Show your child the calendar for a month with a special day or holiday. Ask your child to point out 1, 2, and 3 days after that special day or holiday.

Name ______________________

Extend Your Thinking 2-4

Decision Making

Every fact below stands for a letter.
Think of a secret word.
Then write the related fact for each letter of your word.
The related fact stands for the same letter.

A	9 + 3 = 12	P	7 + 5 = 12
E	9 + 2 = 11	O	7 + 4 = 11
H	8 + 4 = 12	S	7 + 3 = 10
I	8 + 3 = 11	T	6 + 5 = 11
M	8 + 2 = 10	Y	6 + 4 = 10

Ask a classmate to find your secret word by writing the letter above each fact.

Example: H: 4 + 8 = 12   I: 3 + 8 = 11

Write the related facts here.

Notes for Home Your child discovered a coded message by matching related addition facts. *Home Activity:* Help your child create a new coded message using the same facts and letters.

Name ______________________

Extend Your Thinking 2-5

Critical Thinking

Cross out the set that does not belong in each group.
Write a fact telling how many things are similar in each group.

3 + 2 = 5

4 + 6 = 10

3 + 5 = 8

Notes for Home Your child wrote addition facts describing groups of similar items. *Home Activity:* Ask your child to explain why he or she crossed out certain items in each group.

Name ______________________

Extend Your Thinking 2-6

Visual Thinking

Begin with the numbers in the center circle.
Add the number in the ring to each number.
Write the answer in the next ring.
Color parts with odd numbers red.

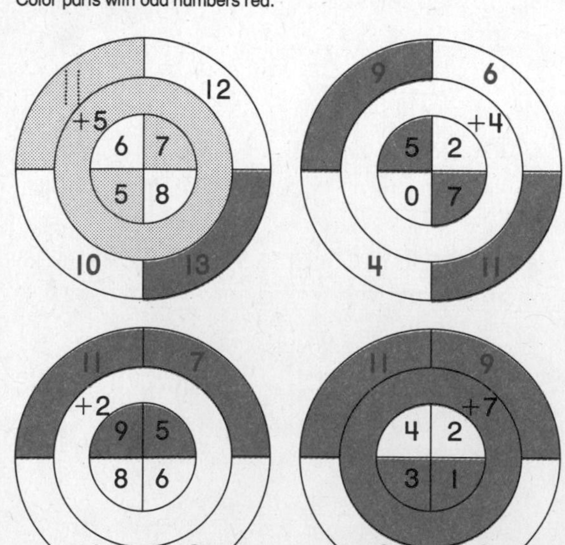

Notes for Home Your child completed addition facts through 12, and identified odd and even numbers. *Home Activity:* Ask your child to tell what the answers would be if you changed the number in the ring of one of the circles to 3.

Name ______________________

Extend Your Thinking 2-7

Decision Making

The city zoo must sell 10 animals in all to another zoo.
Decide how many animals to sell from each group.
Write 5 subtraction sentences to show your choices.

The zoo has nine big cats. __9__ – _____ = _____

The zoo also has ten apes. _____ – _____ = _____

Five elephants live at the zoo. _____ – _____ = _____

Eight zebras live together at the zoo. _____ – _____ = _____

Seven snakes slither in the snake house.

_____ – _____ = _____

Complete this sentence. Tell what you will sell.

_____ cats + _____ apes + _____ elephants +

_____ zebras + _____ snakes = 10 animals in all

Answers will vary.

Notes for Home Your child wrote subtraction sentences and completed an addition sentence to show that his or her answers were correct. *Home Activity:* Ask your child to explain his or her choices.

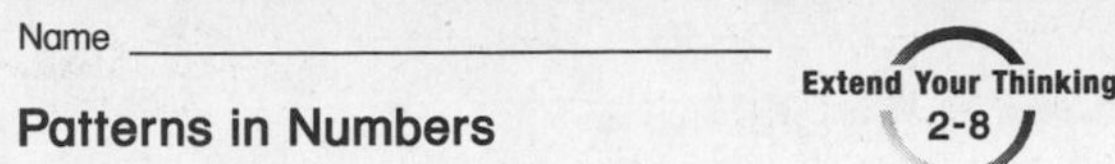

Name ______________________

Extend Your Thinking 2-8

Patterns in Numbers

Count back by 1s from 12 to 0 across each column.
Then connect the dots of the numbers with a pencil.

12•	12•	12•	12•	12•	12•	12•	12•	12•	12•	12•	12•	12•
11•	11•	11•	11•	11•	11•	11•	11•	11•	11•	11•	11•	11•
10•	10•	10•	10•	10•	10•	10•	10•	10•	10•	10•	10•	10•
9•	9•	9•	9•	9•	9•	9•	9•	9•	9•	9•	9•	9•
8•	8•	8•	8•	8•	8•	8•	8•	8•	8•	8•	8•	8•
7•	7•	7•	7•	7•	7•	7•	7•	7•	7•	7•	7•	7•
6•	6•	6•	6•	6•	6•	6•	6•	6•	6•	6•	6•	6•
5•	5•	5•	5•	5•	5•	5•	5•	5•	5•	5•	5•	5•
4•	4•	4•	4•	4•	4•	4•	4•	4•	4•	4•	4•	4•
3•	3•	3•	3•	3•	3•	3•	3•	3•	3•	3•	3•	3•
2•	2•	2•	2•	2•	2•	2•	2•	2•	2•	2•	2•	2•
1•	1•	1•	1•	1•	1•	1•	1•	1•	1•	1•	1•	1•
0•	0•	0•	0•	0•	0•	0•	0•	0•	0•	0•	0•	0•

Begin at the same spot. Count back by 2s from 12 to 0. Connect the dots of the numbers with a red crayon.

Which line is longer? **The pencil line (for counting back by 1s) is longer.**

Notes for Home Your child compared the patterns made on a grid while counting back by 1s and 2s. *Home Activity:* Ask your child to use two more colors to mark the lines formed while counting back by 3s and by 4s. Compare the lines.

Use with pages 57–58. **17**

Name ______________________

Extend Your Thinking 2-9

Visual Thinking

These children were at a fair.
They hit a mark with a big hammer to ring the bell.
Circle the answer to each question.

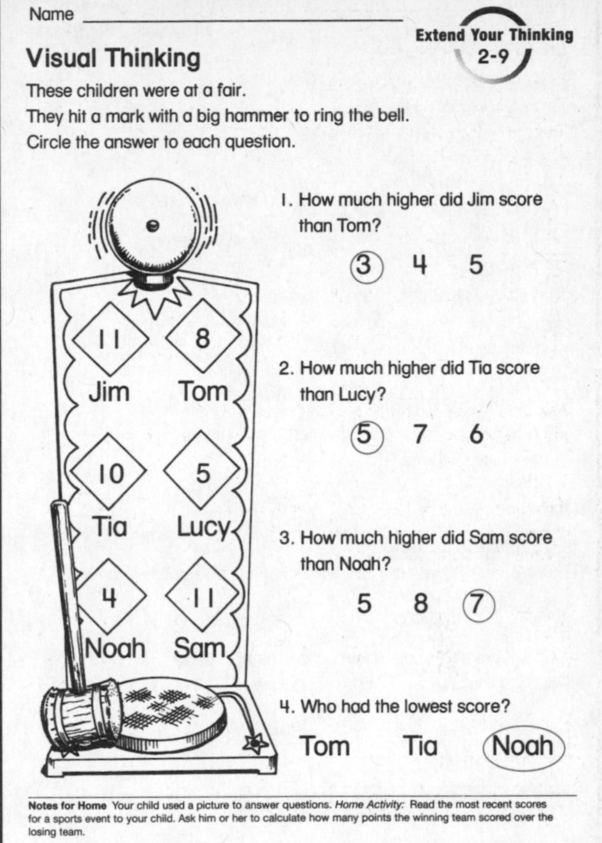

1. How much higher did Jim score than Tom?
   (3) 4 5
2. How much higher did Tia score than Lucy?
   (5) 7 6
3. How much higher did Sam score than Noah?
   5 8 (7)
4. Who had the lowest score?
   Tom Tia (Noah)

Notes for Home Your child used a picture to answer questions. *Home Activity:* Read the most recent scores for a sports event to your child. Ask him or her to calculate how many points the winning team scored over the losing team.

18 Use with pages 59–60.

Name ______________________

Extend Your Thinking 2-10

Decision Making

Draw a path to the beach.
Solve the problems on your path.

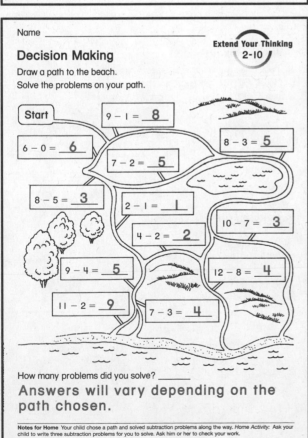

Start

9 − 1 = **8**

6 − 0 = **6**

8 − 3 = **5**

7 − 2 = **5**

8 − 5 = **3**

2 − 1 = **1**

10 − 7 = **3**

4 − 2 = **2**

9 − 4 = **5**

12 − 8 = **4**

11 − 2 = **9**

7 − 3 = **4**

How many problems did you solve? ______

Answers will vary depending on the path chosen.

Notes for Home Your child chose a path and solved subtraction problems along the way. *Home Activity:* Ask your child to write three subtraction problems for you to solve. Ask him or her to check your work.

Use with pages 61–62. **19**

Name ______________________

Extend Your Thinking 2-11

Critical Thinking

Cross out the one that does not belong.
Match the others with a drawing.

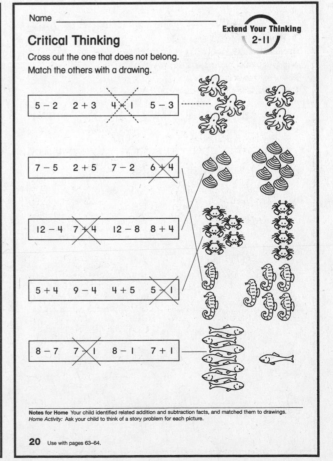

5 − 2 2 + 3 ~~4 + 1~~ 5 − 3

7 − 5 2 + 5 7 − 2 ~~6 + 4~~

12 − 4 ~~7 + 4~~ 12 − 8 8 + 4

5 + 4 9 − 4 4 + 5 ~~5 + 1~~

8 − 7 ~~7 + 1~~ 8 − 1 7 + 1

Notes for Home Your child identified related addition and subtraction facts, and matched them to drawings. *Home Activity:* Ask your child to think of a story problem for each picture.

20 Use with pages 63–64.

Name ______________________

Extend Your Thinking 2-12

Critical Thinking

Read the problem.
Solve the number sentence that goes with the problem.

1. One pirate put 8 gold pieces into a chest. Another put in 4 gold pieces. How many gold pieces are there all together?

   8 − 4 = ____ 8 + 4 = <u>12</u>

2. The pirates sailed on 5 ships. Then 2 ships sank. How many ships are left?

   5 − 2 = <u>3</u> 5 + 2 = ____

3. One pirate saw 9 trees on the island. The other saw 3 trees. How many more did the first pirate see?

   9 − 3 = <u>6</u> 9 + 3 = ____

4. One pirate dug a hole 5 feet deep. The next pirate dug it 2 feet deeper. How deep was the hole all together?

   5 − 2 = ____ 5 + 2 = <u>7</u>

Notes for Home Your child chose and completed operations to solve story problems. *Home Activity:* Ask your child to explain the reasoning behind his or her choices.

Name ______________________

Extend Your Thinking 3-1

Patterns in Data

Which award is better?
Award A: You get $3 each day for 4 days.
Award B: You get $1 the first day. On each of the next 3 days, the award is double what it was the day before.

Award A: $3 per day

	Day 1	Day 2	Day 3	Day 4
Today's Award	$3	$3	$ 3	$ 3
Total So Far	$3	Yesterday's Total + Today: $6	Yesterday's Total + Today: $ 9	Yesterday's Total + Today: $ 12

Award B: Doubling yesterday's award

	Day 1	Day 2	Day 3	Day 4
Today's Award	$1	$2	$4	$ 8
Total So Far	$1	Yesterday's Total + Today: $3	Yesterday's Total + Today: $ 7	Yesterday's Total + Today: $ 15

Which award is better, A or B? <u>B</u>

Notes for Home Your child extended two number patterns to determine quantity. *Home Activity:* Help your child to extend both patterns one more day. (Award A: Day 4 - $15; Award B: Day 4 - $31.)

Name ______________________

Extend Your Thinking 3-2

Critical Thinking

Help the children in each problem share equally.
Write a new fact using doubles.

Tonya has 5 apples. Richard has 3 apples.

5 + 3 = 8 [4] + [4] = 8

Arthur has 8 baseballs. Maria has 6 baseballs.

8 + 6 = <u>14</u> [7] + [7] = <u>14</u>

Tawana has 2 pencils. Suli has 4 pencils.

2 + 4 = <u>6</u> [3] + [3] = <u>6</u>

Anna has 7 blocks. Laura has 5 blocks.

7 + 5 = <u>12</u> [6] + [6] = <u>12</u>

Notes for Home Your child matched addition facts with related doubles facts and solved both problems. *Home Activity:* Arrange 6 objects on a table, with 2 in one pile and 4 in another. Ask your child to rearrange the objects to represent a doubles fact (3 + 3). Repeat the process with 8 and 10 objects. (4 + 4; 5 + 5)

Name ______________________

Extend Your Thinking 3-3

Visual Thinking

First finish the number sentence on each birdhouse roof to tell you how many birds belong.
Then match the birds to the house where they belong.

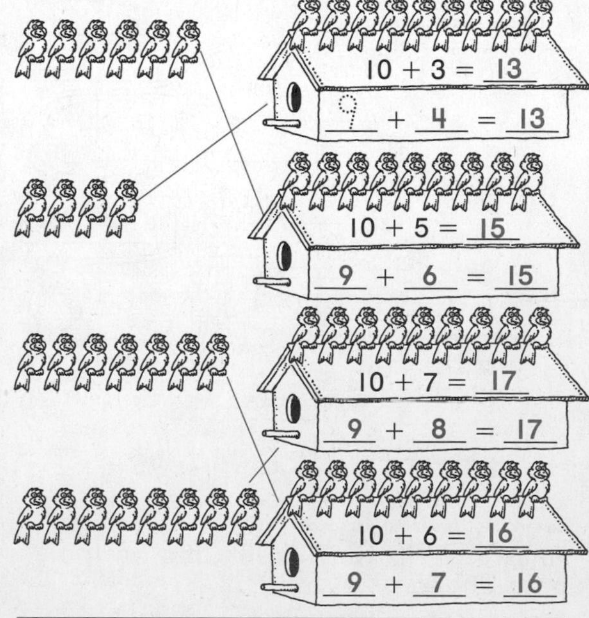

Notes for Home Your child practiced adding with 10 in problems where one addend is 9. *Home Activity:* Try some mental math with your child. Ask him or her for the answers to these problems: 9 + 4 (13), 9 + 7 (16), 9 + 6 (15), and 9 + 2 (11).

Name

Decision Making

Extend Your Thinking 3-4

Solve every problem.
Then balance each scale by writing a fact on its other side.

7 + 4 = 11
9 + 4 = 13

10 + 3 = 13 9 + 4 = 13

7 + 6 = 13
3 + 9 = 12

10 + 2 = 12 3 + 9 = 12

2 + 9 = 11
3 + 7 = 10

10 + 1 = 11 2 + 9 = 11

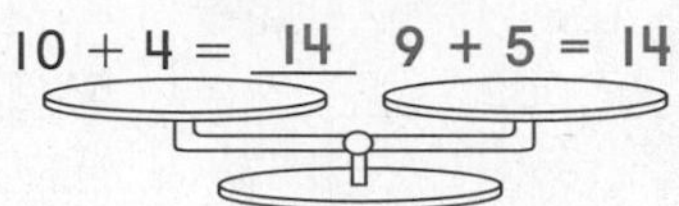

9 + 5 = 14
7 + 8 = 15

10 + 4 = 14 9 + 5 = 14

Notes for Home Your child practiced adding with 10 when one of the numbers in an addition problem is 9. *Home Activity:* Ask your child to balance a scale with a number fact using 10 and a number fact using 9.

Use with pages 89–90. **25**

Name

Critical Thinking

Extend Your Thinking 3-5

Solve these problems.
Write a number sentence for each.

Detective Fox: Your bucket is gone. How many fish were in it?
Bear: I fished for 5 hours. **Otter:** I put 7 fish in the bucket.
Bear: I put 6 fish in the bucket. **Wildcat:** I was here at 9 A.M.

Detective Fox: My answer is 7 + 6 = 13.

Detective Fox: The safe won't open. How much is in it?
Crocodile: I put in \$50. **Zebra:** I put in \$10.
Kangaroo: I have \$30 in my pocket.

Detective Fox: My answer is 50 + 10 = \$60.

Detective Fox: How many birds flew away?
Ostrich: These 2 cages are old. **Eagle:** 9 were in this cage.
Finch: 6 of the birds were blue. **Robin:** 5 were in that cage.

Detective Fox: My answer is 9 + 5 = 14.

Notes for Home Your child solved word problems by identifying necessary information. *Home Activity:* Ask your child to make up another word problem for you to solve.

26 Use with pages 91–92.

Name

Decision Making

Extend Your Thinking 3-6

Solve these problems.
On the last line of each problem write the addition and subtraction number sentences your used.

Mark has 8 dollars. How much will 2 caps cost? \$8
How much money will he have left if he only buys 1 cap? \$4
4 + 4 = 8 dollars; 8 − 4 = 4 dollars

Kris and Carol have 6 dollars. How much will 2 sandwiches cost? \$6
How much money will they have left if they only buy 1? \$3
3 + 3 = 6 dollars; 6 − 3 = 3 dollars

Tracy has 19 dollars. How much will 2 dolls cost? \$18
How much money will she have left if she only buys 1? \$10
9 + 9 = 18 dollars; 19 − 9 = 10 dollars

Notes for Home Your child used addition doubles facts to help subtract. *Home Activity:* While in a store, ask your child to double the price of an item. Round each price to a dollar figure from \$1 to \$9.

Use with pages 93–94. **27**

Name

Visual Thinking

Extend Your Thinking 3-7

Rachel folded pieces of paper.
Then she cut out a shape on each fold.
How will the papers look when they are unfolded?
Match each folded paper with an unfolded paper.

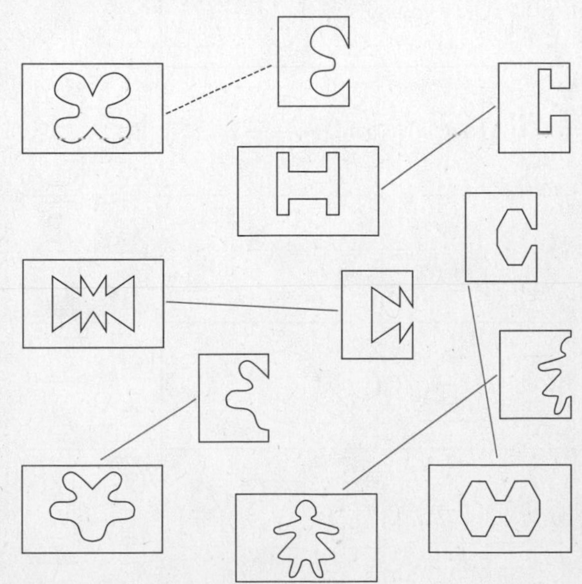

Notes for Home Your child explored symmetry by matching shapes. *Home Activity:* Help your child to cut out an original shape from folded paper. Predict the entire shape before unfolding the paper.

28 Use with pages 97–98.

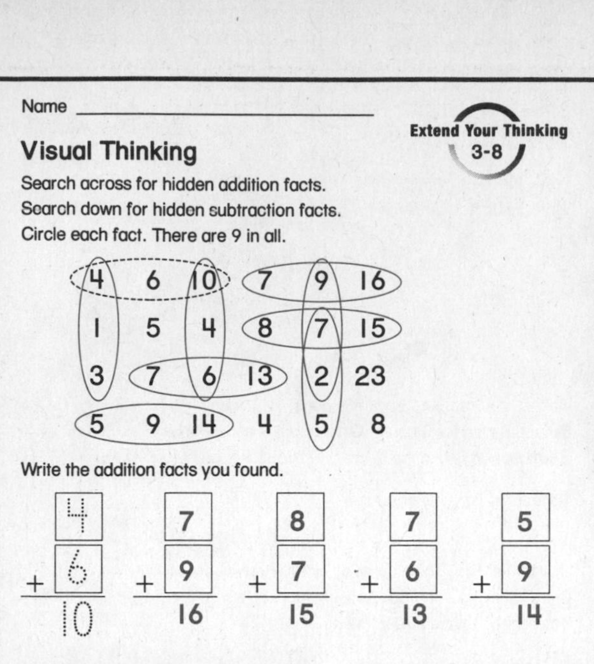

Name ____________________

Extend Your Thinking 3-8

Visual Thinking

Search across for hidden addition facts.
Search down for hidden subtraction facts.
Circle each fact. There are 9 in all.

4	6	10	7	9	16
1	5	4	8	7	15
3	7	6	13	2	23
5	9	14	4	5	8

Write the addition facts you found.

4 + 6 = 10; 7 + 9 = 16; 8 + 7 = 15; 7 + 6 = 13; 5 + 9 = 14

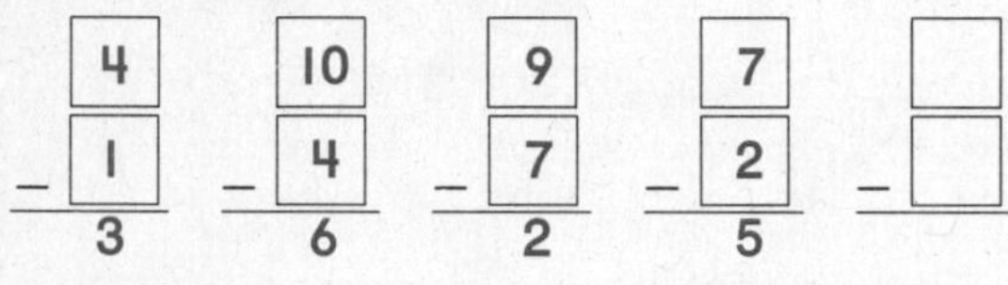

Write the subtraction facts you found.

4 − 1 = 3; 10 − 4 = 6; 9 − 7 = 2; 7 − 2 = 5

Notes for Home Your child found hidden addition and subtraction facts in a puzzle. *Home Activity:* Ask your child to write one more addition fact and one more subtraction fact.

Use with pages 99–100. **29**

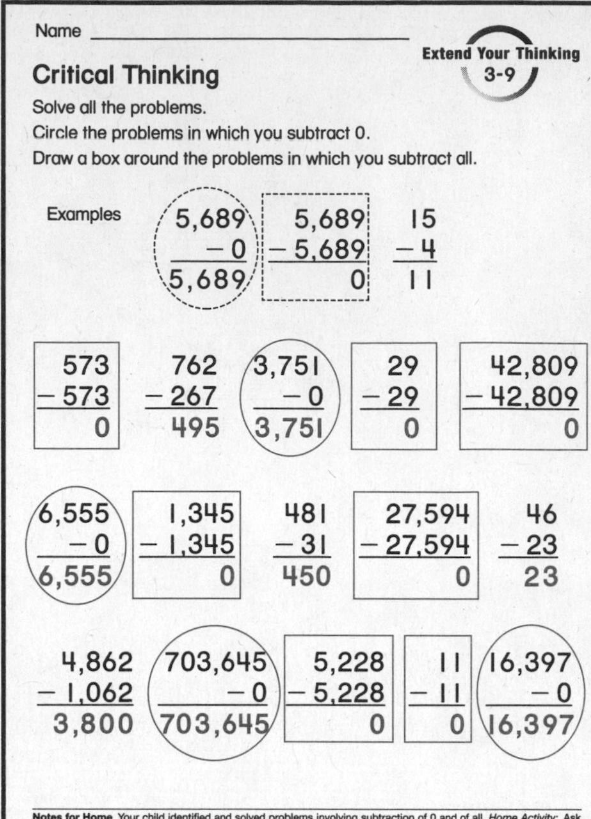

Name ____________________

Extend Your Thinking 3-9

Critical Thinking

Solve all the problems.
Circle the problems in which you subtract 0.
Draw a box around the problems in which you subtract all.

Examples: 5,689 − 0 = 5,689; 5,689 − 5,689 = 0; 15 − 4 = 11

573 − 573 = 0; 762 − 267 = 495; 3,751 − 0 = 3,751; 29 − 29 = 0; 42,809 − 42,809 = 0

6,555 − 0 = 6,555; 1,345 − 1,345 = 0; 481 − 31 = 450; 27,594 − 27,594 = 0; 46 − 23 = 23

4,862 − 1,062 = 3,800; 703,645 − 0 = 703,645; 5,228 − 5,228 = 0; 11 − 11 = 0; 16,397 − 0 = 16,397

Notes for Home Your child identified and solved problems involving subtraction of 0 and of all. *Home Activity:* Ask your child to use mental math and answer a problem in which a very large number is subtracted from itself, such as 87,546 - 87,546.

30 Use with pages 101–102.

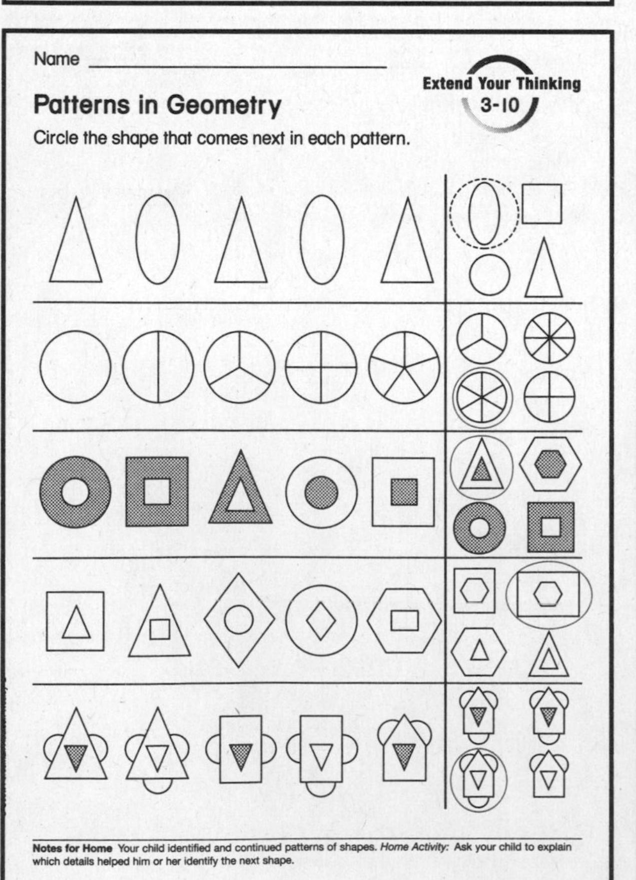

Name ____________________

Extend Your Thinking 3-10

Patterns in Geometry

Circle the shape that comes next in each pattern.

Notes for Home Your child identified and continued patterns of shapes. *Home Activity:* Ask your child to explain which details helped him or her identify the next shape.

Use with pages 105–106. **31**

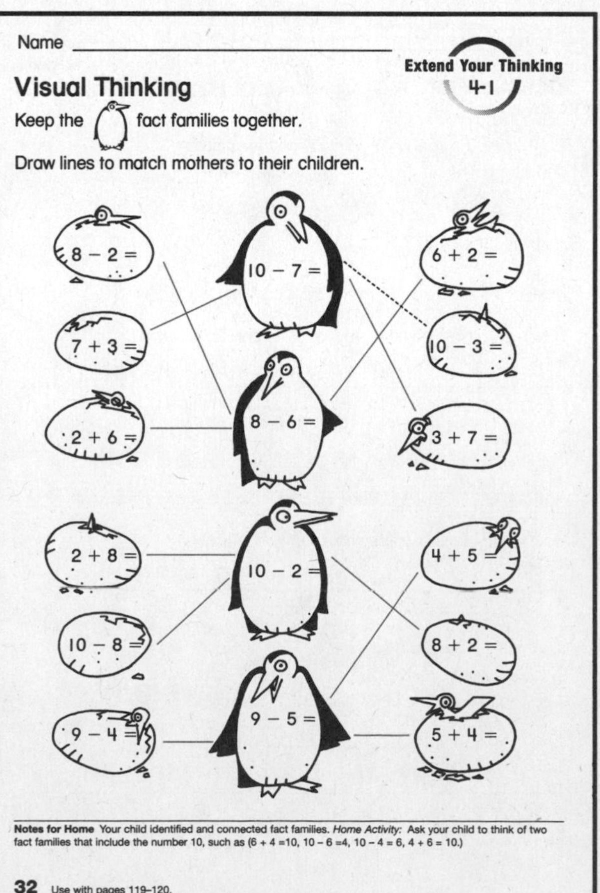

Name ____________________

Extend Your Thinking 4-1

Visual Thinking

Keep the fact families together.

Draw lines to match mothers to their children.

Notes for Home Your child identified and connected fact families. *Home Activity:* Ask your child to think of two fact families that include the number 10, such as (6 + 4 =10, 10 − 6 =4, 10 − 4 = 6, 4 + 6 = 10.)

32 Use with pages 119–120.

Name ______________________

Extend Your Thinking 4-2

Critical Thinking

Where did Sam leave his glasses? Find the clue in the 3 code words. Then circle the answer at the bottom of the page.

5-B	6-R	7-K
8-P	9-H	10-W
12-O	15-E	18-S

15 − 5 = 10   10 + 5 = 15

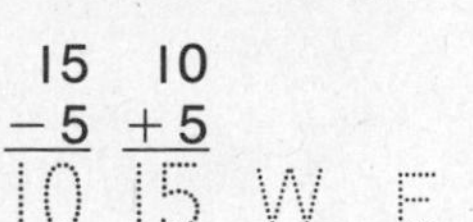

W E

15 − 8 = 7   7 + 8 = 15   8 + 7 = 15   15 − 7 = 8   K E E P

12 − 7 = 5   5 + 7 = 12   7 + 5 = 12   12 − 5 = 7   9 + 9 = 18   B O O K S

15 − 6 = 9   9 + 6 = 15   15 − 9 = 6   6 + 9 = 15   H E R E

Where are the glasses? bed car (shelf) hall kitchen

Notes for Home Your child used his or her knowledge of fact families to solve a puzzle. *Home Activity:* Ask your child to use the code and fact families to develop a one-word message.

Name ______________________

Extend Your Thinking 4-3

Visual Thinking

Complete each number sentence.
Then draw lines to match the shapes that fit together.
Make sure you have all 4 facts in each family.

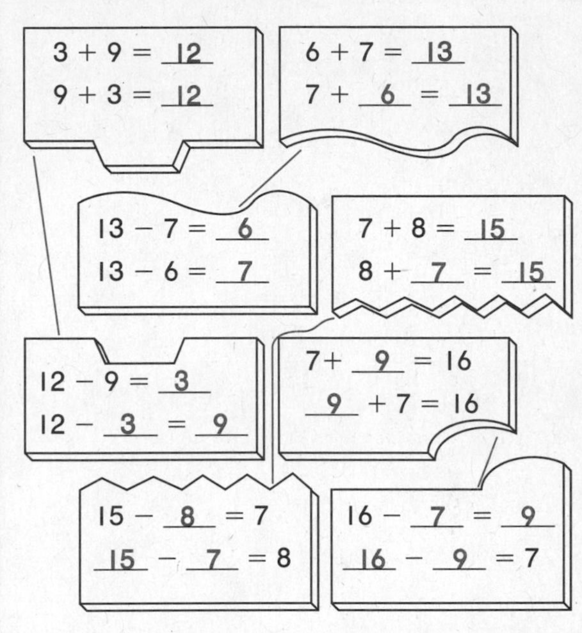

3 + 9 = 12
9 + 3 = 12

6 + 7 = 13
7 + 6 = 13

13 − 7 = 6
13 − 6 = 7

7 + 8 = 15
8 + 7 = 15

12 − 9 = 3
12 − 3 = 9

7 + 9 = 16
9 + 7 = 16

15 − 8 = 7
15 − 7 = 8

16 − 7 = 9
16 − 9 = 7

Notes for Home Your child completed number sentences and matched fact families. *Home Activity:* Ask your child to make up a story problem for one of the fact families.

Name ______________________

Extend Your Thinking 4-4

Critical Thinking

Read the story.
Circle the fact that solves the problem.

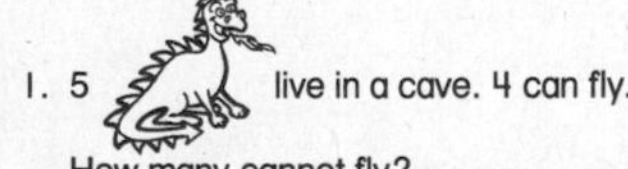

1. 5 [dragons] live in a cave. 4 can fly.
   How many cannot fly?
   5 + 4 = 9   (5 − 4 = 1)

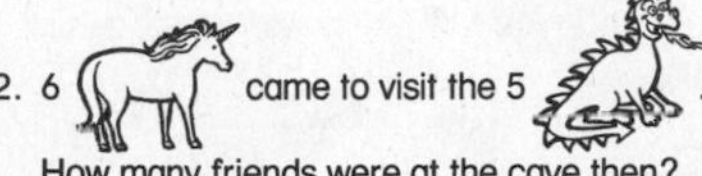

2. 6 [unicorns] came to visit the 5 [dragons].
   How many friends were at the cave then?
   (6 + 5 = 11)   6 − 5 = 1
3. The friends ate 12 pies. 7 of the pies were apple.
   How many pies were different?
   12 + 7 = 19   (12 − 7 = 5)
4. 2 of the 6 [unicorns] went home.
   How many stayed?
   6 + 2 = 8   (6 − 2 = 4)

Notes for Home Your child solved story problems by identifying the fact that solved each problem. *Home Activity:* Ask your child to choose one of the circled facts and state the three other addition and subtraction facts related to it. For example, for the fact 5 − 4 = 1, the related facts are 5 − 1 = 4, 4 + 1 = 5, and 1 + 4 = 5.

Name ______________________

Extend Your Thinking 4-5

Critical Thinking

Find the mystery numbers.

	Fact 1	Fact 2	Mystery Numbers
1.	7 + [9] = 16	5 + [9] = 14	[9]
2.	[8] + 6 = 14	[8] + 3 = 11	[8]
3.	5 + [7] = 12	[7] + △1 = 8	[7] △1
4.	[9] + △8 = 17	[9] − △8 = 1	[9] △8
5.	[5] + [5] = 10	[5] + △7 = 12	[5] △7

Notes for Home Your child identified the missing number(s) in pairs of facts. *Home Activity:* Ask your child to explain how he or she found the missing numbers in one of the rows.

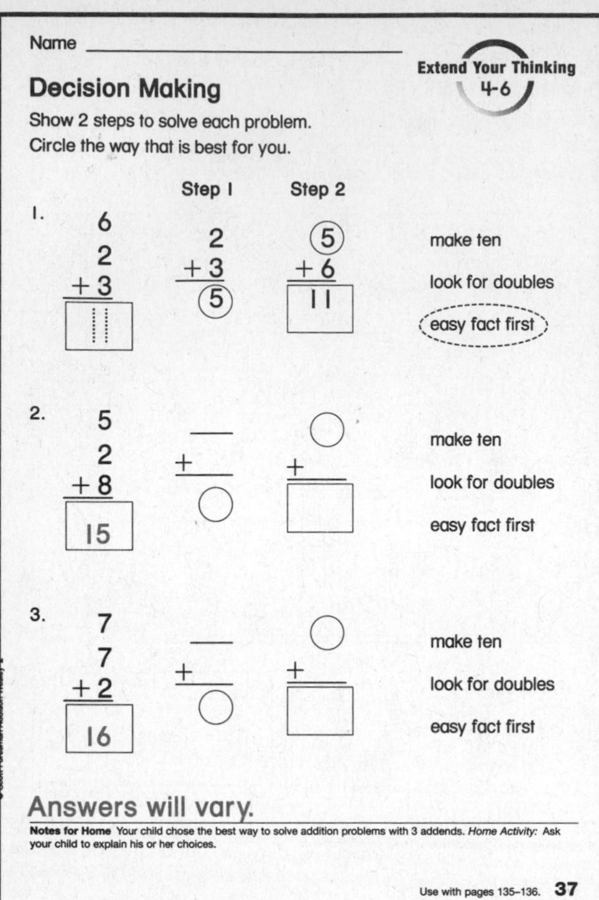

Name ______________________

Extend Your Thinking 4-6

Decision Making

Show 2 steps to solve each problem.
Circle the way that is best for you.

		Step 1	Step 2	
1.	6 + 2 + 3 = 11	2 + 3 = 5	5 + 6 = 11	make ten look for doubles (easy fact first)
2.	5 + 2 + 8 = 15	___ + ___ = ○	○ + ___ = ☐	make ten look for doubles easy fact first
3.	7 + 7 + 2 = 16	___ + ___ = ○	○ + ___ = ☐	make ten look for doubles easy fact first

Answers will vary.

Notes for Home Your child chose the best way to solve addition problems with 3 addends. *Home Activity:* Ask your child to explain his or her choices.

Use with pages 135–136. **37**

Name ______________________

Extend Your Thinking 4-7

Patterns in Numbers

This is a function machine. It changes numbers by adding 7.
Fill in the missing numbers going in and coming out.

In	Out
9	16
4	11
3	10
8	15
1	8
10	17
11	18
5	12
2	9

Notes for Home Your child followed a rule being applied to numbers. *Home Activity:* Ask your child to design a function machine and create a new rule. Work together to apply the rule to the numbers used in this activity.

38 Use with pages 137–138.

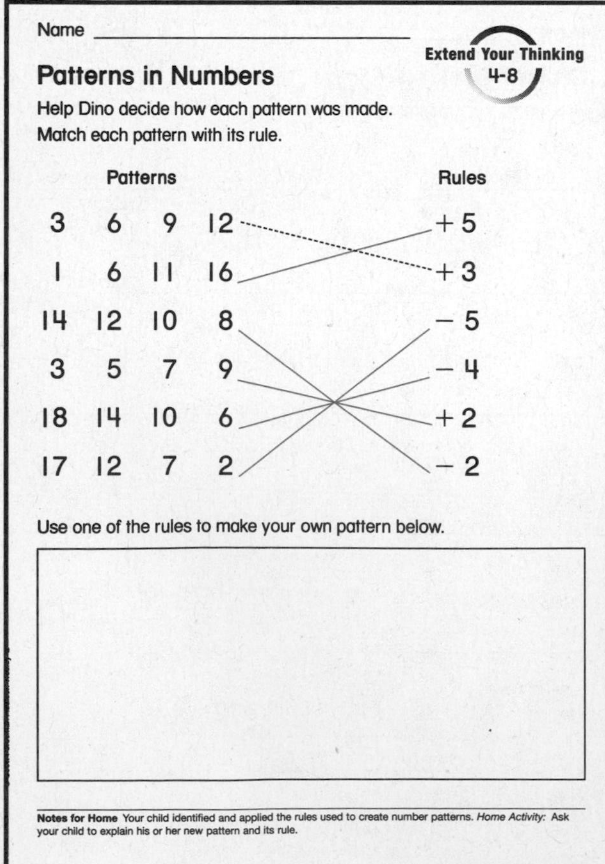

Name ______________________

Extend Your Thinking 4-8

Patterns in Numbers

Help Dino decide how each pattern was made.
Match each pattern with its rule.

Patterns	Rules
3 6 9 12	+5
1 6 11 16	+3
14 12 10 8	−5
3 5 7 9	−4
18 14 10 6	+2
17 12 7 2	−2

Use one of the rules to make your own pattern below.

Notes for Home Your child identified and applied the rules used to create number patterns. *Home Activity:* Ask your child to explain his or her new pattern and its rule.

Use with pages 139–140. **39**

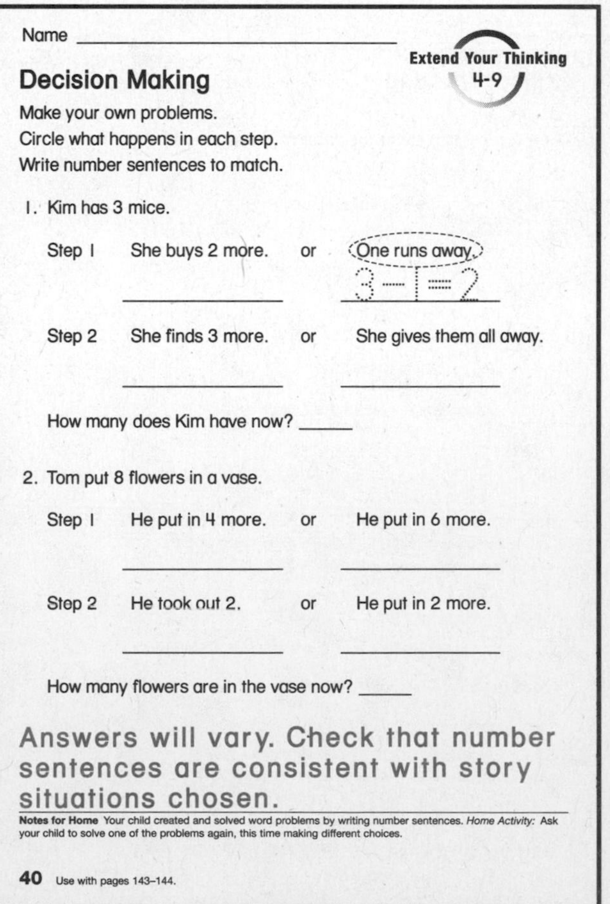

Name ______________________

Extend Your Thinking 4-9

Decision Making

Make your own problems.
Circle what happens in each step.
Write number sentences to match.

1. Kim has 3 mice.

Step 1 She buys 2 more. or (One runs away.)
3 − 1 = 2

Step 2 She finds 3 more. or She gives them all away.

How many does Kim have now? _____

2. Tom put 8 flowers in a vase.

Step 1 He put in 4 more. or He put in 6 more.

Step 2 He took out 2. or He put in 2 more.

How many flowers are in the vase now? _____

Answers will vary. Check that number sentences are consistent with story situations chosen.

Notes for Home Your child created and solved word problems by writing number sentences. *Home Activity:* Ask your child to solve one of the problems again, this time making different choices.

40 Use with pages 143–144.

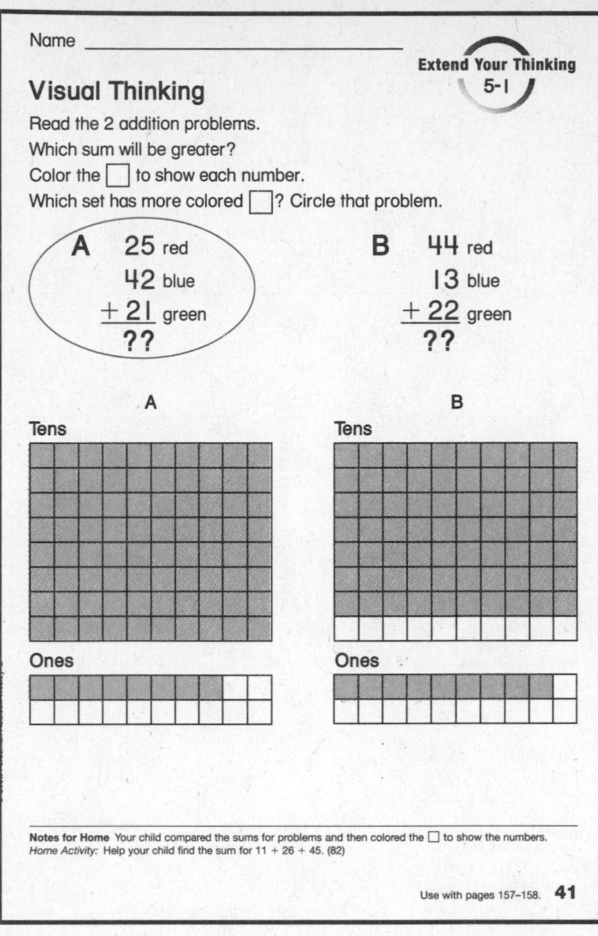

Name ______________________

Extend Your Thinking 5-1

Visual Thinking

Read the 2 addition problems.
Which sum will be greater?
Color the □ to show each number.
Which set has more colored □? Circle that problem.

A		B	
25	red	44	red
42	blue	13	blue
+ 21	green	+ 22	green
??		??	

A — Tens, Ones

B — Tens, Ones

Notes for Home Your child compared the sums for problems and then colored the □ to show the numbers.
Home Activity: Help your child find the sum for 11 + 26 + 45. (82)

Use with pages 157–158. **41**

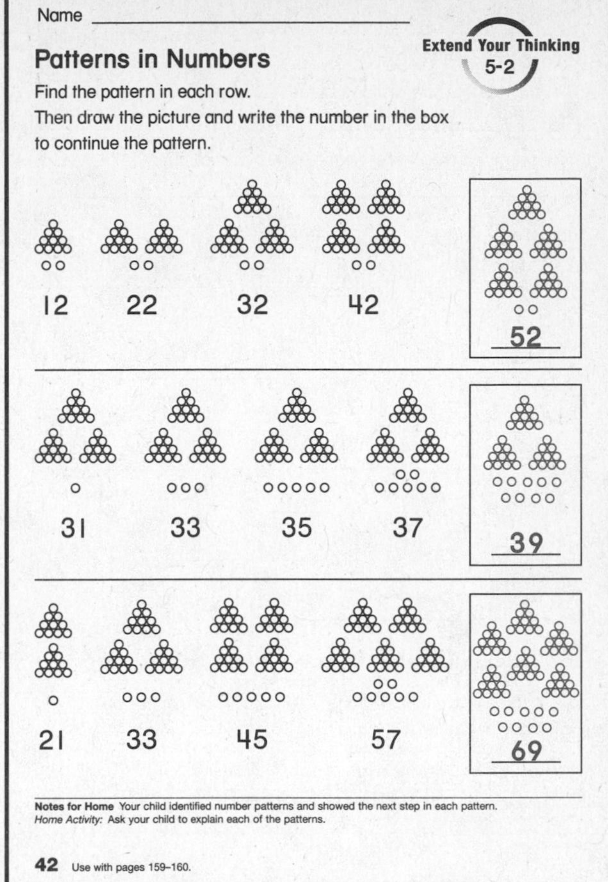

Name ______________________

Extend Your Thinking 5-2

Patterns in Numbers

Find the pattern in each row.
Then draw the picture and write the number in the box to continue the pattern.

12 22 32 42 52

31 33 35 37 39

21 33 45 57 69

Notes for Home Your child identified number patterns and showed the next step in each pattern.
Home Activity: Ask your child to explain each of the patterns.

42 Use with pages 159–160.

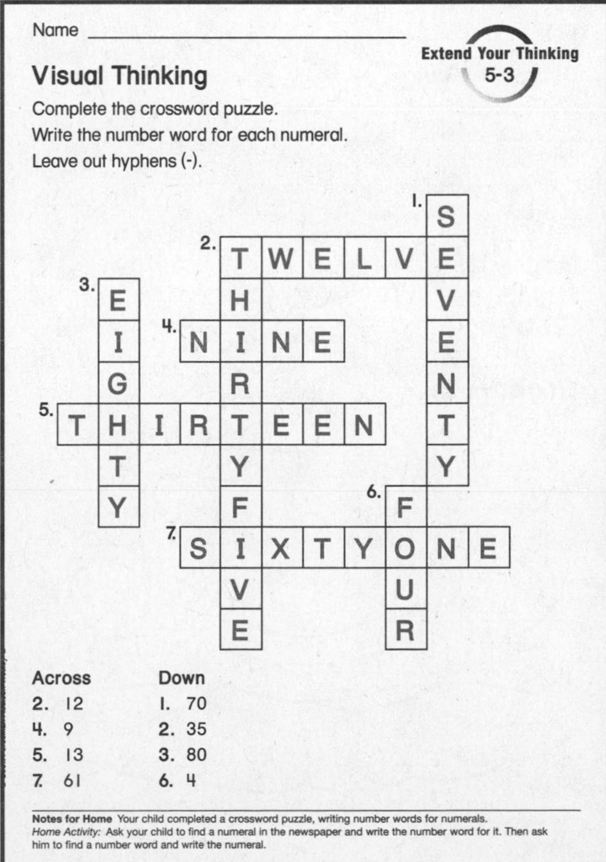

Name ______________________

Extend Your Thinking 5-3

Visual Thinking

Complete the crossword puzzle.
Write the number word for each numeral.
Leave out hyphens (-).

Across	Down
2. 12	1. 70
4. 9	2. 35
5. 13	3. 80
7. 61	6. 4

Notes for Home Your child completed a crossword puzzle, writing number words for numerals.
Home Activity: Ask your child to find a numeral in the newspaper and write the number word for it. Then ask him to find a number word and write the numeral.

Use with pages 161–162. **43**

Name ______________________

Extend Your Thinking 5-4

Decision Making

Circle the things you might buy in groups of 100.

Circle the things you are likely to see in groups of 100.

Notes for Home Your child showed an awareness of the concept of 100 by identifying objects that would be likely to be bought in groups of 100 or seen in groups of 100. *Home Activity:* Ask your child to explain his or her choices.

44 Use with pages 163–164.

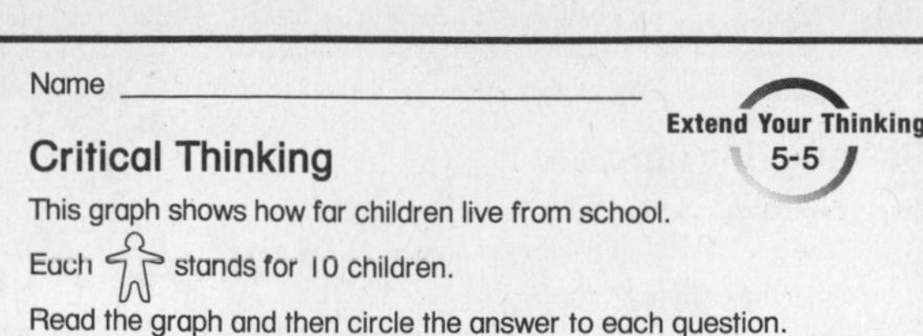

Name ______________________

Extend Your Thinking 5-5

Critical Thinking

This graph shows how far children live from school.

Each (person symbol) stands for 10 children.

Read the graph and then circle the answer to each question.

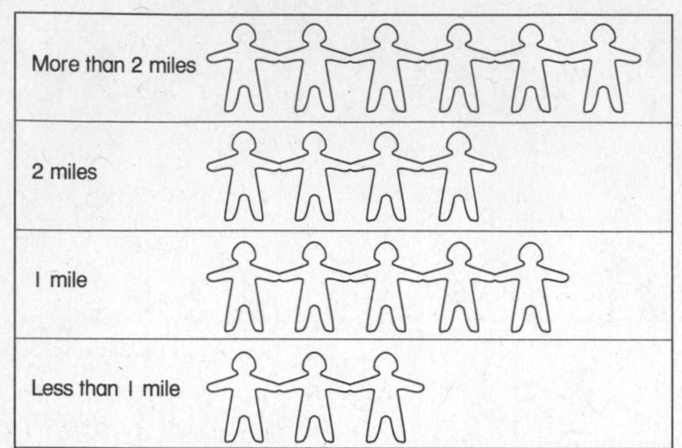

How far do most students live from school?

(2 miles or more) I mile or less

How many students live less than a mile from school? 50 (30)

The children who live more than I mile from school ride the bus.
How many children ride the bus? (100) 50

How many children must get to school in other ways? 30 (80)

Notes for Home Your child used information in a pictograph to answer questions. *Home Activity:* Work with your child to create a pictograph that describes your family in some way. Each symbol should represent ten items. The pictograph could show how many shoes each person has, or how many rocks each person collected on a recent trip to the park.

Use with pages 165–166. **45**

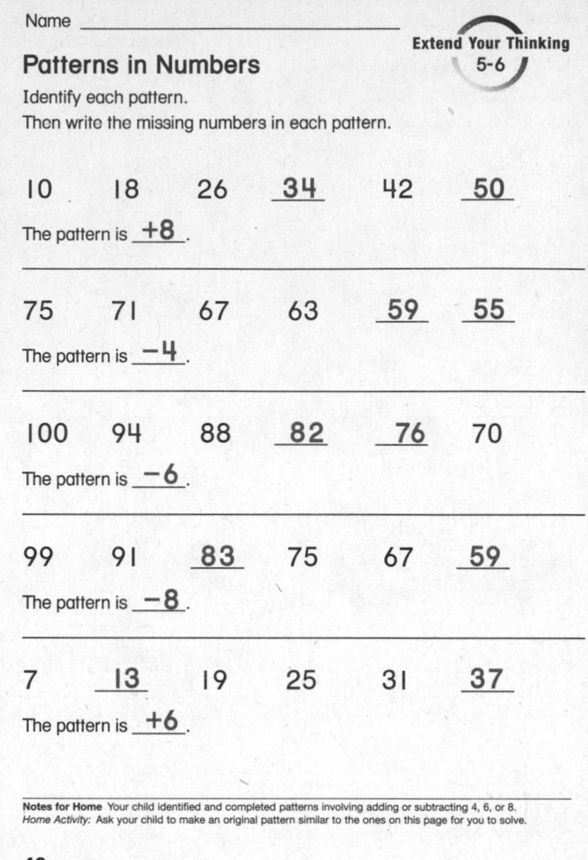

Name ______________________

Extend Your Thinking 5-6

Patterns in Numbers

Identify each pattern.
Then write the missing numbers in each pattern.

10 18 26 __34__ 42 __50__

The pattern is __+8__.

75 71 67 63 __59__ __55__

The pattern is __−4__.

100 94 88 __82__ __76__ 70

The pattern is __−6__.

99 91 __83__ 75 67 __59__

The pattern is __−8__.

7 __13__ 19 25 31 __37__

The pattern is __+6__.

Notes for Home Your child identified and completed patterns involving adding or subtracting 4, 6, or 8. *Home Activity:* Ask your child to make an original pattern similar to the ones on this page for you to solve.

46 Use with pages 169–170.

Name ______________________

Extend Your Thinking 5-7

Critical Thinking

Some children tried to guess the number that was in the hat.
Write **A** under each guess that is after 58.
Write **B** under each guess that is before 58.
Circle the guess that is closest to 58.

Beth 36	Sanji 67	Lou 15	Nancy 13
B	A	B	B
Able 92	Frances 29	Sue 38	James 74
A	B	B	A
Carl 60	(Maria 57)	Steve 86	Dawn 41
A	(B)	A	B

Each phrase below tells about a number above. Write it.

between 28 and 30	29	just before 42	41
between 37 and 39	38	just after 73	74
just before 14	13	just after 14	15
between 59 and 61	60	just before 37	36
between 66 and 68	67	just after 91	92

Notes for Home Your child identified numbers that are between, before, or after given numbers. *Home Activity:* Say a number. Have your child tell the number that is immediately before and immediately after that number.

Use with pages 170–171. **47**

Name ______________________

Extend Your Thinking 5-8

Visual Thinking

Color each part that is close to 10 red.
Color each part that is close to 20 blue.
Color each part that is close to 30 green.
Color each part that is close to 40 yellow.
Color each part that is close to 50 purple.

Red—11, 12, 13
Blue—17, 18, 21, 22
Green—28, 32, 33
Yellow—38, 42, 43
Purple—48, 49, 51

42 22 18 38 11 43 17 21 11 13 12 48 32 51 28 49 33

Notes for Home Your child decided whether each number was closer to the decade number before or after it. *Home Activity:* With your child, look at newspaper ads and decide whether each price is closer to the decade number before or after it.

48 Use with pages 173–174.

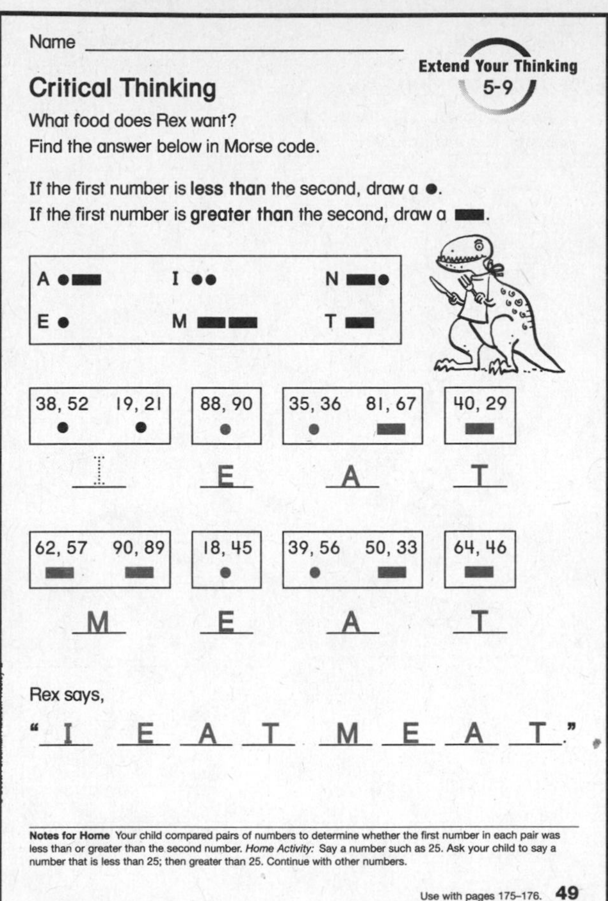

Name ______________________

Extend Your Thinking 5-9

Critical Thinking

What food does Rex want?
Find the answer below in Morse code.

If the first number is **less than** the second, draw a ●.
If the first number is **greater than** the second, draw a ▬.

A ●▬	I ●●	N ▬●
E ●	M ▬▬	T ▬

38, 52 19, 21	88, 90	35, 36 81, 67	40, 29
● ●	●	● ▬	▬
I	E	A	T

62, 57 90, 89	18, 45	39, 56 50, 33	64, 46
▬ ▬	●	● ▬	▬
M	E	A	T

Rex says,

"I E A T M E A T"

Notes for Home Your child compared pairs of numbers to determine whether the first number in each pair was less than or greater than the second number. *Home Activity:* Say a number such as 25. Ask your child to say a number that is less than 25; then greater than 25. Continue with other numbers.

Use with pages 175–176. **49**

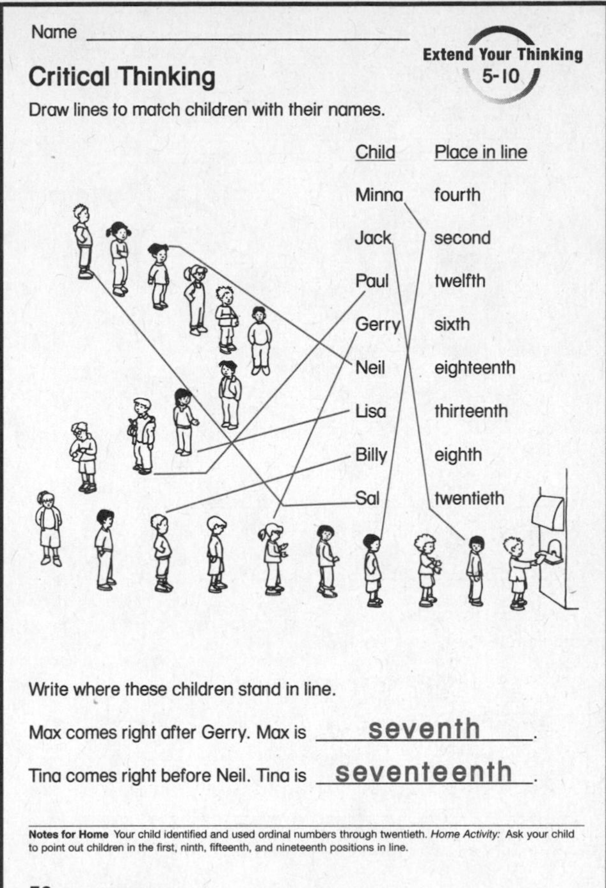

Name ______________________

Extend Your Thinking 5-10

Critical Thinking

Draw lines to match children with their names.

Child	Place in line
Minna	fourth
Jack	second
Paul	twelfth
Gerry	sixth
Neil	eighteenth
Lisa	thirteenth
Billy	eighth
Sal	twentieth

Write where these children stand in line.

Max comes right after Gerry. Max is **seventh**.

Tina comes right before Neil. Tina is **seventeenth**.

Notes for Home Your child identified and used ordinal numbers through twentieth. *Home Activity:* Ask your child to point out children in the first, ninth, fifteenth, and nineteenth positions in line.

50 Use with pages 179–180.

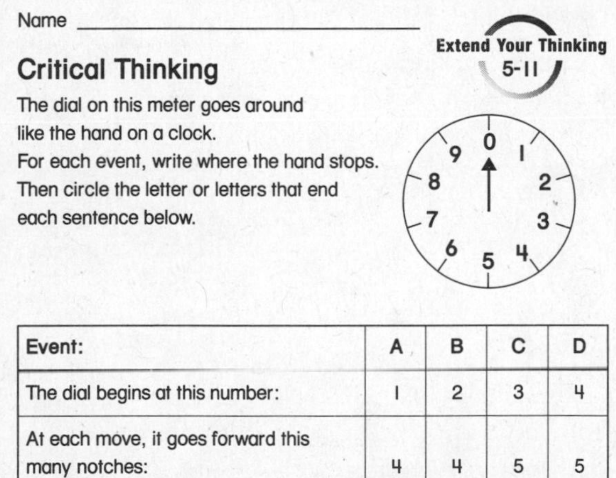

Name ______________________

Extend Your Thinking 5-11

Critical Thinking

The dial on this meter goes around like the hand on a clock.
For each event, write where the hand stops.
Then circle the letter or letters that end each sentence below.

Event:	A	B	C	D
The dial begins at this number:	1	2	3	4
At each move, it goes forward this many notches:	4	4	5	5
It moves this many times:	3	3	3	3
It ends here:	3	4	8	9

1. The dial starts and ends on an even number in event A (B) C D
2. The dial starts on an even number and ends on an odd number in event A B C (D)
3. The dial starts on an odd number and ends on an even number in event A B (C) D

Notes for Home Your child followed patterns and identified even and odd numbers. *Home Activity:* Ask your child to extend each event one more turn. Where does the dial end each time? (7, 8, 3, 4)

Use with pages 181–182. **51**

Name ______________________

Extend Your Thinking 5-12

Critical Thinking

Each box has three names for the same number.
It also has one name that does not belong.
Draw a line through the name that does not belong.

1. forty-nine ~~39~~ 4 tens 9 ones 49	**2.** 27 2 tens 7 ones ~~29~~ twenty-seven
3. 75 ~~57~~ 7 tens 5 ones seventy-five	**4.** ninety-three 93 ~~3 tens 9 ones~~ 9 tens 3 ones
5. eighteen ~~8 tens 0 ones~~ 18 1 ten 8 ones	**6.** 5 tens 4 ones 54 ~~forty-five~~ fifty-four
7. 6 tens 2 ones sixty-two ~~2 tens 6 ones~~ 62	**8.** ~~ninety-eight~~ 8 tens 9 ones 89 eighty-nine

Notes for Home Your child identified three names for the same number. *Home Activity:* Ask your child to write another name for the number he or she crossed out in each box.

52 Use with pages 185–186.

Name ______________________

Extend Your Thinking 6-1

Visual Thinking

Tina and Joe put their money together to buy a gift.
Circle the coins that Tina may have put in.
Draw an X on the coins that Joe may have put in.

Answers will vary, but should total 43¢ and 56¢.

Notes for Home Your child selected coins that together equaled given amounts of money. *Home Activity:* Ask your child to count the dimes, nickels, and pennies in your change purse or pocket.

Use with pages 199–200. **53**

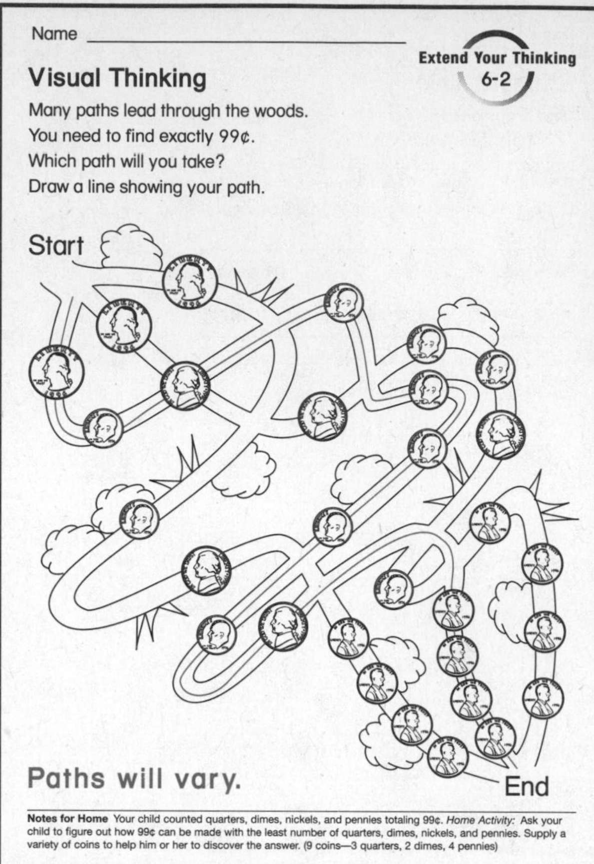

Name ______________________

Extend Your Thinking 6-2

Visual Thinking

Many paths lead through the woods.
You need to find exactly 99¢.
Which path will you take?
Draw a line showing your path.

Paths will vary.

Notes for Home Your child counted quarters, dimes, nickels, and pennies totaling 99¢. *Home Activity:* Ask your child to figure out how 99¢ can be made with the least number of quarters, dimes, nickels, and pennies. Supply a variety of coins to help him or her to discover the answer. (9 coins—3 quarters, 2 dimes, 4 pennies)

54 Use with pages 201–202.

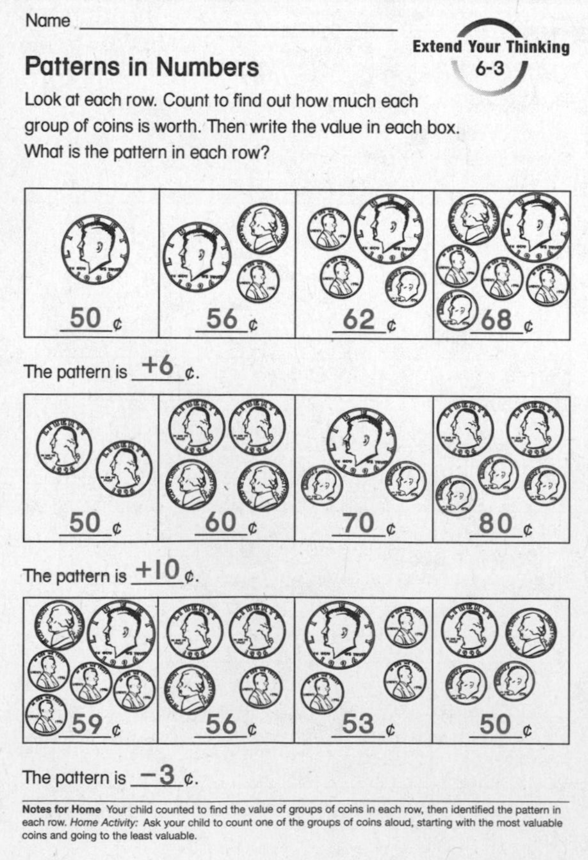

Name ______________________

Extend Your Thinking 6-3

Patterns in Numbers

Look at each row. Count to find out how much each group of coins is worth. Then write the value in each box.
What is the pattern in each row?

50 ¢	56 ¢	62 ¢	68 ¢

The pattern is +6 ¢.

50 ¢	60 ¢	70 ¢	80 ¢

The pattern is +10 ¢.

59 ¢	56 ¢	53 ¢	50 ¢

The pattern is −3 ¢.

Notes for Home Your child counted to find the value of groups of coins in each row, then identified the pattern in each row. *Home Activity:* Ask your child to count one of the groups of coins aloud, starting with the most valuable coins and going to the least valuable.

Use with pages 205–206. **55**

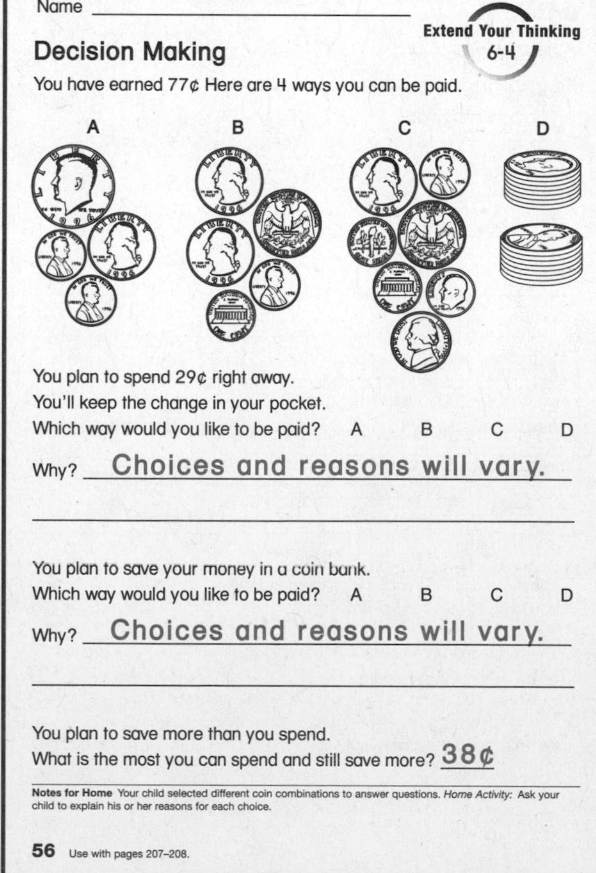

Name ______________________

Extend Your Thinking 6-4

Decision Making

You have earned 77¢ Here are 4 ways you can be paid.

A B C D

You plan to spend 29¢ right away.
You'll keep the change in your pocket.
Which way would you like to be paid? A B C D

Why? Choices and reasons will vary.

You plan to save your money in a coin bank.
Which way would you like to be paid? A B C D

Why? Choices and reasons will vary.

You plan to save more than you spend.
What is the most you can spend and still save more? 38¢

Notes for Home Your child selected different coin combinations to answer questions. *Home Activity:* Ask your child to explain his or her reasons for each choice.

56 Use with pages 207–208.

Name ______________________

Extend Your Thinking 6-5

Decision Making

You want to earn $5.00.
Circle the jobs you would do.

$3.00 $1.00 $2.00 $4.00

Answers will vary, but should total $5.00.

Circle what you would buy with $5.00.

$3.00 50¢ $2.00 75¢ 75¢ $1.00 50¢ 25¢

How much money is left over? **Answers will vary.**

Notes for Home Your child chose jobs to earn a total of $5.00; then chose how he or she would spend the $5.00. *Home Activity:* Ask your child to suggest a job around the house that he or she could do to earn $5.00.

Use with pages 211–212. **57**

Name ______________________

Extend Your Thinking 6-6

Critical Thinking

Draw lines to match the children with their change.
Each child bought the same thing. It cost 39¢.

I paid with a half dollar.
I paid with 4 dimes.
I paid with a quarter and 2 dimes.

Each child bought the same thing. It cost 57¢.

I paid with a dollar bill.
I paid with 6 dimes.
I paid with 3 quarters.

Notes for Home Home Your child identified the value of each coin combination and the correct change from each. *Home Activity:* Help your child to figure out the correct change from $1.00 if it was used to buy a 39¢ item. (61¢)

58 Use with pages 213–214.

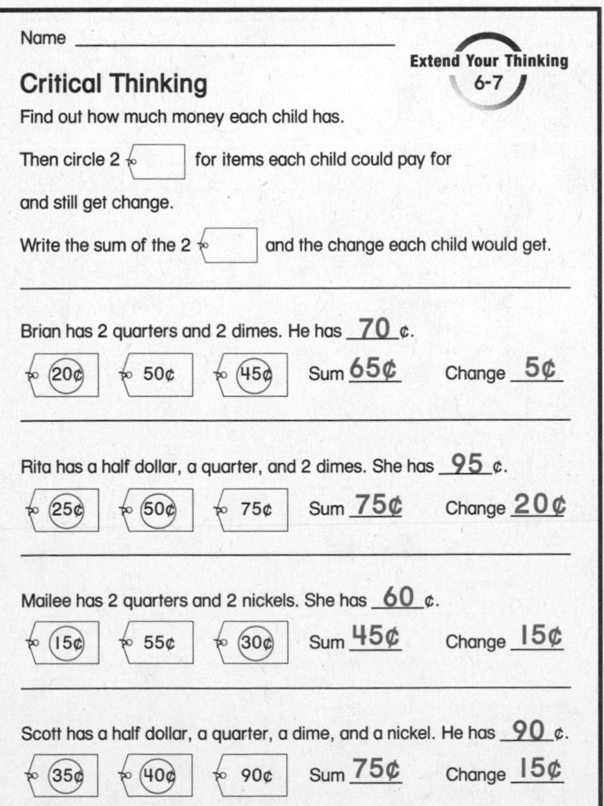

Name ______________________

Extend Your Thinking 6-7

Critical Thinking

Find out how much money each child has.

Then circle 2 [price tags] for items each child could pay for and still get change.

Write the sum of the 2 [price tags] and the change each child would get.

Brian has 2 quarters and 2 dimes. He has **70** ¢.

(20¢) 50¢ (45¢) Sum **65¢** Change **5¢**

Rita has a half dollar, a quarter, and 2 dimes. She has **95** ¢.

(25¢) (50¢) 75¢ Sum **75¢** Change **20¢**

Mailee has 2 quarters and 2 nickels. She has **60** ¢.

(15¢) 55¢ (30¢) Sum **45¢** Change **15¢**

Scott has a half dollar, a quarter, a dime, and a nickel. He has **90** ¢.

(35¢) (40¢) 90¢ Sum **75¢** Change **15¢**

Notes for Home Your child solved problems by making change. *Home Activity:* Select one or two rows and ask your child to tell you how much more each child would need to spend to all of his or her money. (The answers will be the amount of change each child got.)

Use with pages 219–220. **59**

Name ______________________

Extend Your Thinking 7-1

Visual Thinking

Play Tic-Tac-Time. Mark each picture with X or O.

X The action takes a minute or less to do.

O The action takes more than a minute to do.

Draw a line to show the winner.

Ann

Circle the winner. (O) X

Notes for Home Your child classified activities according to how much time they require. *Home Activity:* Ask your child to pantomime 2 activities pictured that take a minute or less to do.

60 Use with pages 233–234.

Name ______________________

Extend Your Thinking 7-2

Decision Making

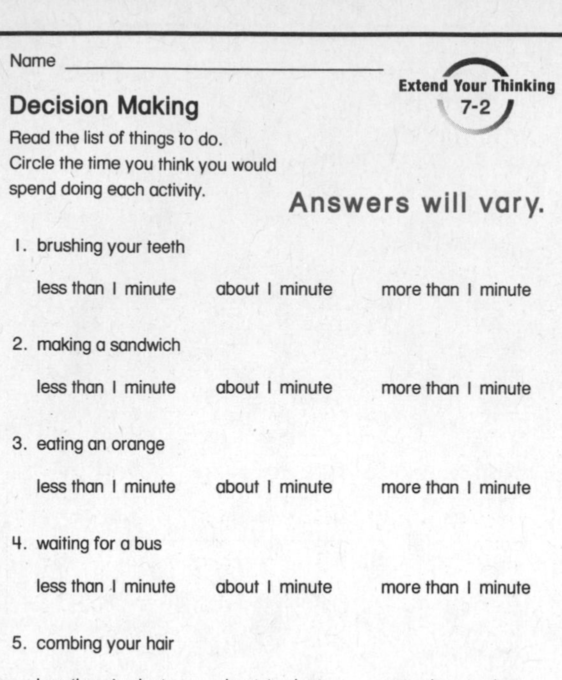

Read the list of things to do.
Circle the time you think you would spend doing each activity.

Answers will vary.

1. brushing your teeth
   less than 1 minute   about 1 minute   more than 1 minute
2. making a sandwich
   less than 1 minute   about 1 minute   more than 1 minute
3. eating an orange
   less than 1 minute   about 1 minute   more than 1 minute
4. waiting for a bus
   less than 1 minute   about 1 minute   more than 1 minute
5. combing your hair
   less than 1 minute   about 1 minute   more than 1 minute
6. putting on a sweater
   less than 1 minute   about 1 minute   more than 1 minute

Notes for Home Your child decided how much time he or she would spend doing a variety of activities, using a duration of less than 1 minute, about 1 minute, and more than 1 minute. *Home Activity:* Ask your child to measure the time it takes for him or her to complete everyday activities such as dressing, setting the table, etc.

Name ______________________

Extend Your Thinking 7-3

Visual Thinking

Look at the clocks.
A letter is in the place of 12.
Decide the time each clock shows.
Find the matching clock below.
Write the letter on the line. Then find the message.

11:00	1:00	7:00	6:00
T	I	C	K
11:00	3:00	7:00	6:00
T	O	C	K

Notes for Home Your child told time to the hour on analog clocks and matched each clock with a digital clock showing the same time. *Home Activity:* Ask your child to read a clock on the hour in your home.

Name ______________________

Extend Your Thinking 7-4

Critical Thinking

Match each child with what he or she spent time doing.

Notes for Home Your child matched pictured activities having specific beginning and ending times. *Home Activity:* Ask your child to record beginning and ending times to keep track of how many hours he or she spends sleeping, watching TV, and reading during a 2-day period.

Name ______________________

Extend Your Thinking 7-5

Critical Thinking

Complete the timetable.
Then answer the questions.

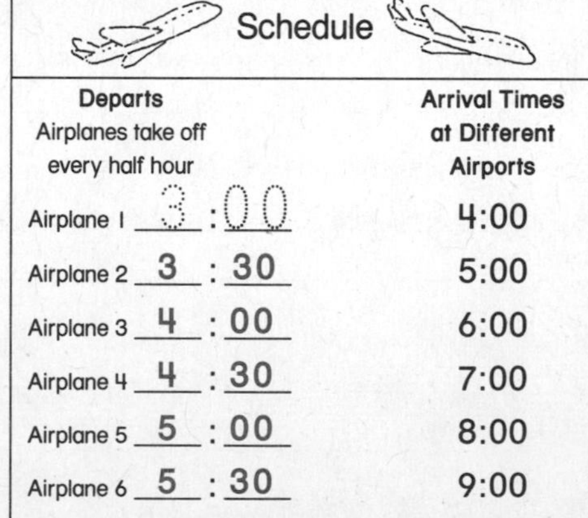

Schedule

Departs Airplanes take off every half hour	Arrival Times at Different Airports
Airplane 1 3 : 00	4:00
Airplane 2 3 : 30	5:00
Airplane 3 4 : 00	6:00
Airplane 4 4 : 30	7:00
Airplane 5 5 : 00	8:00
Airplane 6 5 : 30	9:00

1. How long is Airplane 4 in the air? 2 1/2 hours
2. How long is Airplane 5 in the air? 3 hours
3. Which airplane has the shortest flying time? 1
4. When would airplane 7 take off? 6:00

Notes for Home Your child completed a timetable using half-hour and hour times. *Home Activity:* Ask your child: *How many hours after Airplane 1 did Airplane 6 take off?* (2 1/2 hours later)

Name ______________________

Extend Your Thinking 7-6

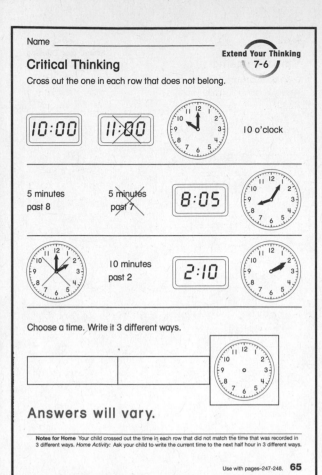

Critical Thinking

Cross out the one in each row that does not belong.

10:00 ~~11:00~~  10 o'clock

5 minutes past 8 ~~5 minutes past 7~~ 8:05 

 10 minutes past 2 2:10 

Choose a time. Write it 3 different ways.

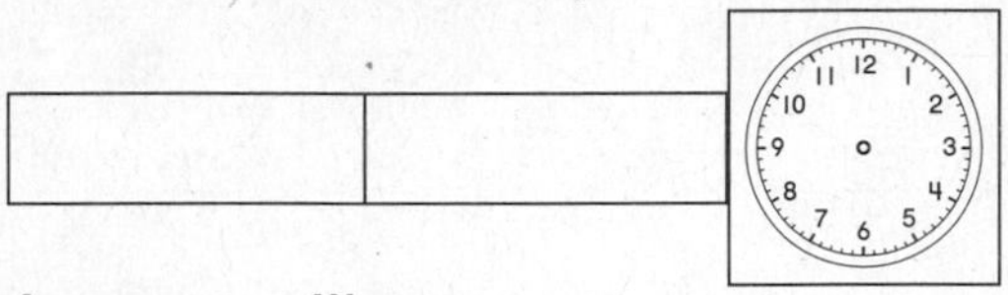

Answers will vary.

Notes for Home Your child crossed out the time in each row that did not match the time that was recorded in 3 different ways. *Home Activity:* Ask your child to write the current time to the next half hour in 3 different ways.

Name ______________________

Extend Your Thinking 7-7

Patterns in Data

Two buses leave City Square at the same times.
One bus goes east to East Town Mall.
The ride to East Town Mall takes 15 minutes.
The other bus goes west to West Market.
The ride to West Market takes 5 minutes.
Fill in the missing times on these schedules.

Leave City Square	Arrive East Town Mall
9:00	9:15
9:30	9:45
10:00	**10:15**
10:20	**10:35**
10:40	**10:55**
10:50	**11:05**
11:05	**11:20**
11:15	**11:30**
11:30	**11:45**

Leave City Square	Arrive West Market
9:00	9:05
9:30	9:35
10:00	**10:05**
10:20	**10:25**
10:40	**10:45**
10:50	**10:55**
11:05	**11:10**
11:15	**11:20**
11:30	**11:35**

Notes for Home Your child found the arrival times in a bus schedule by adding either 5 or 15 minutes to departure times. *Home Activity:* Show your child a bus (or other) timetable and ask him or her to read a column of starting times and relate it to the first column in these tables.

Name ______________________

Extend Your Thinking 7-8

Patterns in Numbers

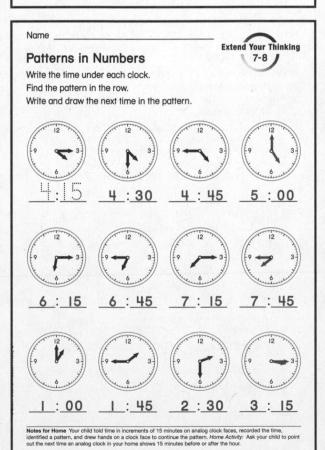

Write the time under each clock.
Find the pattern in the row.
Write and draw the next time in the pattern.

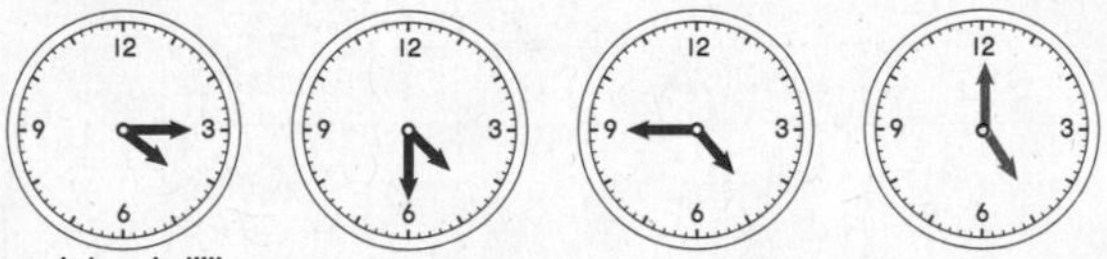

4:15 4 : 30 4 : 45 5 : 00

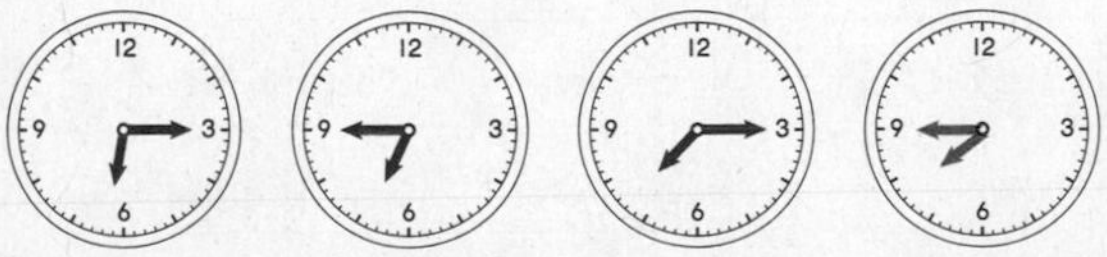

6 : 15 6 : 45 7 : 15 7 : 45

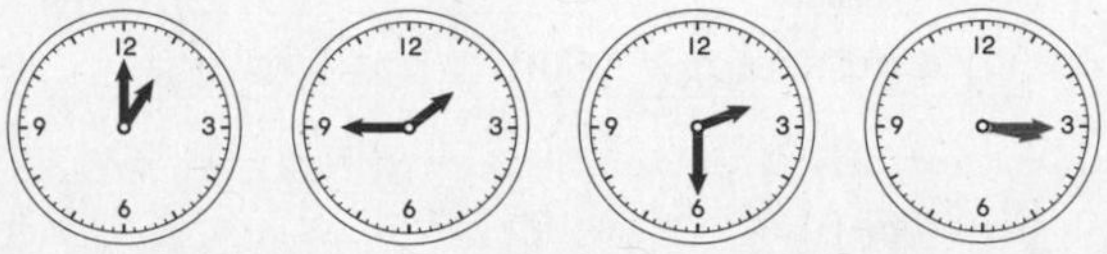

1 : 00 1 : 45 2 : 30 3 : 15

Notes for Home Your child told time in increments of 15 minutes on analog clock faces, recorded the time, identified a pattern, and drew hands on a clock face to continue the pattern. *Home Activity:* Ask your child to point out the next time an analog clock in your home shows 15 minutes before or after the hour.

Name ______________________

Extend Your Thinking 7-9

Decision Making

You are at the zoo.
Decide what to do there. Decide when to do it.
Write what you will do next to the time.

These tips will help.

You have not eaten lunch yet.
If you like, you may do something twice.

Zoo Schedule

Meet the Zookeeper	1:00 to 3:30
Big Cat building open	2:00 to 4:00
Zoo shop open	1:30 to 4:30
Monkeys are fed	2:00 to 2:30
Lunchroom open	12:00 to 2:00

1:00 ______________________
1:30 ______________________
2:00 ______________________
2:30 ______________________
3:00 ______________________
3:30 Go home. **Answers will vary.**

Notes for Home Your child decided on a schedule for a zoo visit, taking into account opening and closing times and personal preferences. *Home Activity:* Ask your child to help you schedule a shopping trip or a trip to a museum, based on real-life time considerations.

Name ________________

Extend Your Thinking 8-1

Critical Thinking

Find the plane that each skydiver jumped from.
Draw a line from each skydiver to the plane with the correct sum.

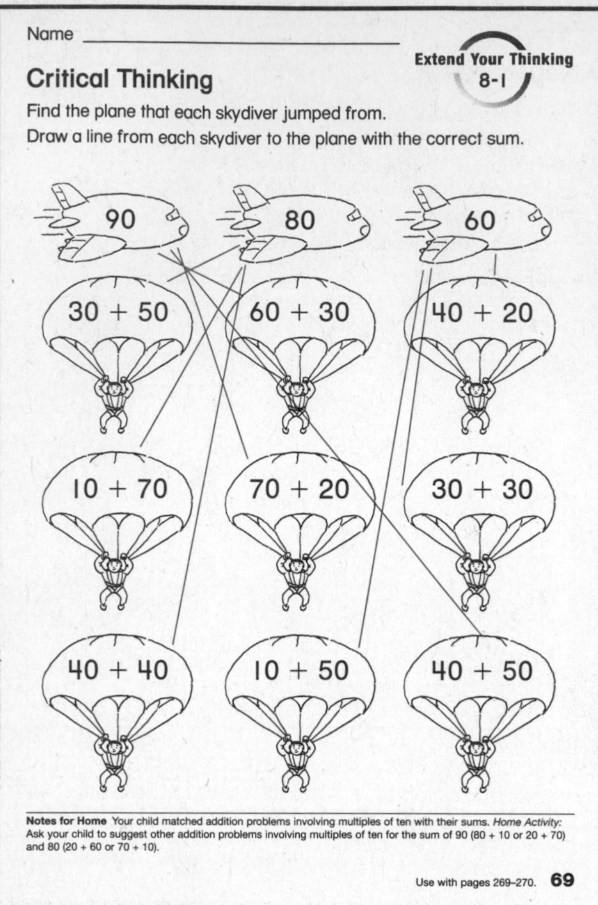

Notes for Home Your child matched addition problems involving multiples of ten with their sums. *Home Activity:* Ask your child to suggest other addition problems involving multiples of ten for the sum of 90 (80 + 10 or 20 + 70) and 80 (20 + 60 or 70 + 10).

Use with pages 269–270. **69**

Name ________________

Extend Your Thinking 8-2

Visual Thinking

Solve each addition problem.
Write the sum in the outer circle.

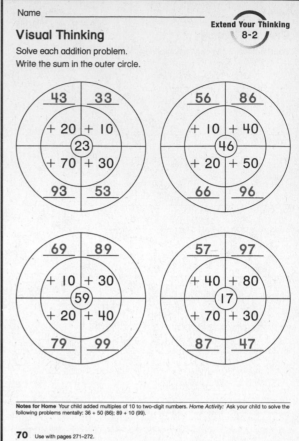

Center	Problem	Sum
23	+ 20	43
23	+ 10	33
23	+ 70	93
23	+ 30	53
46	+ 10	56
46	+ 40	86
46	+ 20	66
46	+ 50	96
59	+ 10	69
59	+ 30	89
59	+ 20	79
59	+ 40	99
17	+ 40	57
17	+ 80	97
17	+ 70	87
17	+ 30	47

Notes for Home Your child added multiples of 10 to two-digit numbers. *Home Activity:* Ask your child to solve the following problems mentally: 36 + 50 (86); 89 + 10 (99).

70 Use with pages 271–272.

Name ________________

Extend Your Thinking 8-3

Decision Making

Sometimes it's useful to have an **exact count** of things, such as the number of people in your family.
Sometimes it's useful to **count by 10s**, such as finding the number of children in your grade.
Other times, it's useful to **count in larger groups**, such as finding the number of window panes in your school.

Decide how to count the things below. Write **E** for exact count.
Write **10** for groups of 10. Write **L** for larger groups.

1. in a forest L
2. in your desk 10
3. in a library L
4. in a restaurant 10
5. in your closet E
6. in a post office L
7. in a parking lot L
8. in a supermarket L

Possible responses are shown.

Notes for Home Your child classified items for which it would be useful to have an exact count, a count by tens, or an even less exact count by larger groups. *Home Activity:* Ask your child to explain the reasons for several of his or her decisions.

Use with pages 273–274. **71**

Name ________________

Extend Your Thinking 8-4

Patterns in Data

Jill spends 1 hour at the gym every day.
This chart tells how Jill plans to use her time for 6 days.
Jill will keep up the pattern she began in the first 2 days.
Fill in the missing numbers.

	Running	Swimming
Monday	10 minutes	50 minutes
Tuesday	20 minutes	40 minutes
Wednesday	30 minutes	30 minutes
Thursday	40 minutes	20 minutes
Friday	50 minutes	10 minutes
Saturday	60 minutes	0 minutes

What is Jill's pattern? Each day Jill runs 10 minutes more and swims 10 minutes less.

On which day does Jill spend equal times running and swimming?
Wednesday

On which day does Jill not swim? Saturday

Notes for Home Your child read a chart which recorded a pattern and then made a prediction about future events based on that pattern. *Home Activity:* Ask your child to explain his or her reasoning.

72 Use with pages 275–276.

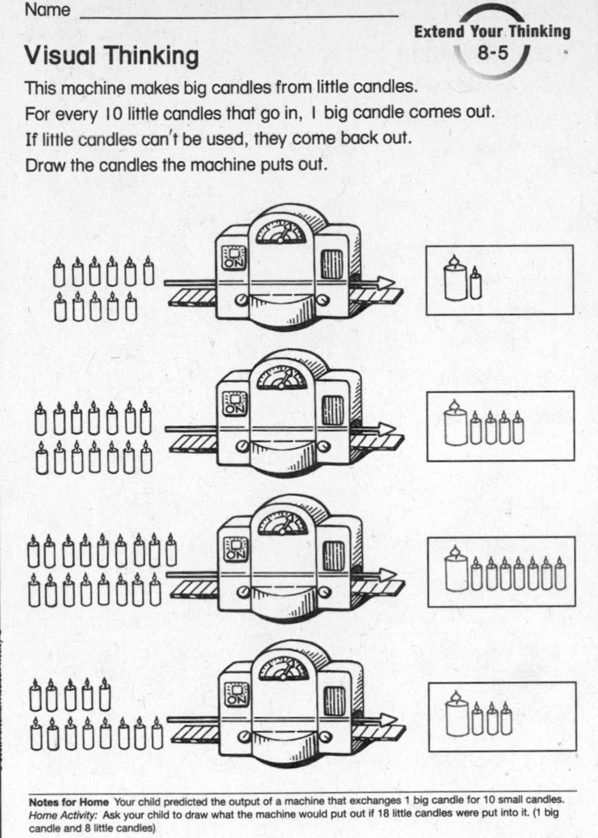

Name ______________________

Extend Your Thinking 8-5

Visual Thinking

This machine makes big candles from little candles.
For every 10 little candles that go in, 1 big candle comes out.
If little candles can't be used, they come back out.
Draw the candles the machine puts out.

Notes for Home Your child predicted the output of a machine that exchanges 1 big candle for 10 small candles. *Home Activity:* Ask your child to draw what the machine would put out if 18 little candles were put into it. (1 big candle and 8 little candles)

Use with pages 279–280. **73**

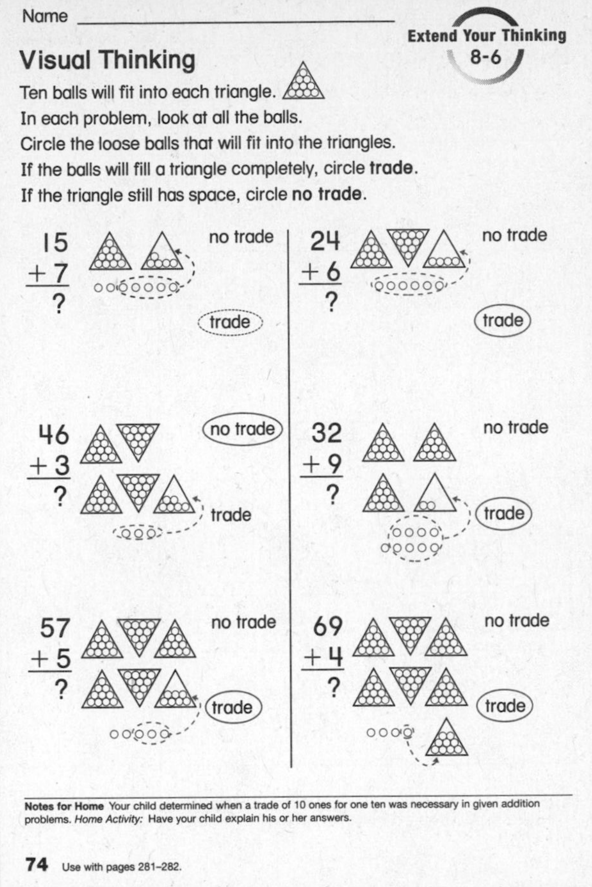

Name ______________________

Extend Your Thinking 8-6

Visual Thinking

Ten balls will fit into each triangle.
In each problem, look at all the balls.
Circle the loose balls that will fit into the triangles.
If the balls will fill a triangle completely, circle **trade**.
If the triangle still has space, circle **no trade**.

15 + 7 = ? — no trade / trade

24 + 6 = ? — no trade / trade

46 + 3 = ? — no trade / trade

32 + 9 = ? — no trade / trade

57 + 5 = ? — no trade / trade

69 + 4 = ? — no trade / trade

Notes for Home Your child determined when a trade of 10 ones for one ten was necessary in given addition problems. *Home Activity:* Have your child explain his or her answers.

74 Use with pages 281–282.

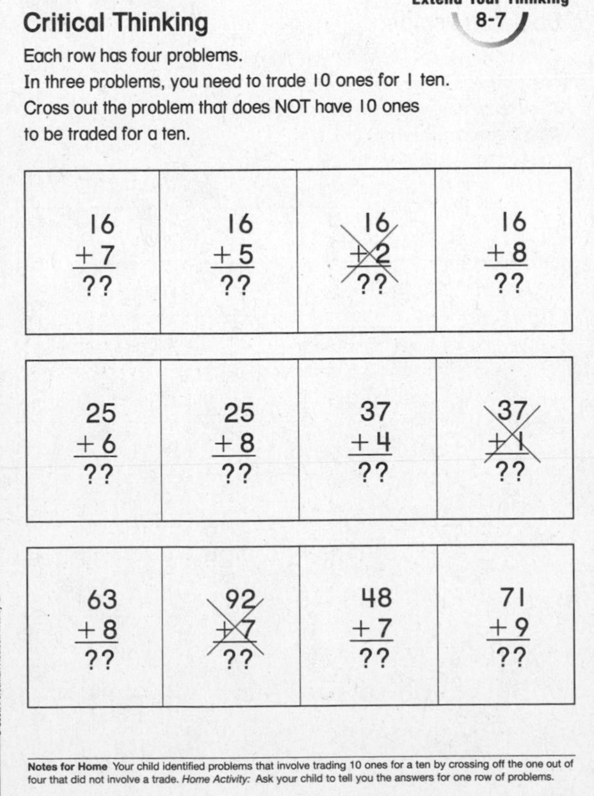

Name ______________________

Extend Your Thinking 8-7

Critical Thinking

Each row has four problems.
In three problems, you need to trade 10 ones for 1 ten.
Cross out the problem that does NOT have 10 ones to be traded for a ten.

16 + 7 = ??	16 + 5 = ??	16 + 2 = ??	16 + 8 = ??
25 + 6 = ??	25 + 8 = ??	37 + 4 = ??	37 + 1 = ??
63 + 8 = ??	92 + 7 = ??	48 + 7 = ??	71 + 9 = ??

Notes for Home Your child identified problems that involve trading 10 ones for a ten by crossing off the one out of four that did not involve a trade. *Home Activity:* Ask your child to tell you the answers for one row of problems.

Use with pages 283–284. **75**

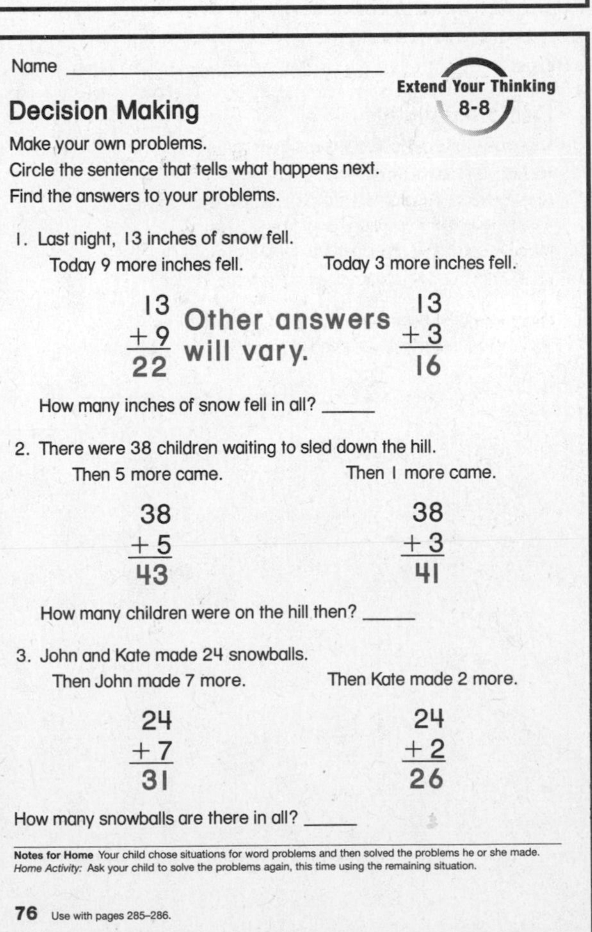

Name ______________________

Extend Your Thinking 8-8

Decision Making

Make your own problems.
Circle the sentence that tells what happens next.
Find the answers to your problems.

1. Last night, 13 inches of snow fell.
   Today 9 more inches fell. — 13 + 9 = 22
   Today 3 more inches fell. — 13 + 3 = 16

   Other answers will vary.

   How many inches of snow fell in all? _____

2. There were 38 children waiting to sled down the hill.
   Then 5 more came. — 38 + 5 = 43
   Then 1 more came. — 38 + 3 = 41

   How many children were on the hill then? _____

3. John and Kate made 24 snowballs.
   Then John made 7 more. — 24 + 7 = 31
   Then Kate made 2 more. — 24 + 2 = 26

   How many snowballs are there in all? _____

Notes for Home Your child chose situations for word problems and then solved the problems he or she made. *Home Activity:* Ask your child to solve the problems again, this time using the remaining situation.

76 Use with pages 285–286.

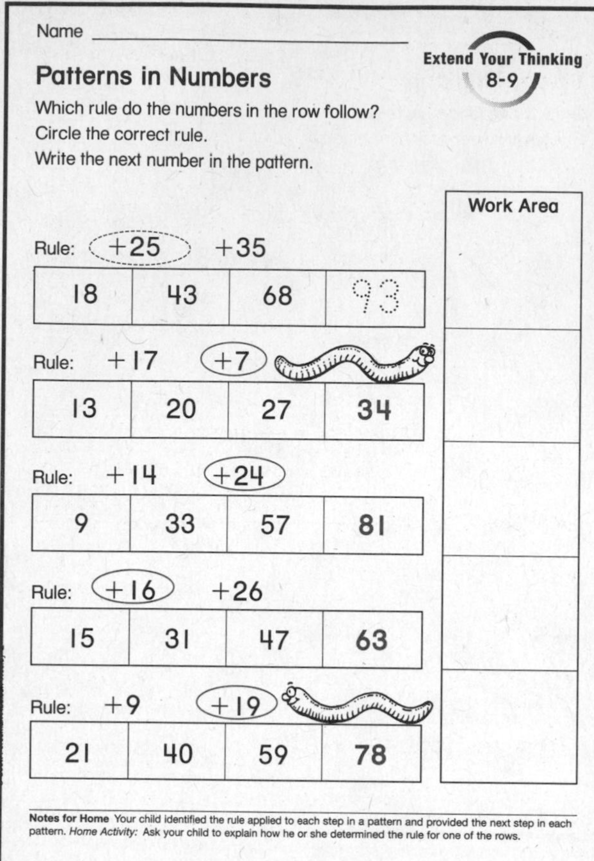

Name ______________________

Extend Your Thinking 8-9

Patterns in Numbers

Which rule do the numbers in the row follow?
Circle the correct rule.
Write the next number in the pattern.

Work Area

Rule: (+25) +35

18	43	68	93

Rule: +17 (+7)

13	20	27	34

Rule: +14 (+24)

9	33	57	81

Rule: (+16) +26

15	31	47	63

Rule: +9 (+19)

21	40	59	78

Notes for Home Your child identified the rule applied to each step in a pattern and provided the next step in each pattern. *Home Activity:* Ask your child to explain how he or she determined the rule for one of the rows.

Use with pages 289–290. **77**

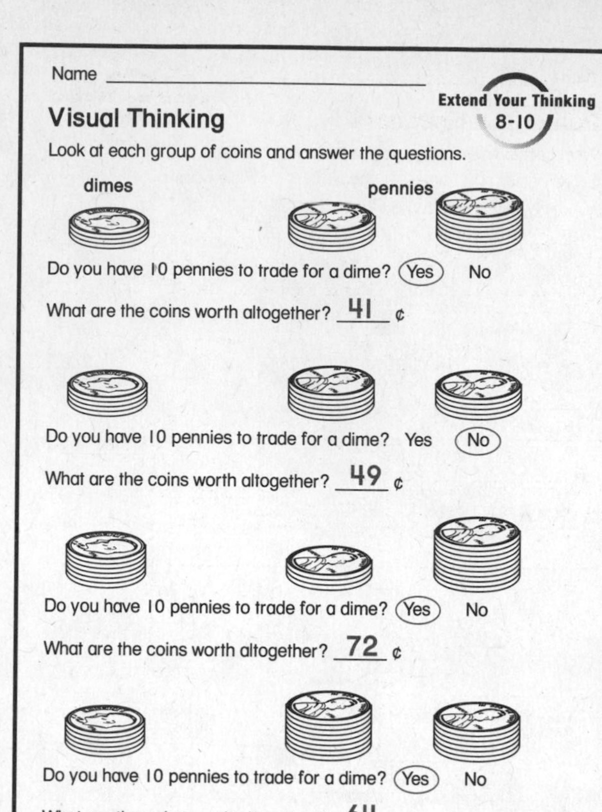

Name ______________________

Extend Your Thinking 8-10

Visual Thinking

Look at each group of coins and answer the questions.

dimes pennies

Do you have 10 pennies to trade for a dime? (Yes) No

What are the coins worth altogether? 41 ¢

Do you have 10 pennies to trade for a dime? Yes (No)

What are the coins worth altogether? 49 ¢

Do you have 10 pennies to trade for a dime? (Yes) No

What are the coins worth altogether? 72 ¢

Do you have 10 pennies to trade for a dime? (Yes) No

What are the coins worth altogether? 64 ¢

Notes for Home Your child added the values of groups of coins and decided whether it was possible to trade in 10 pennies for 1 dime. *Home Activity:* Ask your child to set up a similar problem, using real dimes and pennies, for you to solve.

78 Use with pages 291–292.

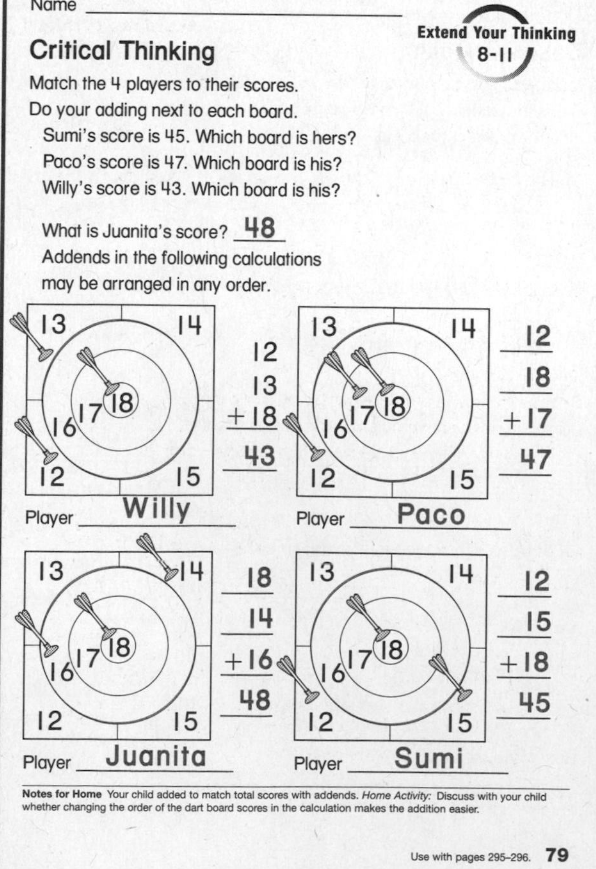

Name ______________________

Extend Your Thinking 8-11

Critical Thinking

Match the 4 players to their scores.
Do your adding next to each board.
Sumi's score is 45. Which board is hers?
Paco's score is 47. Which board is his?
Willy's score is 43. Which board is his?

What is Juanita's score? 48

Addends in the following calculations may be arranged in any order.

12
13
+ 18
43

Player Willy

12
18
+ 17
47

Player Paco

18
14
+ 16
48

Player Juanita

12
15
+ 18
45

Player Sumi

Notes for Home Your child added to match total scores with addends. *Home Activity:* Discuss with your child whether changing the order of the dart board scores in the calculation makes the addition easier.

Use with pages 295–296. **79**

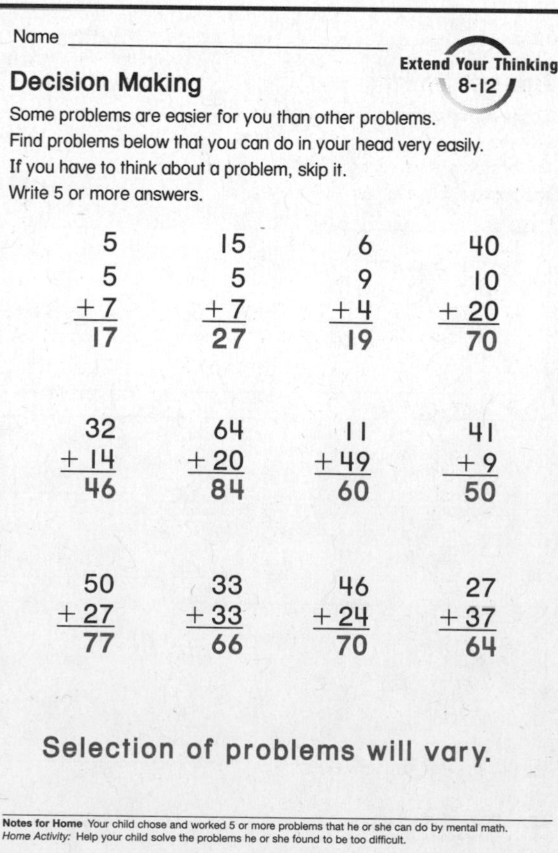

Name ______________________

Extend Your Thinking 8-12

Decision Making

Some problems are easier for you than other problems.
Find problems below that you can do in your head very easily.
If you have to think about a problem, skip it.
Write 5 or more answers.

$5 + 5 + 7 = 17$ $15 + 5 + 7 = 27$ $6 + 9 + 4 = 19$ $40 + 10 + 20 = 70$

$32 + 14 = 46$ $64 + 20 = 84$ $11 + 49 = 60$ $41 + 9 = 50$

$50 + 27 = 77$ $33 + 33 = 66$ $46 + 24 = 70$ $27 + 37 = 64$

Selection of problems will vary.

Notes for Home Your child chose and worked 5 or more problems that he or she can do by mental math. *Home Activity:* Help your child solve the problems he or she found to be too difficult.

80 Use with pages 297–298.

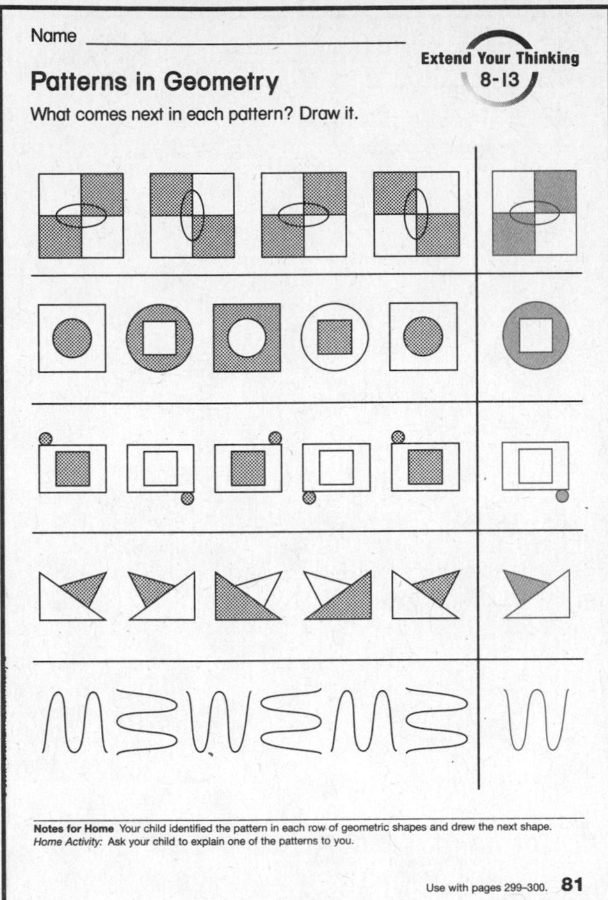
Name ____________________

Extend Your Thinking 8-13

Patterns in Geometry

What comes next in each pattern? Draw it.

Notes for Home Your child identified the pattern in each row of geometric shapes and drew the next shape. *Home Activity:* Ask your child to explain one of the patterns to you.

Use with pages 299–300. **81**

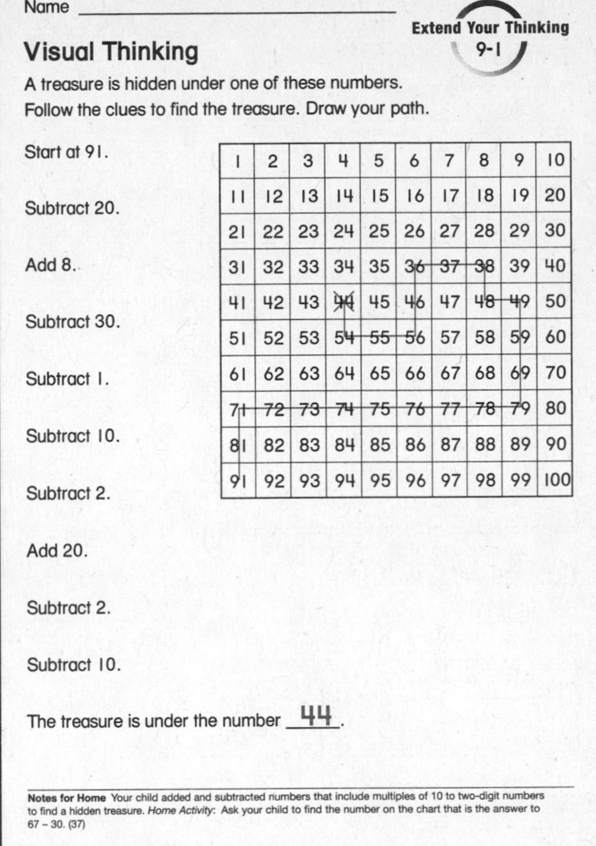
Name ____________________

Extend Your Thinking 9-1

Visual Thinking

A treasure is hidden under one of these numbers.
Follow the clues to find the treasure. Draw your path.

Start at 91.

Subtract 20.

Add 8.

Subtract 30.

Subtract 1.

Subtract 10.

Subtract 2.

Add 20.

Subtract 2.

Subtract 10.

1	2	3	4	5	6	7	8	9	10
11	12	13	14	15	16	17	18	19	20
21	22	23	24	25	26	27	28	29	30
31	32	33	34	35	36	37	38	39	40
41	42	43	44	45	46	47	48	49	50
51	52	53	54	55	56	57	58	59	60
61	62	63	64	65	66	67	68	69	70
71	72	73	74	75	76	77	78	79	80
81	82	83	84	85	86	87	88	89	90
91	92	93	94	95	96	97	98	99	100

The treasure is under the number 44.

Notes for Home Your child added and subtracted numbers that include multiples of 10 to two-digit numbers to find a hidden treasure. *Home Activity:* Ask your child to find the number on the chart that is the answer to 67 – 30. (37)

82 Use with pages 315–316.

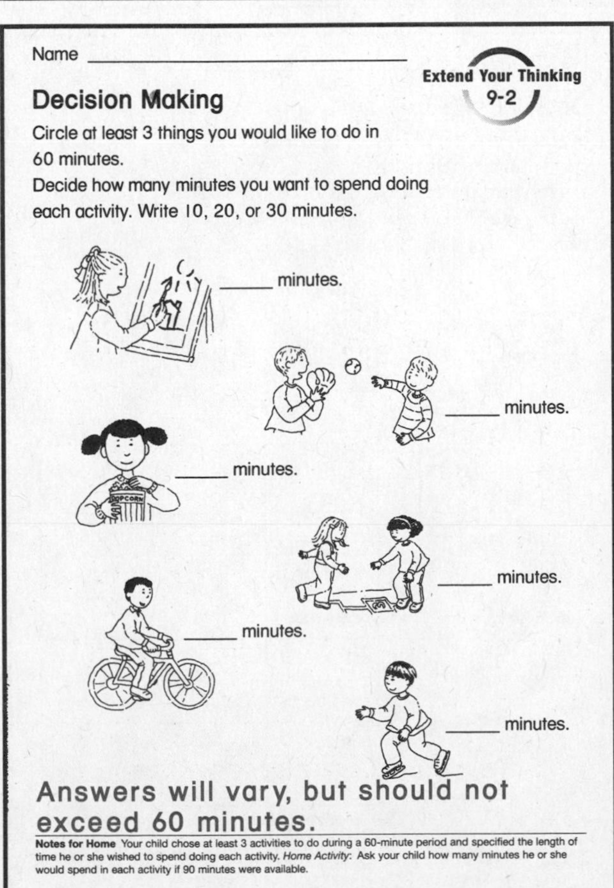
Name ____________________

Extend Your Thinking 9-2

Decision Making

Circle at least 3 things you would like to do in 60 minutes.
Decide how many minutes you want to spend doing each activity. Write 10, 20, or 30 minutes.

_____ minutes.

_____ minutes.

_____ minutes.

_____ minutes.

_____ minutes.

_____ minutes.

Answers will vary, but should not exceed 60 minutes.

Notes for Home Your child chose at least 3 activities to do during a 60-minute period and specified the length of time he or she wished to spend doing each activity. *Home Activity:* Ask your child how many minutes he or she would spend in each activity if 90 minutes were available.

Use with pages 317–318. **83**

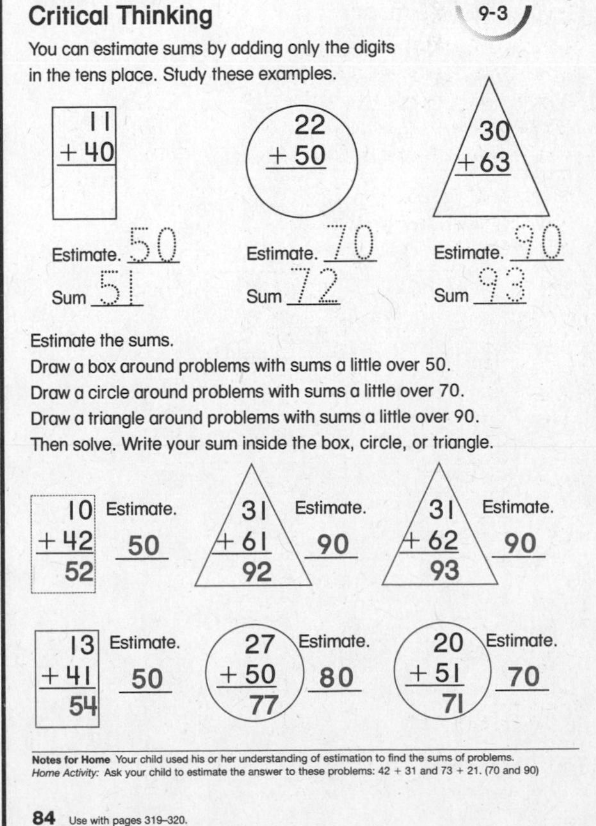
Name ____________________

Extend Your Thinking 9-3

Critical Thinking

You can estimate sums by adding only the digits in the tens place. Study these examples.

11 + 40 — Estimate. 50 — Sum 51

22 + 50 — Estimate. 70 — Sum 72

30 + 63 — Estimate. 90 — Sum 93

Estimate the sums.
Draw a box around problems with sums a little over 50.
Draw a circle around problems with sums a little over 70.
Draw a triangle around problems with sums a little over 90.
Then solve. Write your sum inside the box, circle, or triangle.

10 + 42 = 52 — Estimate. 50

31 + 61 = 92 — Estimate. 90

31 + 62 = 93 — Estimate. 90

13 + 41 = 54 — Estimate. 50

27 + 50 = 77 — Estimate. 80

20 + 51 = 71 — Estimate. 70

Notes for Home Your child used his or her understanding of estimation to find the sums of problems. *Home Activity:* Ask your child to estimate the answer to these problems: 42 + 31 and 73 + 21. (70 and 90)

84 Use with pages 319–320.

Name ______________________

Extend Your Thinking 9-4

Critical Thinking

Find the one that does not belong.
Cross it out.

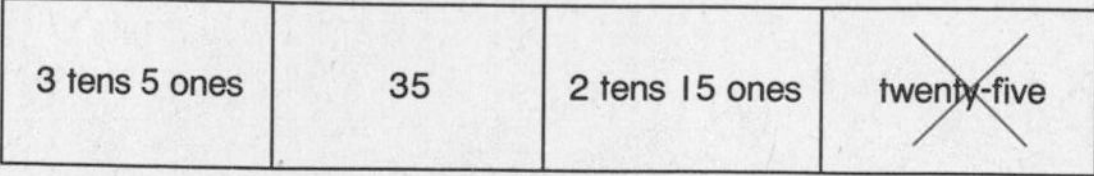

3 tens 5 ones	35	2 tens 15 ones	twenty-five

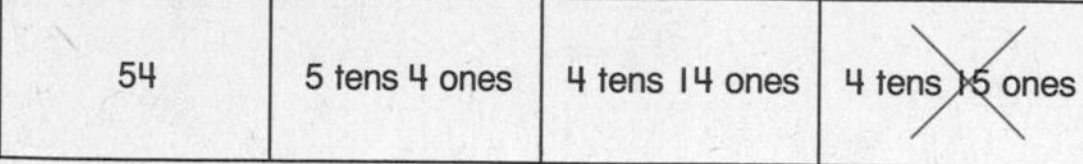

54	5 tens 4 ones	4 tens 14 ones	4 tens 15 ones

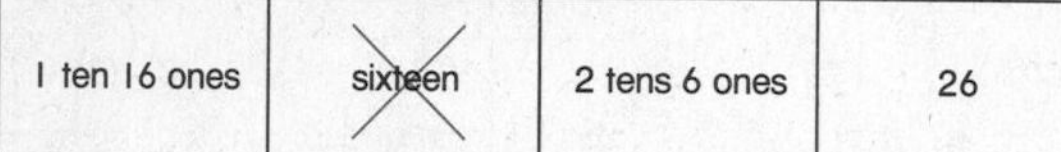

1 ten 16 ones	sixteen	2 tens 6 ones	26

7 tens 18 ones	seventy-eight	78	7 tens 8 ones

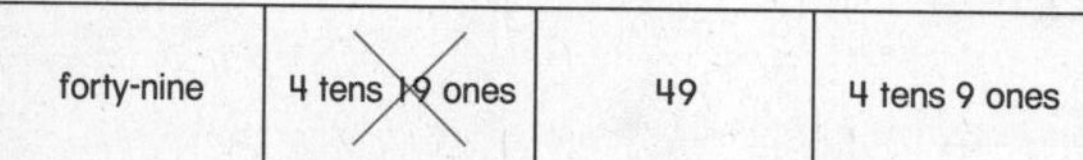

forty-nine	4 tens 19 ones	49	4 tens 9 ones

Notes for Home Your child recognized different ways of naming the same number and crossed out the name that did not belong in each row. *Home Activity:* Ask your child to write the number 53 in 3 different ways. (fifty-three, 53, five tens and 3 ones, or 4 tens and 13 ones)

Use with pages 321–322. **85**

Name ______________________

Extend Your Thinking 9-5

Critical Thinking

Decide if you need to trade.
Look at the ones in each problem.
Draw a box around the larger number.

If the box is here, a trade is needed. → 73 − 28

If the box is here, a trade is not needed. → 67 − 24

Circle **Trade** or **No Trade**.

1. 63 − 57 Trade No Trade
2. 45 − 14 Trade No Trade
3. 92 − 36 Trade No Trade
4. 88 − 57 Trade No Trade
5. 45 − 29 Trade No Trade
6. 51 − 24 Trade No Trade
7. 99 − 72 Trade No Trade
8. 40 − 21 Trade No Trade

Notes for Home Your child identified and compared the numbers in the ones place of subtraction problems, and marked when regrouping (or a trade) is needed. *Home Activity:* Ask your child to explain why a trade is needed when the second amount of ones is larger than the first amount of ones.

86 Use with pages 323–324.

Name ______________________

Extend Your Thinking 9-6

Patterns in Numbers

Each row follows a rule.
Use the rule to find the next 3 numbers.

Rule −6 94 88 82 76 70 64

94 − 6 = 88; 88 − 6 = 82; 82 − 6 = 76; 76 − 6 = 70; 70 − 6 = 64

Rule −7 86 79 72 65 58 51

86 − 7 = 79; 79 − 7 = 72; 72 − 7 = 65; 65 − 7 = 58; 58 − 7 = 51

Rule −9 99 90 81 72 63 54

99 − 9 = 90; 90 − 9 = 81; 81 − 9 = 72; 72 − 9 = 63; 63 − 9 = 54

Notes for Home Your child applied a rule in each row, subtracting a one-digit number from a two-digit number to find the next 3 numbers in the pattern. *Home Activity:* Ask your child to explain when he or she should make a trade of one ten for 10 ones. (when the number being subtracted has a greater ones digit than the other number)

Use with pages 325–326. **87**

Name ______________________

Extend Your Thinking 9-7

Decision Making

Suppose you are in art class and you are asked to design a class flag.
You only can put between 15 and 25 items on your flag.
You can take no more than 9 items from any pack.
Write how many things are left in each pack.

50 Buttons

Materials	How many I took	How many are left
ribbons		
red beads		
blue beads		
gold beads		
silver beads		
buttons		
Total		

Answers will vary.

Notes for Home Your child selected materials and did subtraction involving trades of tens for ten ones to find how many materials were left. *Home Activity:* Using buttons or other small objects, ask your child to take a handful, count them aloud, take out 7, subtract to find how many are left, and then recount to check.

88 Use with pages 329–330.

Name ______________________

Extend Your Thinking 9-8

Critical Thinking

How many letters are in the alphabet?

To answer this riddle, first subtract. Then use the code below.

74	50	44	72	72
− 39	− 20	− 8	− 63	− 29
35	30	36	9	43

61	91	89	95
− 46	− 17	− 77	− 56
15	74	12	39

Code:	1 A	3 E	5 L	7 P	9 T
	2 B	4 H	6 N	8 S	0 V

Copy your answers in order in the top boxes. Write the letters below.

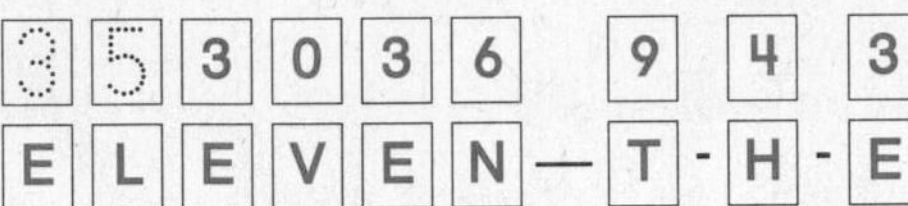

Notes for Home Your child solved subtraction problems involving trading tens for ones to find the coded answer to a riddle. *Home Activity:* Ask your child to identify the problems that involve trades. (74 – 39, 44 – 8, 72 – 63, 72 – 29, 61 – 46, 91 – 17, 95 – 56)

Name ______________________

Extend Your Thinking 9-9

Patterns in Numbers

Which rule do the numbers on the trucks follow?

Draw a box around the rule.

Write the next number in the pattern.

Work Area

Rule: −14 −16 [−18]

Rule: −23 [−25] −27

Rule: −15 [−19] −28

Rule: −17 −23 [−27]

Rule: [−9] −16 −21

Notes for Home Your child identified the rule applied to each step in a pattern and provided the next step in each subtraction pattern. *Home Activity:* Ask your child to explain one of the patterns to you.

Name ______________________

Extend Your Thinking 9-10

Visual Thinking

If you need to trade 1 ten for 10 ones, color the square red.

If you don't need to trade, do not color the square.

The colored squares will answer the riddle.

Which 2 letters scare teeth the most? DK

50−9	42−3	29−20	62−21	30−7	77−30	69−20	23−5
60−3	41−30	50−4	34−10	20−19	82−41	74−58	94−50
45−26	67−30	70−35	93−40	63−27	90−38	68−40	45−20
30−14	58−20	80−38	63−12	40−14	29−10	85−47	79−53
96−69	30−17	36−20	75−30	60−39	96−24	41−10	80−54

Notes for Home Your child decided when it was necessary to trade 10 ones for 1 ten to solve subtraction problems, especially those involving zero. *Home Activity:* Ask your child which is easier to solve and why: 47 – 20 or 40 – 27.

Name ______________________

Extend Your Thinking 9-11

Critical Thinking

Which addition problem helps you check your subtraction?

Solve the subtraction problems.

Solve the addition problems.

Then match each subtraction problem with an addition problem.

Write a subtraction problem of your own.
Then write the addition problem you used to check the subtraction problem.

Answers will vary.

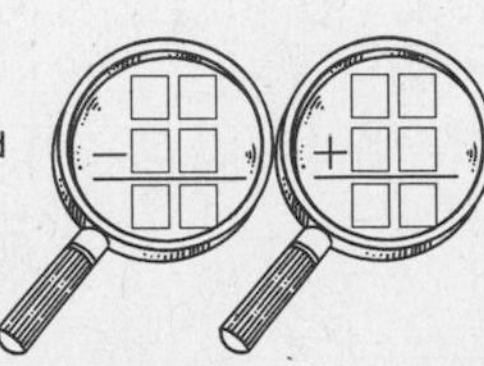

Notes for Home Your child subtracted 2 two-digit numbers and then identified the addition problem that could be used to check the subtraction. *Home Activity:* Show your child how you use addition to check subtraction in everyday life, such as when you check your subtraction in a checkbook.

Name ______________________

Extend Your Thinking 9-12

Critical Thinking

Sometimes you have to add and subtract to find the answer to a problem.
Circle the steps you need to find each answer.
Then find the answer.

1. Martin has a quarter and 2 dimes. He buys a pen for 39¢.
   How much change does he get? 6¢

   25¢ + 39¢ = 64¢ | (25¢ + 20¢ = 45¢) | 39¢ − 25¢ = 14¢ | (45¢ − 39¢ = 6¢)

2. Pencils cost 10¢ each or 3 for a quarter. If you have 40¢, how many pencils can you buy? 4

   10¢ + 40¢ = 50¢ | (40¢ − 25¢ = 15¢) | 40¢ − 38¢ = 2¢ | (15¢ − 10¢ = 5¢) | (3 + 1 = 4)

3. A small notepad is 43¢. A large one is 75¢. Which costs more, 2 small pads or 1 large pad? By how much? 2 small pads. 11¢

   43¢ + 2¢ = 45¢ | (43¢ + 43¢ = 86¢) | 75¢ − 45¢ = 30¢ | (86¢ − 75¢ = 11¢) | 43¢ − 1¢ = 42¢

Notes for Home Your child identified addition and subtraction problems that are part of multi-step story problems, and answered the problems. *Home Activity:* Ask your child to explain his or her reasoning.

Use with pages 341–342. **93**

Name ______________________

Extend Your Thinking 9-13

Visual Thinking

Circle the facts that you use.
Cross off the facts you do not use.
Solve the problems about some of the items in this grocery ad.

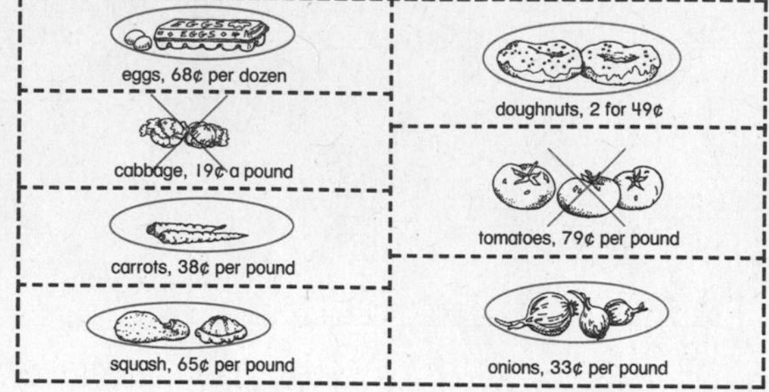

1. Katie has 3 quarters. She buys a dozen eggs. How much change does she get? 7¢
2. Steve has 90¢. Can he buy 4 doughnuts? No
3. How much more does one pound of squash cost than one pound of carrots? 27¢
4. Anna has 95¢. She buys a pound each of carrots and onions. How much change does she get? 24¢

Notes for Home Your child identified details given in an ad that were relevant to story problems and crossed off unneeded information. *Home Activity:* Ask your child to find and compare the number of calories listed on two different cereal boxes.

94 Use with pages 345–346.

Name ______________________

Extend Your Thinking 10-1

Visual Thinking

Count the items in each set.
Circle each group of 100. Cross out extra items.
If a set has less than 100, draw enough to fill it with 100.

Notes for Home Your child identified or completed pictures of groups of 100. *Home Activity:* Ask your child to name items in your home which may number 100, such as pins, paper clips, rubber bands.

Use with pages 357–358. **95**

Name ______________________

Extend Your Thinking 10-2

Decision Making

Suppose you can get prizes for your school by collecting these things. Fill in the lists and answer the question below.

Thing to be collected	Number needed for prize	Prize
cereal box tops	800	set of storybooks
labels from flour bags	500	art supplies
soup can labels	700	basketball

Smallest to greatest number of things	Easiest to hardest things to collect	Prizes in the order I want them
flour bag labels	Answers will vary.	
soup can labels		
cereal box tops		

Which one of the three things would you choose to collect? Why?

Notes for Home Your child listed 3 items in 3 different orders: from smallest to greatest quantities, from most available to least available, and from most desired personally to least desired. *Home Activity:* Ask your child to explain his or her reasons for the order in column 2 and in column 3.

96 Use with pages 359–360.

Name ____________________

Extend Your Thinking 10-3

Visual Thinking

Help Kate get to Grandma's house.
Draw a line to show her the way.

Count how many hundreds ■, tens ▲, and ones □ she passed.

6 hundreds 4 tens 5 ones

Now write the number that says the same amount. 645

Notes for Home Your child drew a path through a maze and counted hundred, tens, and ones that were passed. *Home Activity:* Ask your child to open a book with more than one hundred pages at random, read the page number, and then tell how many hundreds, tens, and ones that number represents.

Name ____________________

Extend Your Thinking 10-4

Critical Thinking

Five pets came with their owners to a hotel.
Use the clues to match the animals with their room numbers.
Draw a line from each door to the correct animal.

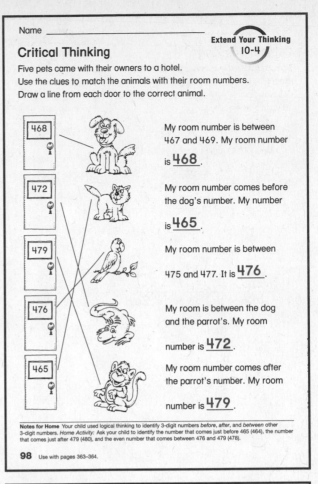

468
472
479
476
465

My room number is between 467 and 469. My room number is 468.

My room number comes before the dog's number. My number is 465.

My room number is between 475 and 477. It is 476.

My room is between the dog and the parrot's. My room number is 472.

My room number comes after the parrot's number. My room number is 479.

Notes for Home Your child used logical thinking to identify 3-digit numbers *before*, *after*, and *between* other 3-digit numbers. *Home Activity:* Ask your child to identify the number that comes just before 465 (464), the number that comes just after 479 (480), and the even number that comes between 476 and 479 (478).

Name ____________________

Extend Your Thinking 10-5

Critical Thinking

These charts show how much skating 3 children did in 2 months.
Each skate stands for skating around the rink 20 times.

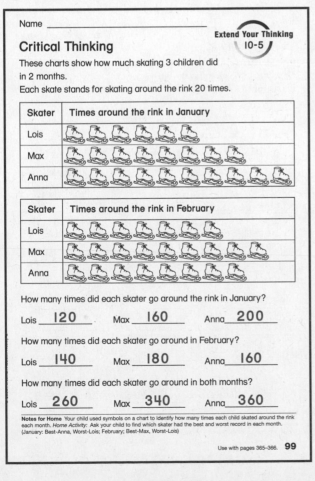

Skater	Times around the rink in January
Lois	
Max	
Anna	

Skater	Times around the rink in February
Lois	
Max	
Anna	

How many times did each skater go around the rink in January?

Lois 120 Max 160 Anna 200

How many times did each skater go around in February?

Lois 140 Max 180 Anna 160

How many times did each skater go around in both months?

Lois 260 Max 340 Anna 360

Notes for Home Your child used symbols on a chart to identify how many times each child skated around the rink each month. *Home Activity:* Ask your child to find which skater had the best and worst record in each month. (January: Best-Anna, Worst-Lois; February; Best-Max, Worst-Lois)

Name ____________________

Extend Your Thinking 10-6

Visual Thinking

Find the answer to this riddle.
Count by 100s to complete the dot-to-dot puzzle.

Riddle:
I am full when I am away, and I am empty when I am home.
What am I?

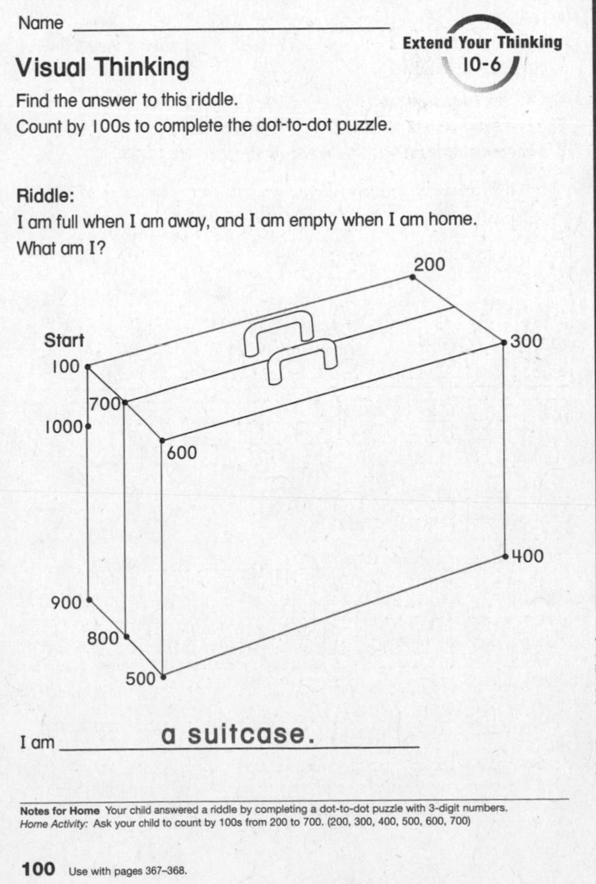

I am a suitcase.

Notes for Home Your child answered a riddle by completing a dot-to-dot puzzle with 3-digit numbers. *Home Activity:* Ask your child to count by 100s from 200 to 700. (200, 300, 400, 500, 600, 700)

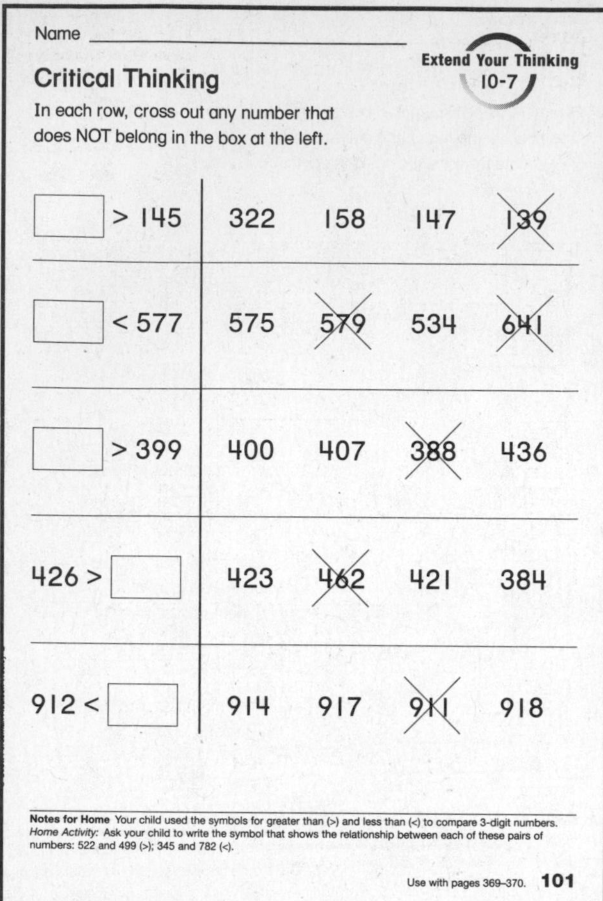

Name ______________________

Extend Your Thinking 10-7

Critical Thinking

In each row, cross out any number that does NOT belong in the box at the left.

☐ > 145	322	158	147	~~139~~
☐ < 577	575	~~579~~	534	~~641~~
☐ > 399	400	407	~~388~~	436
426 > ☐	423	~~462~~	421	384
912 < ☐	914	917	~~911~~	918

Notes for Home Your child used the symbols for greater than (>) and less than (<) to compare 3-digit numbers. *Home Activity:* Ask your child to write the symbol that shows the relationship between each of these pairs of numbers: 522 and 499 (>); 345 and 782 (<).

Use with pages 369–370. **101**

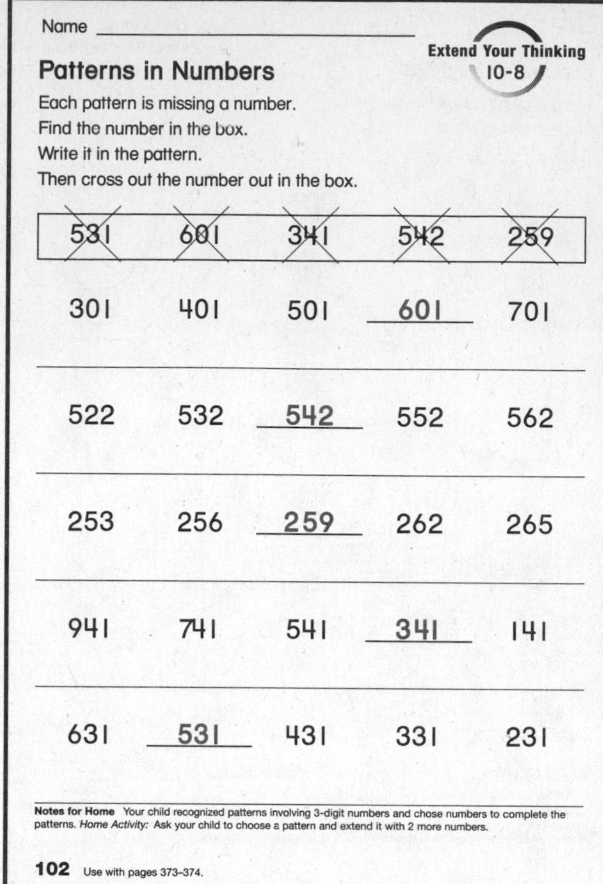

Name ______________________

Extend Your Thinking 10-8

Patterns in Numbers

Each pattern is missing a number.
Find the number in the box.
Write it in the pattern.
Then cross out the number out in the box.

~~531~~	~~601~~	~~341~~	~~542~~	~~259~~
301	401	501	601	701
522	532	542	552	562
253	256	259	262	265
941	741	541	341	141
631	531	431	331	231

Notes for Home Your child recognized patterns involving 3-digit numbers and chose numbers to complete the patterns. *Home Activity:* Ask your child to choose a pattern and extend it with 2 more numbers.

102 Use with pages 373–374.

Name ______________________

Extend Your Thinking 10-9

Decision Making

Each time you visit King Park, you stop at only 2 places.
Where would you go on your first 2 visits?
Draw 2 paths from the gate. Each path may go to 2 places.

Bridge
424 feet
Berry bushes
223 feet
132 feet
141 feet
170 feet
Swings
120 feet
Fountain
204 feet
Statue
224 feet
352 feet
405 feet
Gate

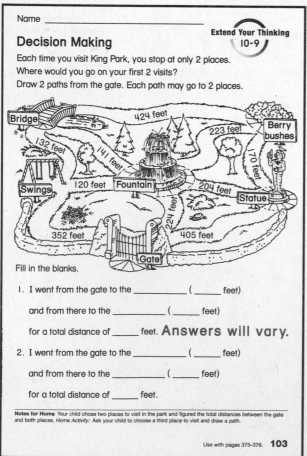

Fill in the blanks.

1. I went from the gate to the __________ (_____ feet)
   and from there to the __________ (_____ feet)
   for a total distance of _____ feet. **Answers will vary.**
2. I went from the gate to the __________ (_____ feet)
   and from there to the __________ (_____ feet)
   for a total distance of _____ feet.

Notes for Home Your child chose two places to visit in the park and figured the total distances between the gate and both places. *Home Activity:* Ask your child to choose a third place to visit and draw a path.

Use with pages 375–376. **103**

Name ______________________

Extend Your Thinking 10-10

Visual Thinking

Play Tic-Tac-Add. First, write the numbers.
Then draw a line to connect the two numbers that show the sum given in the center.

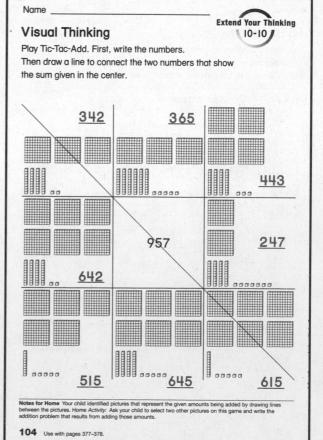

342	365	443
642	957	247
515	645	615

Notes for Home Your child identified pictures that represent the given amounts being added by drawing lines between the pictures. *Home Activity:* Ask your child to select two other pictures on this game and write the addition problem that results from adding those amounts.

104 Use with pages 377–378.

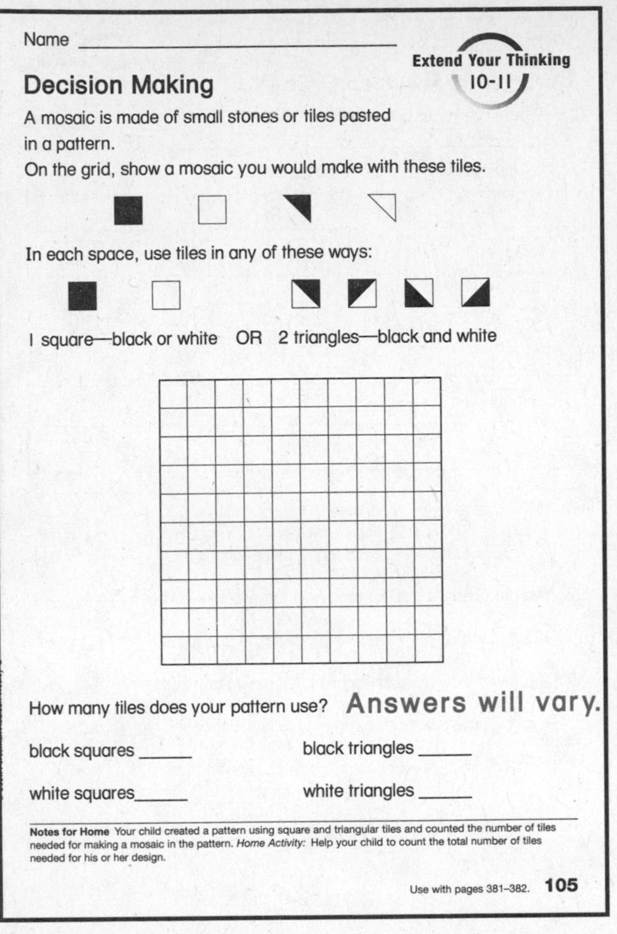

Name ______________________

Extend Your Thinking 10-11

Decision Making

A mosaic is made of small stones or tiles pasted in a pattern.
On the grid, show a mosaic you would make with these tiles.

In each space, use tiles in any of these ways:

1 square—black or white OR 2 triangles—black and white

How many tiles does your pattern use? Answers will vary.

black squares ______ black triangles ______

white squares ______ white triangles ______

Notes for Home Your child created a pattern using square and triangular tiles and counted the number of tiles needed for making a mosaic in the pattern. *Home Activity:* Help your child to count the total number of tiles needed for his or her design.

Use with pages 381–382. **105**

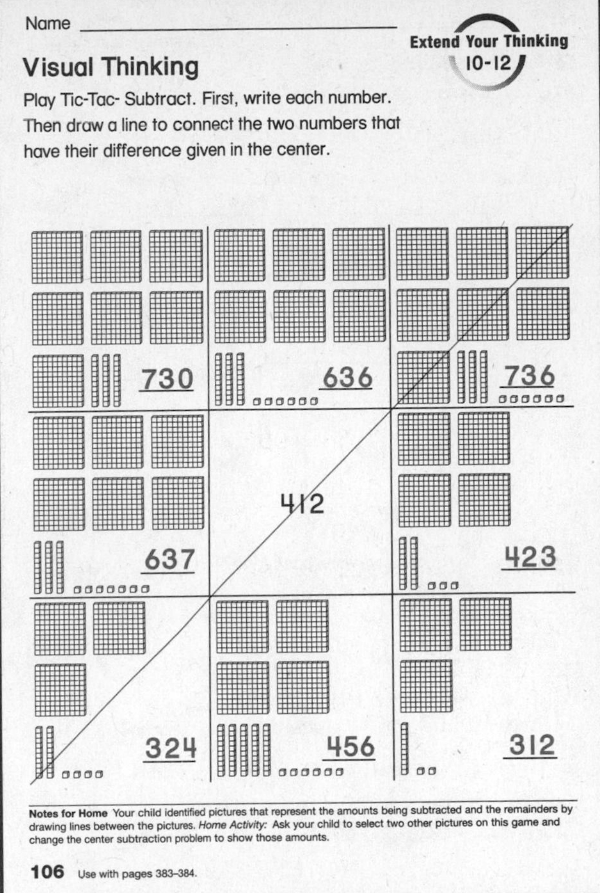

Name ______________________

Extend Your Thinking 10-12

Visual Thinking

Play Tic-Tac- Subtract. First, write each number.
Then draw a line to connect the two numbers that have their difference given in the center.

730	636	736
637	412	423
324	456	312

Notes for Home Your child identified pictures that represent the amounts being subtracted and the remainders by drawing lines between the pictures. *Home Activity:* Ask your child to select two other pictures on this game and change the center subtraction problem to show those amounts.

106 Use with pages 383–384.

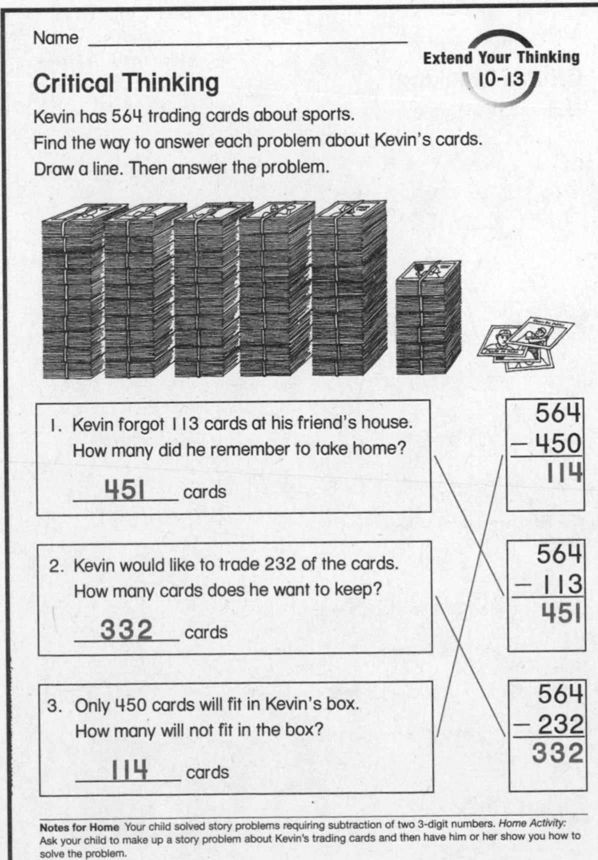

Name ______________________

Extend Your Thinking 10-13

Critical Thinking

Kevin has 564 trading cards about sports.
Find the way to answer each problem about Kevin's cards.
Draw a line. Then answer the problem.

1. Kevin forgot 113 cards at his friend's house. How many did he remember to take home?
   451 cards
2. Kevin would like to trade 232 of the cards. How many cards does he want to keep?
   332 cards
3. Only 450 cards will fit in Kevin's box. How many will not fit in the box?
   114 cards

564 − 450 = 114
564 − 113 = 451
564 − 232 = 332

Notes for Home Your child solved story problems requiring subtraction of two 3-digit numbers. *Home Activity:* Ask your child to make up a story problem about Kevin's trading cards and then have him or her show you how to solve the problem.

Use with pages 387–388. **107**

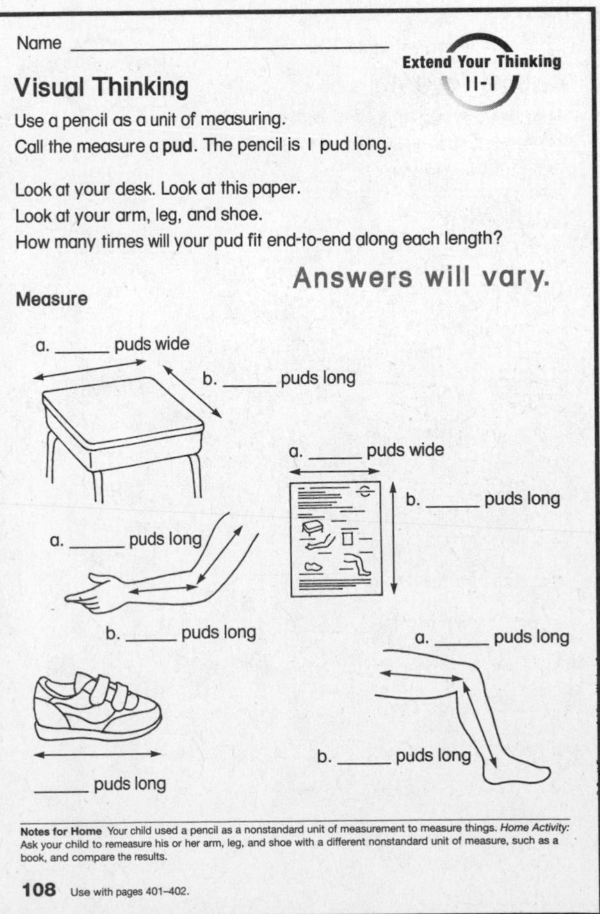

Name ______________________

Extend Your Thinking 11-1

Visual Thinking

Use a pencil as a unit of measuring.
Call the measure a **pud**. The pencil is 1 pud long.

Look at your desk. Look at this paper.
Look at your arm, leg, and shoe.
How many times will your pud fit end-to-end along each length?

Answers will vary.

Measure

a. ______ puds wide
b. ______ puds long

a. ______ puds wide
b. ______ puds long

a. ______ puds long
b. ______ puds long

a. ______ puds long
b. ______ puds long

______ puds long

Notes for Home Your child used a pencil as a nonstandard unit of measurement to measure things. *Home Activity:* Ask your child to remeasure his or her arm, leg, and shoe with a different nonstandard unit of measure, such as a book, and compare the results.

108 Use with pages 401–402.

Name ______________________

Extend Your Thinking 11-2

Visual Thinking

How long is the path out of this maze? Guess.

_____ inches **Answers will vary.**

Now draw the path. Use straight lines so you can measure.

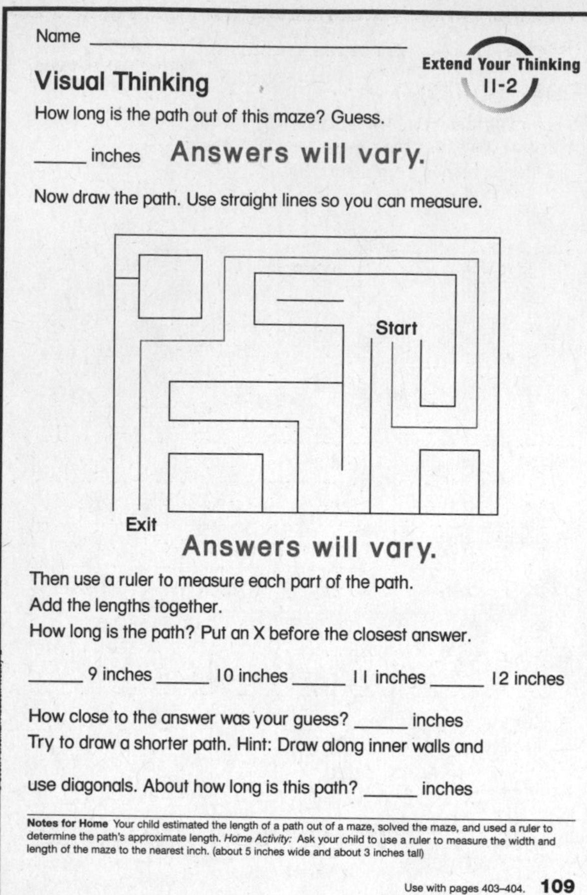

Answers will vary.

Then use a ruler to measure each part of the path.
Add the lengths together.
How long is the path? Put an X before the closest answer.

_____ 9 inches _____ 10 inches _____ 11 inches _____ 12 inches

How close to the answer was your guess? _____ inches
Try to draw a shorter path. Hint: Draw along inner walls and use diagonals. About how long is this path? _____ inches

Notes for Home Your child estimated the length of a path out of a maze, solved the maze, and used a ruler to determine the path's approximate length. *Home Activity:* Ask your child to use a ruler to measure the width and length of the maze to the nearest inch. (about 5 inches wide and about 3 inches tall)

Name ______________________

Extend Your Thinking 11-3

Patterns in Data

Fill in the missing numbers in this chart.

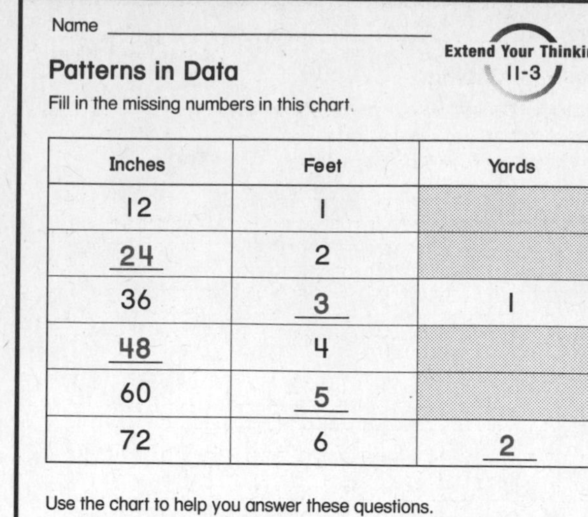

Inches	Feet	Yards
12	1	
24	2	
36	3	1
48	4	
60	5	
72	6	2

Use the chart to help you answer these questions.

1. If a rug is 6 feet long, how many yards long is it? __2__ yards
2. If a ribbon is 48 inches long, how many feet is it? __4__ feet
3. If you jump 6 feet, how many inches did you jump? __72__ inches
4. If a row of flowers is 60 inches long, how many feet is it? __5__ feet
5. If a hole is 2 yards deep, how deep is it in inches? __72__ inches
6. If a blanket is 84 inches long, how many feet is it? __7__ feet

Notes for Home Your child figured out the pattern in a chart converting inches to feet and yards. *Home Activity:* Ask your child which is longer: 72 inches or 3 yards; 4 feet or 2 yards; 6 feet or 60 inches. (3 yards; 2 yards; 6 feet)

Name ______________________

Extend Your Thinking 11-4

Critical Thinking

Andy has a string that is 15 centimeters long.
Circle the shapes that Andy can make with his string.

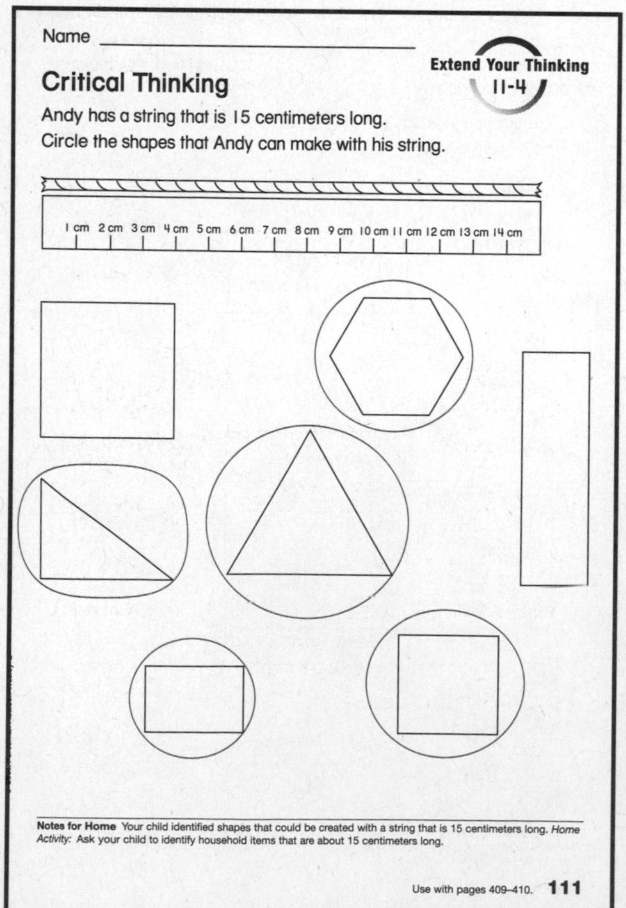

Notes for Home Your child identified shapes that could be created with a string that is 15 centimeters long. *Home Activity:* Ask your child to identify household items that are about 15 centimeters long.

Name ______________________

Extend Your Thinking 11-5

Critical Thinking

Study the large figure.

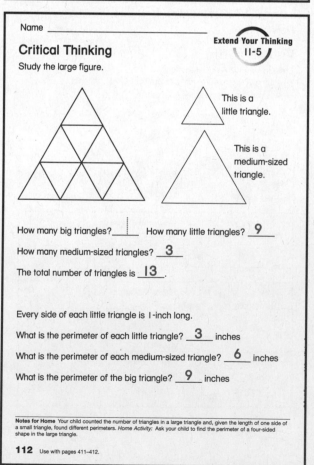

This is a little triangle.

This is a medium-sized triangle.

How many big triangles? __1__ How many little triangles? __9__

How many medium-sized triangles? __3__

The total number of triangles is __13__.

Every side of each little triangle is 1-inch long.

What is the perimeter of each little triangle? __3__ inches

What is the perimeter of each medium-sized triangle? __6__ inches

What is the perimeter of the big triangle? __9__ inches

Notes for Home Your child counted the number of triangles in a large triangle and, given the length of one side of a small triangle, found different perimeters. *Home Activity:* Ask your child to find the perimeter of a four-sided shape in the large triangle.

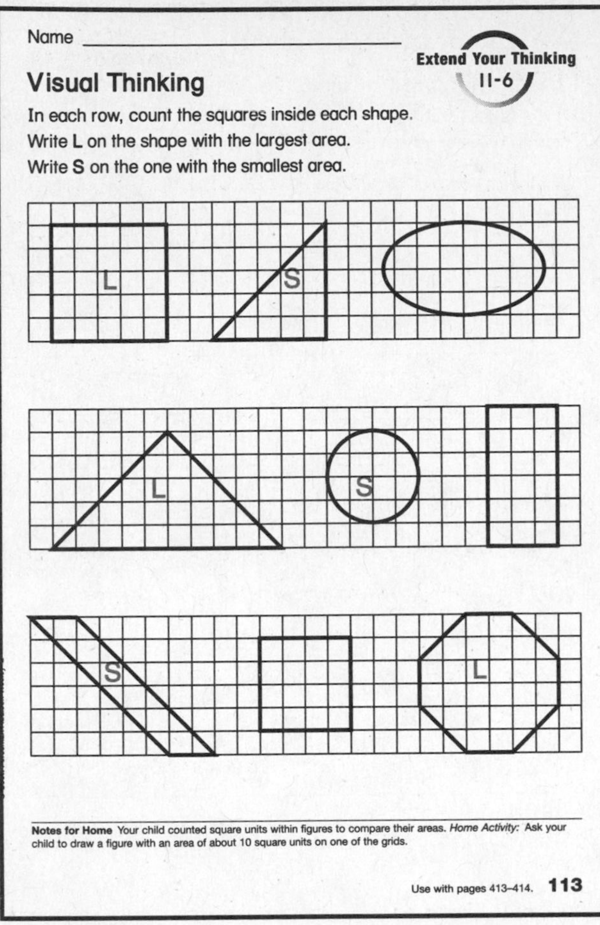

Name ______________________

Extend Your Thinking 11-6

Visual Thinking

In each row, count the squares inside each shape.
Write L on the shape with the largest area.
Write S on the one with the smallest area.

Notes for Home Your child counted square units within figures to compare their areas. *Home Activity:* Ask your child to draw a figure with an area of about 10 square units on one of the grids.

Use with pages 413–414. **113**

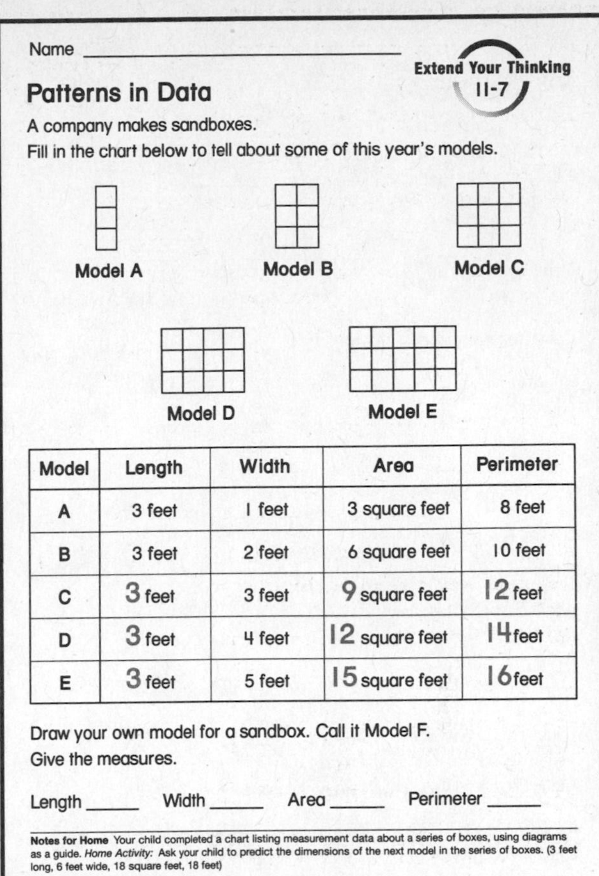

Name ______________________

Extend Your Thinking 11-7

Patterns in Data

A company makes sandboxes.
Fill in the chart below to tell about some of this year's models.

Model	Length	Width	Area	Perimeter
A	3 feet	1 feet	3 square feet	8 feet
B	3 feet	2 feet	6 square feet	10 feet
C	3 feet	3 feet	9 square feet	12 feet
D	3 feet	4 feet	12 square feet	14 feet
E	3 feet	5 feet	15 square feet	16 feet

Draw your own model for a sandbox. Call it Model F.
Give the measures.

Length _____ Width _____ Area _____ Perimeter _____

Notes for Home Your child completed a chart listing measurement data about a series of boxes, using diagrams as a guide. *Home Activity:* Ask your child to predict the dimensions of the next model in the series of boxes. (3 feet long, 6 feet wide, 18 square feet, 18 feet)

114 Use with pages 415–416.

Name ______________________

Extend Your Thinking 11-8

Visual Thinking

Each pair will get on the seesaw.
Who will be up?
Circle the animal or the person.

Notes for Home Your child estimated the weight of people and animals, and circled the one in each pair who weighs less. *Home Activity:* Ask your child to explain why the circled person or animal would rise to the top on the seesaw.

Use with pages 419–420. **115**

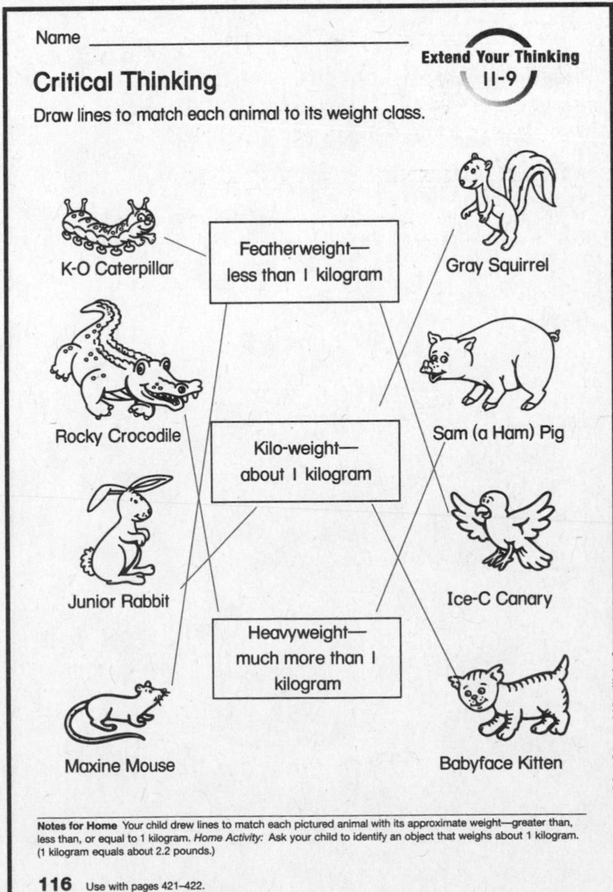

Name ______________________

Extend Your Thinking 11-9

Critical Thinking

Draw lines to match each animal to its weight class.

Notes for Home Your child drew lines to match each pictured animal with its approximate weight—greater than, less than, or equal to 1 kilogram. *Home Activity:* Ask your child to identify an object that weighs about 1 kilogram. (1 kilogram equals about 2.2 pounds.)

116 Use with pages 421–422.

Name ______________________

Extend Your Thinking 11-10

Decision Making

For each punch recipe, write what you need for 2 batches of that punch. Use the chart at the right to help you.

Cups	Pints	Quarts
2	1	
4	2	1

Strawberry Spree

One batch	Amount needed for 2 batches
1 pint frozen strawberry yogurt	2 pints or 1 quarts
2 cups milk	4 cups or 2 pints
	or 1 quarts
1 cup whole strawberries	2 cups or 1 pints

Mix in sliced strawberries. Blend yogurt and milk.

Double Raspberry Drink

One batch	Amount needed for 2 batches
1 cup of raspberries	2 cups or 1 pints
1 quart lemonade	8 cups or 4 pints
	or 2 quarts
3 cups raspberry juice	6 cups or 3 pints

Blend raspberries, lemonade, and juice together.
Add ice cubes. Which punch would you make for a party? Why?

Notes for Home Your child doubled amounts in a recipe and chose containers holding those quantities. *Home Activity:* Help your child make a drink from a mix or concentrate requiring cups or pints of water.

Use with pages 423–424. **117**

Name ______________________

Extend Your Thinking 11-11

Visual Thinking

Find the 8 hidden objects.
Color the objects that can hold more than 1 liter red.
Color the objects that can only hold less than 1 liter green.

Hidden Objects

cup G	barrel R	thimble G	kitchen sink R
glass G	bucket R	eye dropper G	bathtub R

TAXI

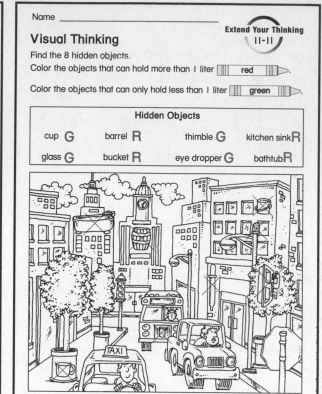

Notes for Home Your child found 8 objects hidden in a picture and estimated the capacity of those objects in comparison to 1 liter. *Home Activity:* Ask your child to look in your refrigerator and find one container that holds less than 1 liter and one that holds more than 1 liter.

118 Use with pages 425–426.

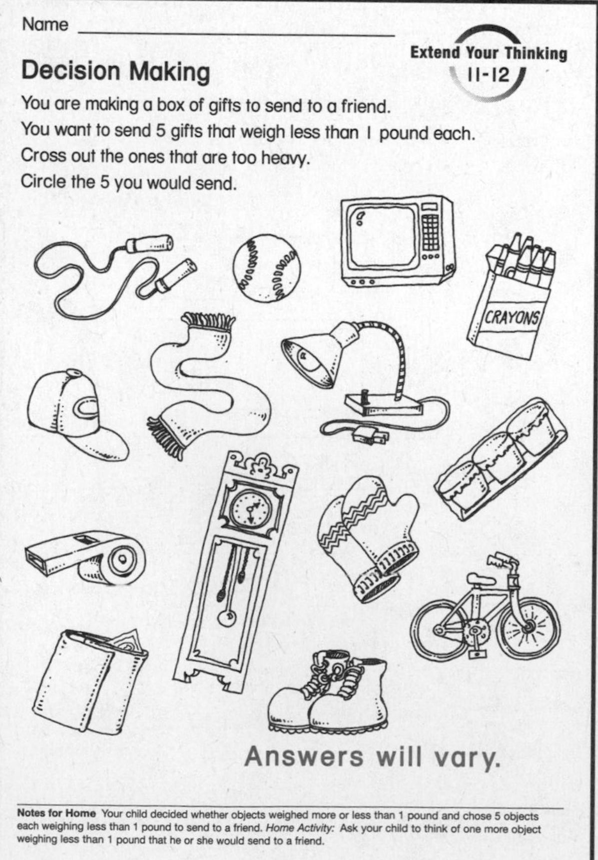

Name ______________________

Extend Your Thinking 11-12

Decision Making

You are making a box of gifts to send to a friend.
You want to send 5 gifts that weigh less than 1 pound each.
Cross out the ones that are too heavy.
Circle the 5 you would send.

Answers will vary.

Notes for Home Your child decided whether objects weighed more or less than 1 pound and chose 5 objects each weighing less than 1 pound to send to a friend. *Home Activity:* Ask your child to think of one more object weighing less than 1 pound that he or she would send to a friend.

Use with pages 429–430. **119**

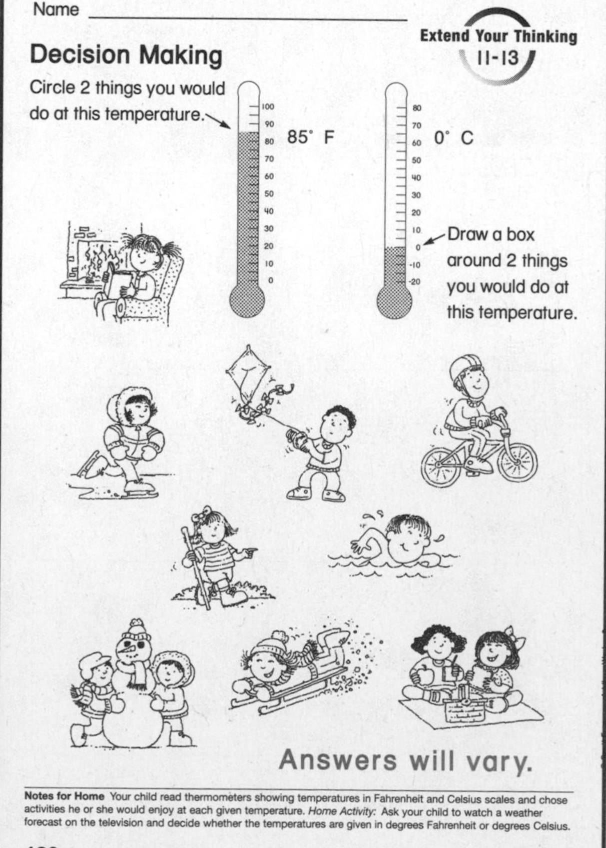

Name ______________________

Extend Your Thinking 11-13

Decision Making

Circle 2 things you would do at this temperature. 85° F

0° C Draw a box around 2 things you would do at this temperature.

Answers will vary.

Notes for Home Your child read thermometers showing temperatures in Fahrenheit and Celsius scales and chose activities he or she would enjoy at each given temperature. *Home Activity:* Ask your child to watch a weather forecast on the television and decide whether the temperatures are given in degrees Fahrenheit or degrees Celsius.

120 Use with pages 431–432.

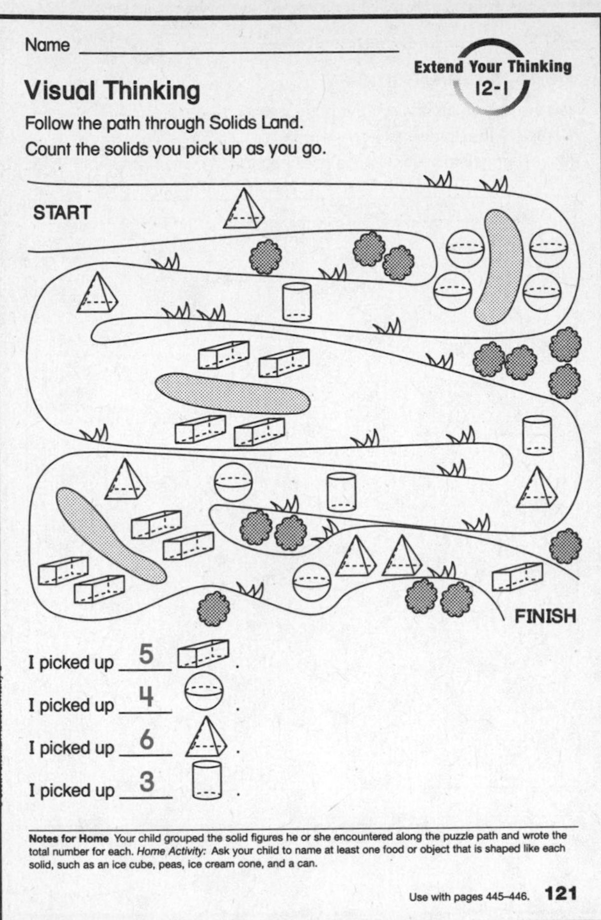

Name ____________________

Extend Your Thinking 12-1

Visual Thinking

Follow the path through Solids Land.
Count the solids you pick up as you go.

I picked up 5 .

I picked up 4 .

I picked up 6 .

I picked up 3 .

Notes for Home Your child grouped the solid figures he or she encountered along the puzzle path and wrote the total number for each. *Home Activity:* Ask your child to name at least one food or object that is shaped like each solid, such as an ice cube, peas, ice cream cone, and a can.

Use with pages 445–446. **121**

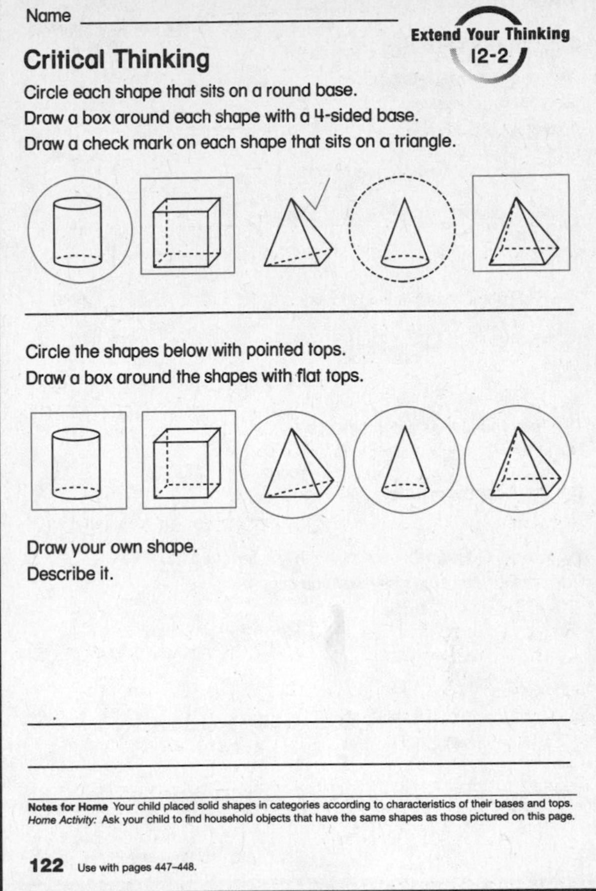

Name ____________________

Extend Your Thinking 12-2

Critical Thinking

Circle each shape that sits on a round base.
Draw a box around each shape with a 4-sided base.
Draw a check mark on each shape that sits on a triangle.

Circle the shapes below with pointed tops.
Draw a box around the shapes with flat tops.

Draw your own shape.
Describe it.

Notes for Home Your child placed solid shapes in categories according to characteristics of their bases and tops. *Home Activity:* Ask your child to find household objects that have the same shapes as those pictured on this page.

122 Use with pages 447–448.

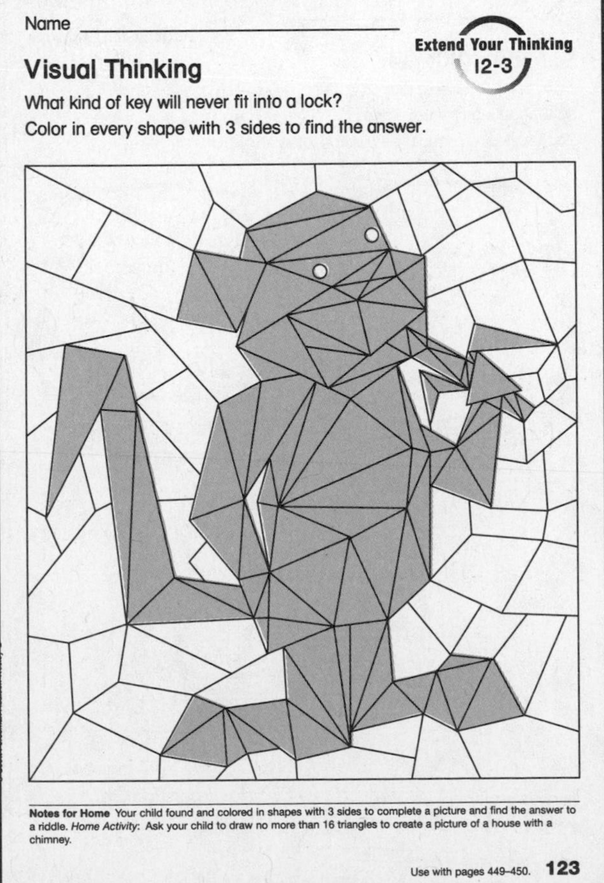

Name ____________________

Extend Your Thinking 12-3

Visual Thinking

What kind of key will never fit into a lock?
Color in every shape with 3 sides to find the answer.

Notes for Home Your child found and colored in shapes with 3 sides to complete a picture and find the answer to a riddle. *Home Activity:* Ask your child to draw no more than 16 triangles to create a picture of a house with a chimney.

Use with pages 449–450. **123**

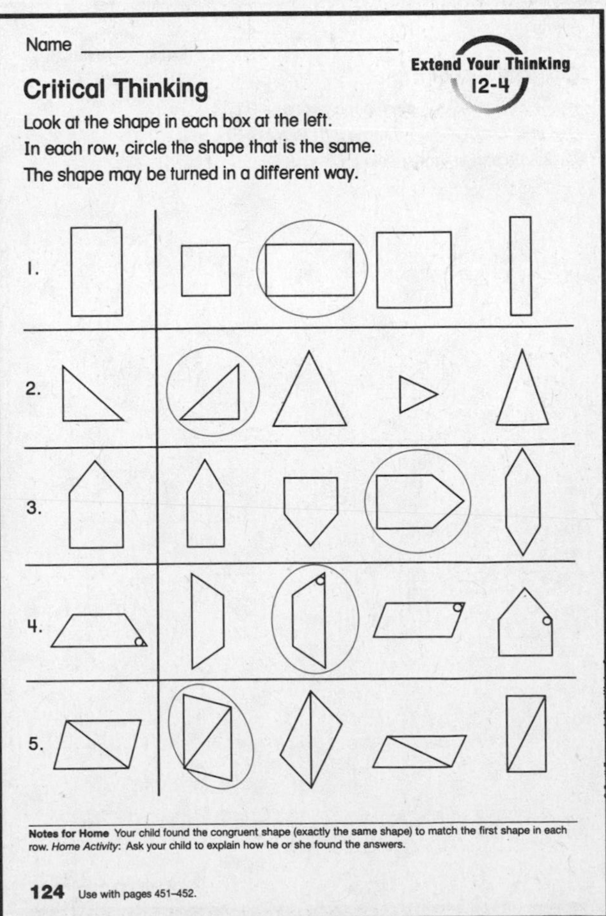

Name ____________________

Extend Your Thinking 12-4

Critical Thinking

Look at the shape in each box at the left.
In each row, circle the shape that is the same.
The shape may be turned in a different way.

Notes for Home Your child found the congruent shape (exactly the same shape) to match the first shape in each row. *Home Activity:* Ask your child to explain how he or she found the answers.

124 Use with pages 451–452.

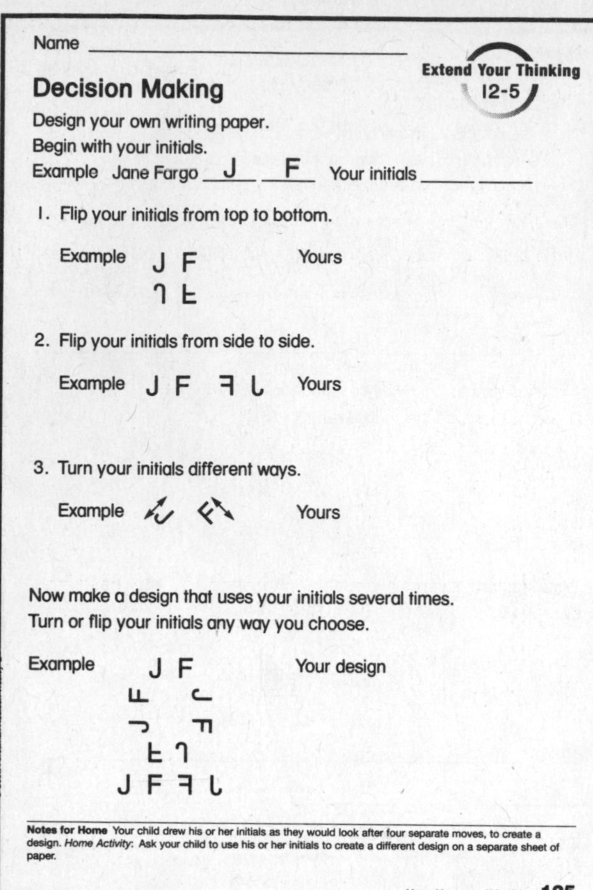

Name ______________________

Extend Your Thinking 12-5

Decision Making

Design your own writing paper.
Begin with your initials.
Example Jane Fargo J F Your initials ____ ____

1. Flip your initials from top to bottom.

Example J F Yours

2. Flip your initials from side to side.

Example J F Yours

3. Turn your initials different ways.

Example Yours

Now make a design that uses your initials several times.
Turn or flip your initials any way you choose.

Example J F Your design

Notes for Home Your child drew his or her initials as they would look after four separate moves, to create a design. *Home Activity:* Ask your child to use his or her initials to create a different design on a separate sheet of paper.

Use with pages 453–454. **125**

Name ______________________

Extend Your Thinking 12-6

Patterns in Geometry

Here is half of the border for a party invitation.
Complete the border.
Make the right half look like the mirror image of the left half.

Notes for Home Your child created a symmetrical pattern by drawing the missing shapes on the right-hand side of an invitation. *Home Activity:* Ask your child to add a shape on the left and draw its matching shape on the right.

126 Use with pages 455–456.

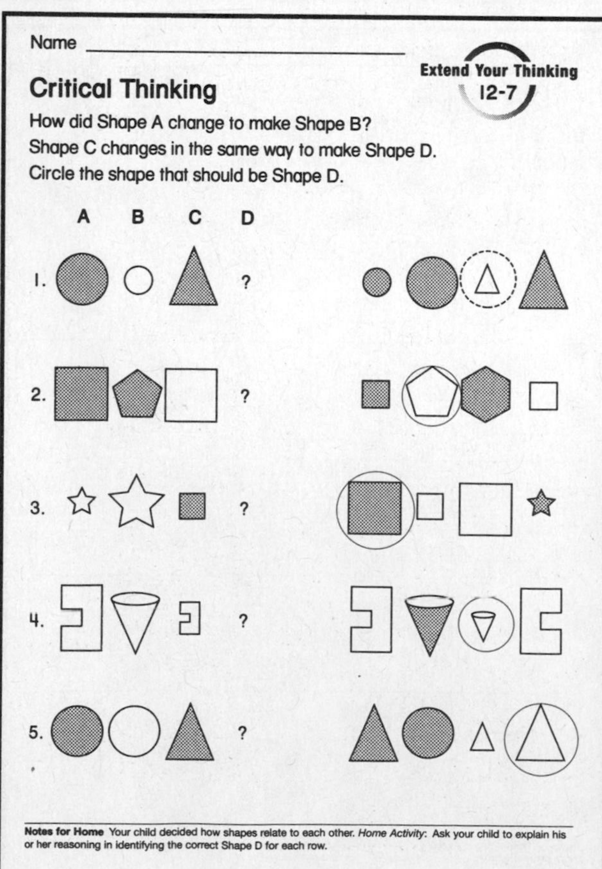

Name ______________________

Extend Your Thinking 12-7

Critical Thinking

How did Shape A change to make Shape B?
Shape C changes in the same way to make Shape D.
Circle the shape that should be Shape D.

A B C D

1. ?

2. ?

3. ?

4. ?

5. ?

Notes for Home Your child decided how shapes relate to each other. *Home Activity:* Ask your child to explain his or her reasoning in identifying the correct Shape D for each row.

Use with pages 459–460. **127**

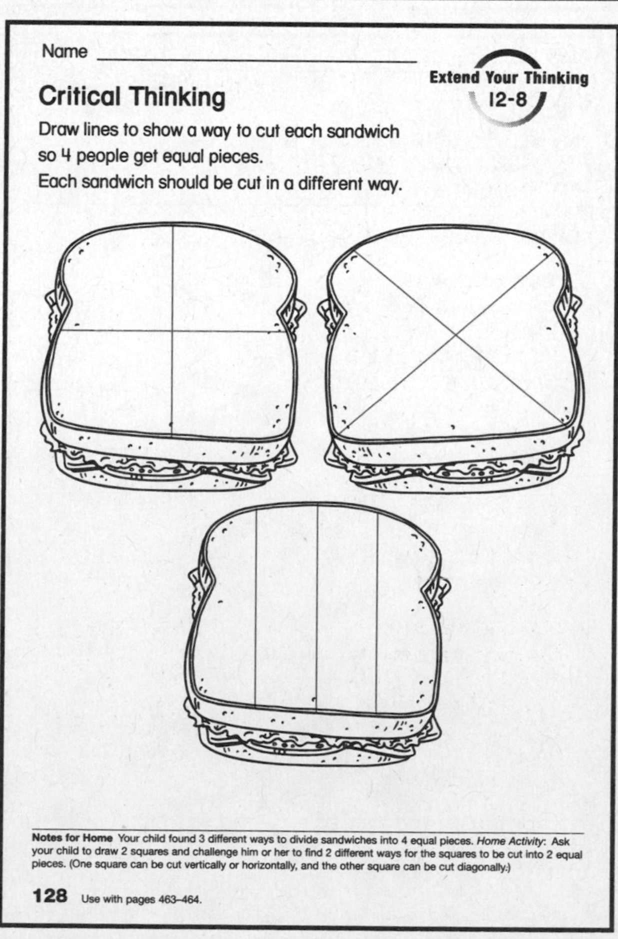

Name ______________________

Extend Your Thinking 12-8

Critical Thinking

Draw lines to show a way to cut each sandwich
so 4 people get equal pieces.
Each sandwich should be cut in a different way.

Notes for Home Your child found 3 different ways to divide sandwiches into 4 equal pieces. *Home Activity:* Ask your child to draw 2 squares and challenge him or her to find 2 different ways for the squares to be cut into 2 equal pieces. (One square can be cut vertically or horizontally, and the other square can be cut diagonally.)

128 Use with pages 463–464.

Name ______________________

Extend Your Thinking 12-9

Decision Making

You get four coupons for free food items.
Draw lines to match each coupon with the food you choose.
On the food, color in the part you get for free.

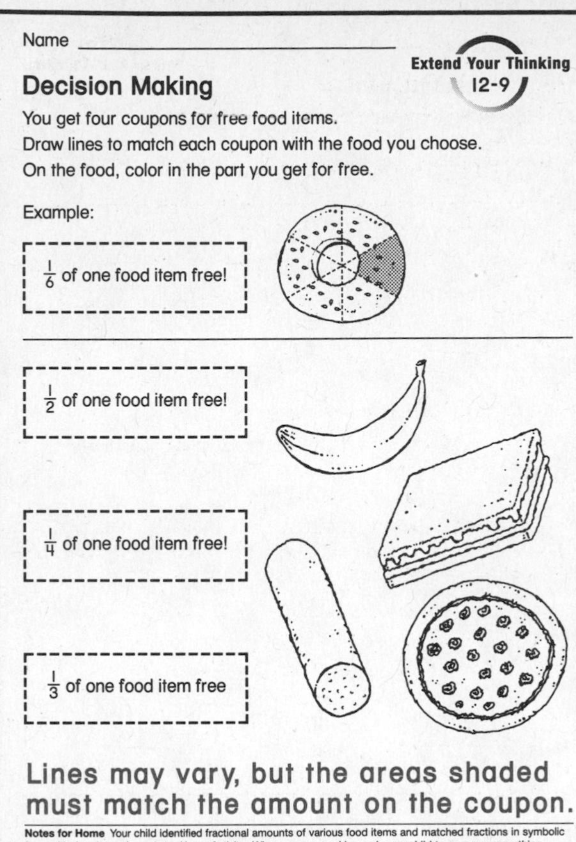

Example:

$\frac{1}{6}$ of one food item free!

$\frac{1}{2}$ of one food item free!

$\frac{1}{4}$ of one food item free!

$\frac{1}{3}$ of one food item free

Lines may vary, but the areas shaded must match the amount on the coupon.

Notes for Home Your child identified fractional amounts of various food items and matched fractions in symbolic form with the pictured amounts. *Home Activity:* When you are cooking, ask your child to measure something simple that involves a fraction, such as a half teaspoon of salt.

Use with pages 465–466. **129**

Name ______________________

Extend Your Thinking 12-10

Patterns in Fractions

Color the number of parts to finish each pattern and write the fraction.

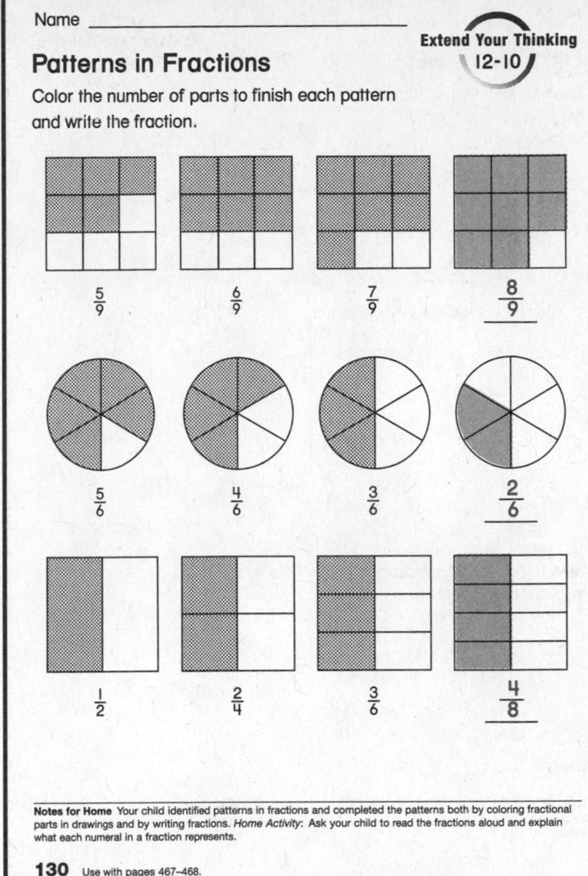

$\frac{5}{9}$ $\frac{6}{9}$ $\frac{7}{9}$ $\frac{8}{9}$

$\frac{5}{6}$ $\frac{4}{6}$ $\frac{3}{6}$ $\frac{2}{6}$

$\frac{1}{2}$ $\frac{2}{4}$ $\frac{3}{6}$ $\frac{4}{8}$

Notes for Home Your child identified patterns in fractions and completed the patterns both by coloring fractional parts in drawings and by writing fractions. *Home Activity:* Ask your child to read the fractions aloud and explain what each numeral in a fraction represents.

130 Use with pages 467–468.

Name ______________________

Extend Your Thinking 12-11

Visual Thinking

Lila puts 16 mushroom slices on each of her pizzas.
These pizzas will be cut into equal pieces.
Draw the cuts that make the number of pieces.
Then draw 16 circles on each pizza for the 16 mushroom slices.
Make the number of mushroom slices per piece equal.

1. Make 2 equal pieces.
   How many slices are on each piece? **8**
   one line cuts pizza in half; 8 circles are on each piece.

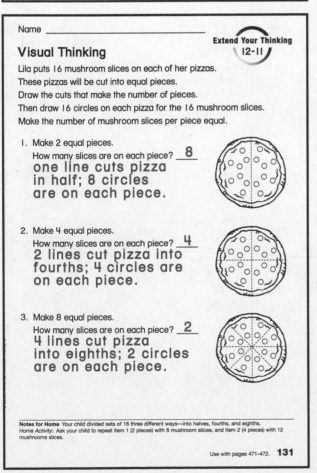

2. Make 4 equal pieces.
   How many slices are on each piece? **4**
   2 lines cut pizza into fourths; 4 circles are on each piece.

3. Make 8 equal pieces.
   How many slices are on each piece? **2**
   4 lines cut pizza into eighths; 2 circles are on each piece.

Notes for Home Your child divided sets of 16 three different ways—into halves, fourths, and eighths. *Home Activity:* Ask your child to repeat item 1 (2 pieces) with 8 mushroom slices, and item 2 (4 pieces) with 12 mushrooms slices.

Use with pages 471–472. **131**

Name ______________________

Extend Your Thinking 12-12

Critical Thinking

Draw a line to match the front of each T-shirt with its back.
Hint: Look for the piece that completes each shape.

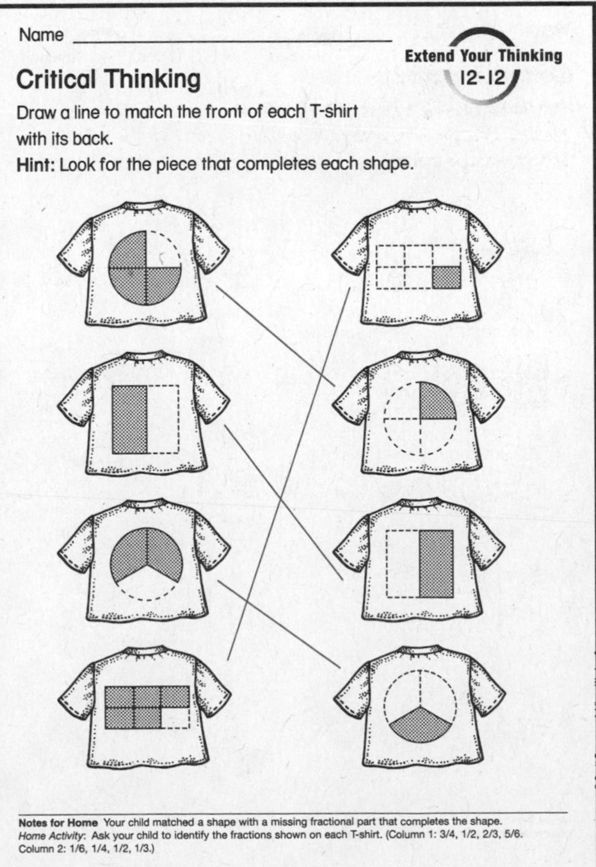

Notes for Home Your child matched a shape with a missing fractional part that completes the shape. *Home Activity:* Ask your child to identify the fractions shown on each T-shirt. (Column 1: 3/4, 1/2, 2/3, 5/6. Column 2: 1/6, 1/4, 1/2, 1/3.)

132 Use with pages 473–474.

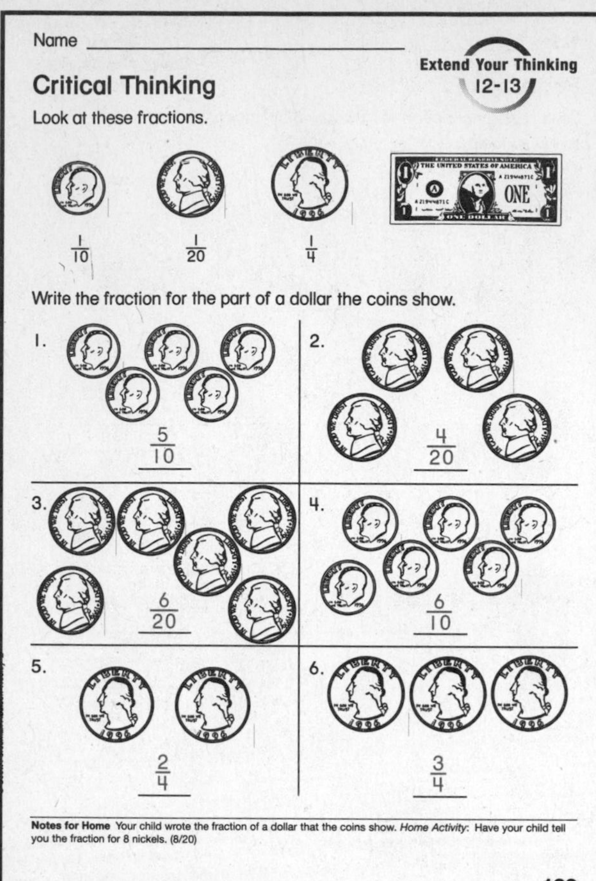

Name ______________________

Extend Your Thinking 12-13

Critical Thinking

Look at these fractions.

$\frac{1}{10}$ $\frac{1}{20}$ $\frac{1}{4}$

Write the fraction for the part of a dollar the coins show.

1. $\frac{5}{10}$
2. $\frac{4}{20}$
3. $\frac{6}{20}$
4. $\frac{6}{10}$
5. $\frac{2}{4}$
6. $\frac{3}{4}$

Notes for Home Your child wrote the fraction of a dollar that the coins show. *Home Activity:* Have your child tell you the fraction for 8 nickels. (8/20)

Use with pages 475–476. **133**

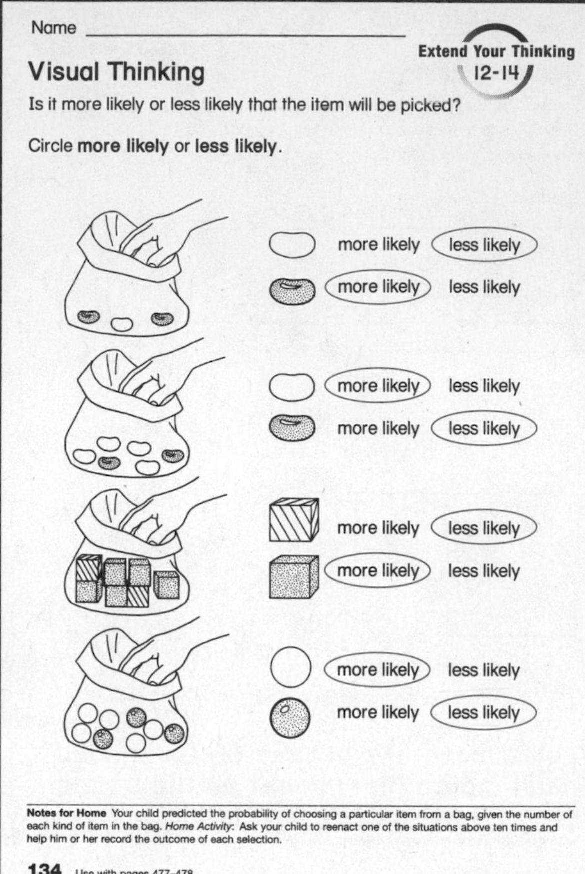

Name ______________________

Extend Your Thinking 12-14

Visual Thinking

Is it more likely or less likely that the item will be picked?

Circle **more likely** or **less likely**.

more likely (less likely)
(more likely) less likely

(more likely) less likely
more likely (less likely)

more likely (less likely)
(more likely) less likely

(more likely) less likely
more likely (less likely)

Notes for Home Your child predicted the probability of choosing a particular item from a bag, given the number of each kind of item in the bag. *Home Activity:* Ask your child to reenact one of the situations above ten times and help him or her record the outcome of each selection.

134 Use with pages 477–478.

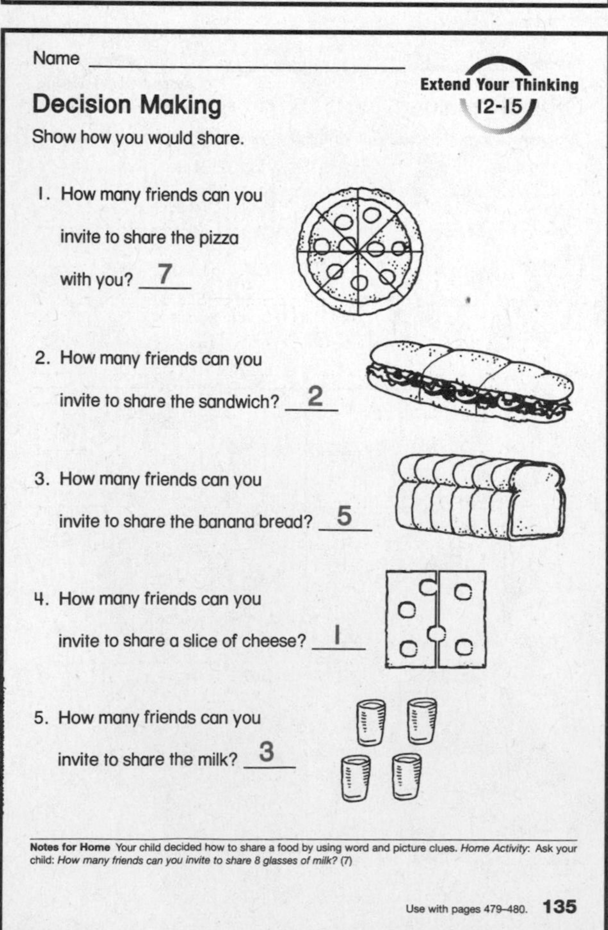

Name ______________________

Extend Your Thinking 12-15

Decision Making

Show how you would share.

1. How many friends can you invite to share the pizza with you? 7
2. How many friends can you invite to share the sandwich? 2
3. How many friends can you invite to share the banana bread? 5
4. How many friends can you invite to share a slice of cheese? 1
5. How many friends can you invite to share the milk? 3

Notes for Home Your child decided how to share a food by using word and picture clues. *Home Activity:* Ask your child: *How many friends can you invite to share 8 glasses of milk?* (7)

Use with pages 479–480. **135**

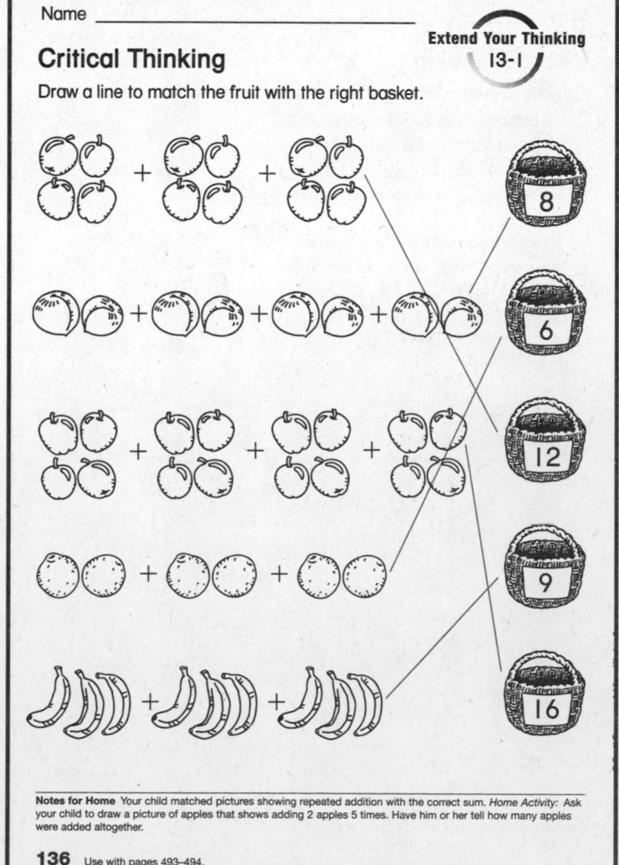

Name ______________________

Extend Your Thinking 13-1

Critical Thinking

Draw a line to match the fruit with the right basket.

Notes for Home Your child matched pictures showing repeated addition with the correct sum. *Home Activity:* Ask your child to draw a picture of apples that shows adding 2 apples 5 times. Have him or her tell how many apples were added altogether.

136 Use with pages 493–494.

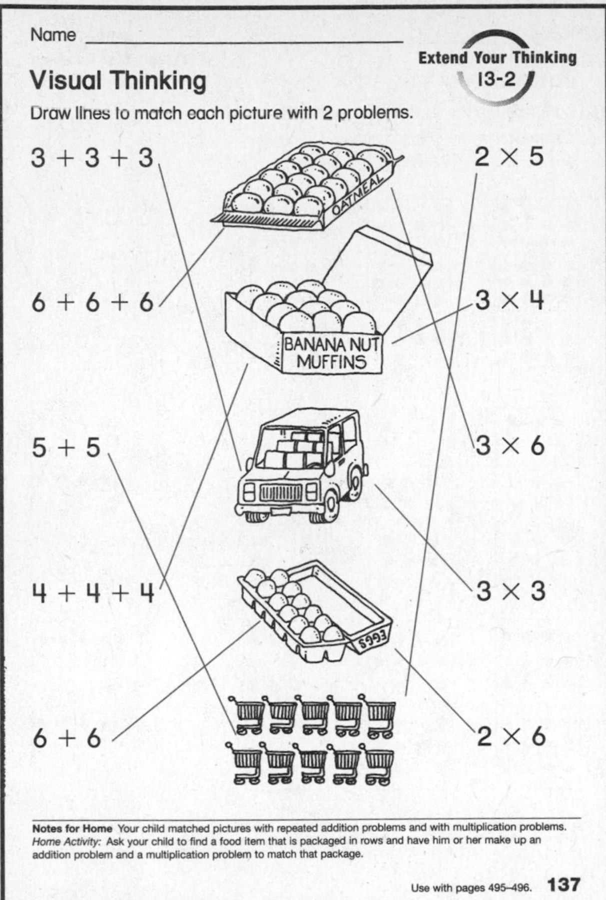

Name ____________________

Extend Your Thinking 13-2

Visual Thinking

Draw lines to match each picture with 2 problems.

3 + 3 + 3	2 × 5
6 + 6 + 6	3 × 4
5 + 5	3 × 6
4 + 4 + 4	3 × 3
6 + 6	2 × 6

Notes for Home Your child matched pictures with repeated addition problems and with multiplication problems. *Home Activity:* Ask your child to find a food item that is packaged in rows and have him or her make up an addition problem and a multiplication problem to match that package.

Use with pages 495–496. **137**

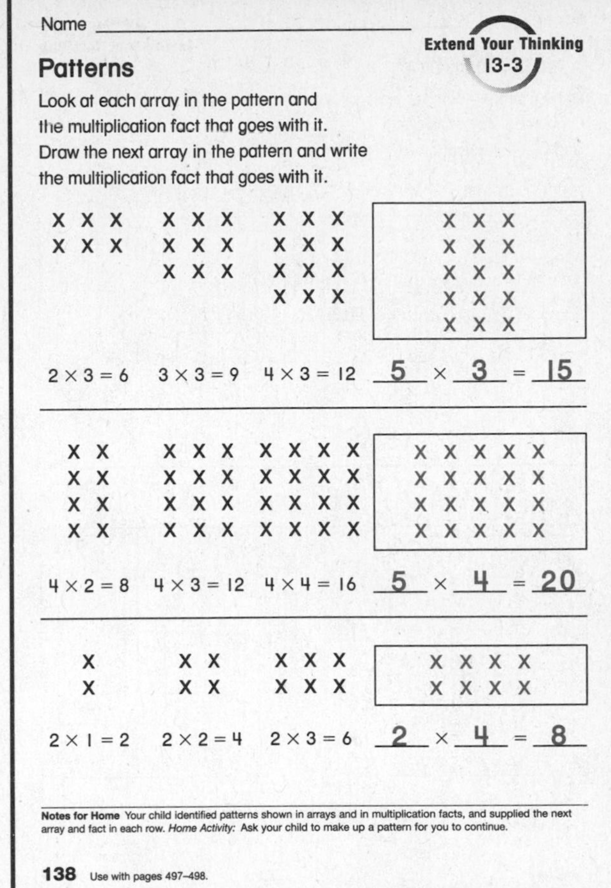

Name ____________________

Extend Your Thinking 13-3

Patterns

Look at each array in the pattern and the multiplication fact that goes with it. Draw the next array in the pattern and write the multiplication fact that goes with it.

$2 \times 3 = 6$ $3 \times 3 = 9$ $4 \times 3 = 12$ 5 × 3 = 15

$4 \times 2 = 8$ $4 \times 3 = 12$ $4 \times 4 = 16$ 5 × 4 = 20

$2 \times 1 = 2$ $2 \times 2 = 4$ $2 \times 3 = 6$ 2 × 4 = 8

Notes for Home Your child identified patterns shown in arrays and in multiplication facts, and supplied the next array and fact in each row. *Home Activity:* Ask your child to make up a pattern for you to continue.

138 Use with pages 497–498.

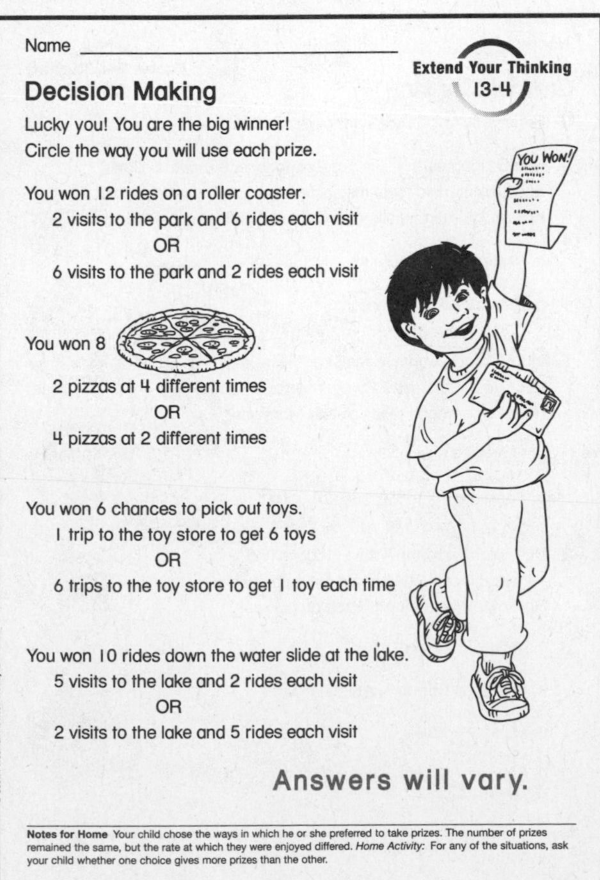

Name ____________________

Extend Your Thinking 13-4

Decision Making

Lucky you! You are the big winner!
Circle the way you will use each prize.

You won 12 rides on a roller coaster.
2 visits to the park and 6 rides each visit
OR
6 visits to the park and 2 rides each visit

You won 8 [pizza].
2 pizzas at 4 different times
OR
4 pizzas at 2 different times

You won 6 chances to pick out toys.
1 trip to the toy store to get 6 toys
OR
6 trips to the toy store to get 1 toy each time

You won 10 rides down the water slide at the lake.
5 visits to the lake and 2 rides each visit
OR
2 visits to the lake and 5 rides each visit

Answers will vary.

Notes for Home Your child chose the ways in which he or she preferred to take prizes. The number of prizes remained the same, but the rate at which they were enjoyed differed. *Home Activity:* For any of the situations, ask your child whether one choice gives more prizes than the other.

Use with pages 499–500. **139**

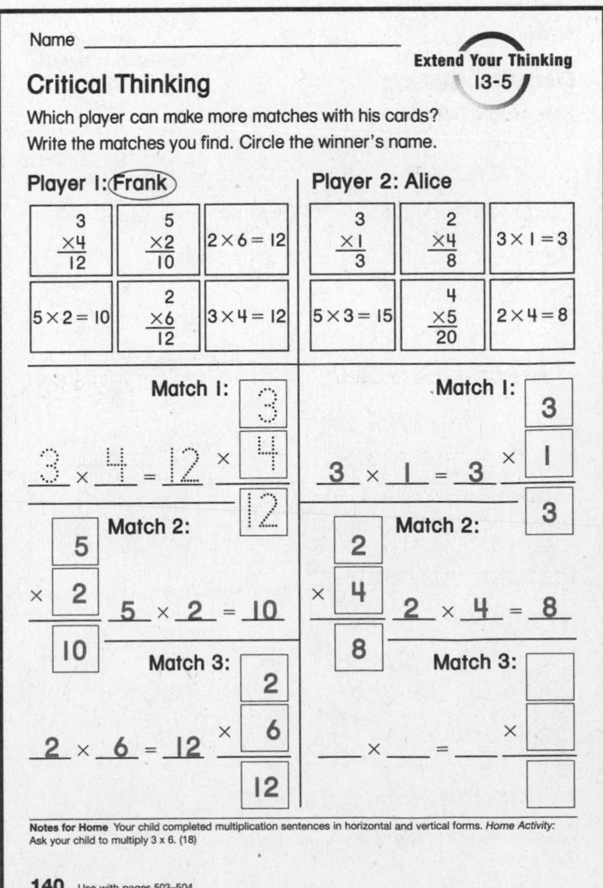

Name ____________________

Extend Your Thinking 13-5

Critical Thinking

Which player can make more matches with his cards?
Write the matches you find. Circle the winner's name.

Player 1: Frank

3 ×4 = 12	5 ×2 = 10	2 × 6 = 12
5 × 2 = 10	2 ×6 = 12	3 × 4 = 12

Match 1: 3 × 4 = 12 ; 3 ×4 = 12
Match 2: 5 ×2 = 10 ; 5 × 2 = 10
Match 3: 2 ×6 = 12 ; 2 × 6 = 12

Player 2: Alice

3 ×1 = 3	2 ×4 = 8	3 × 1 = 3
5 × 3 = 15	4 ×5 = 20	2 × 4 = 8

Match 1: 3 × 1 = 3 ; 3 ×1 = 3
Match 2: 2 ×4 = 8 ; 2 × 4 = 8
Match 3: ___ × ___ = ___

Notes for Home Your child completed multiplication sentences in horizontal and vertical forms. *Home Activity:* Ask your child to multiply 3 x 6. (18)

140 Use with pages 503–504.

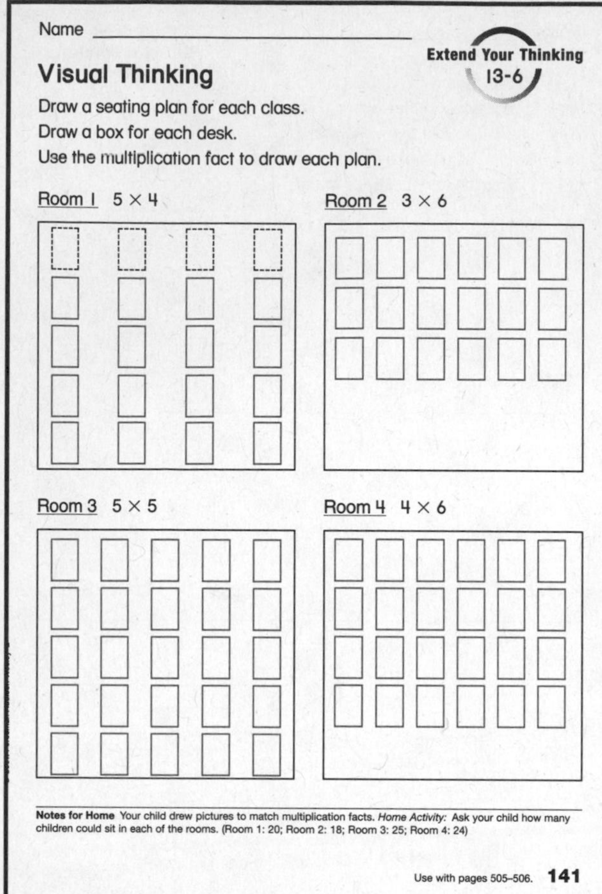
Name ______________________

Extend Your Thinking 13-6

Visual Thinking

Draw a seating plan for each class.
Draw a box for each desk.
Use the multiplication fact to draw each plan.

Room 1 5×4

Room 2 3×6

Room 3 5×5

Room 4 4×6

Notes for Home Your child drew pictures to match multiplication facts. *Home Activity:* Ask your child how many children could sit in each of the rooms. (Room 1: 20; Room 2: 18; Room 3: 25; Room 4: 24)

Use with pages 505–506. **141**

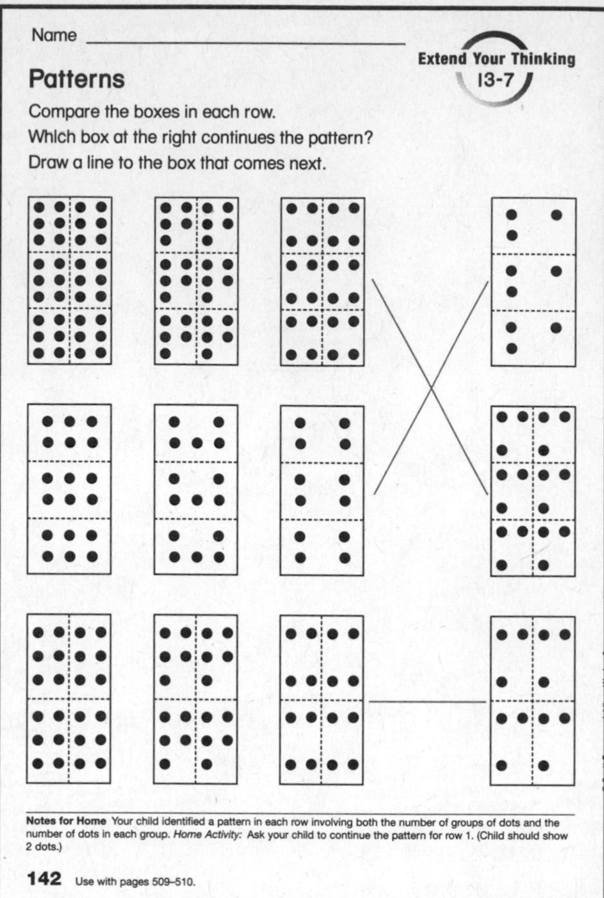
Name ______________________

Extend Your Thinking 13-7

Patterns

Compare the boxes in each row.
Which box at the right continues the pattern?
Draw a line to the box that comes next.

Notes for Home Your child identified a pattern in each row involving both the number of groups of dots and the number of dots in each group. *Home Activity:* Ask your child to continue the pattern for row 1. (Child should show 2 dots.)

142 Use with pages 509–510.

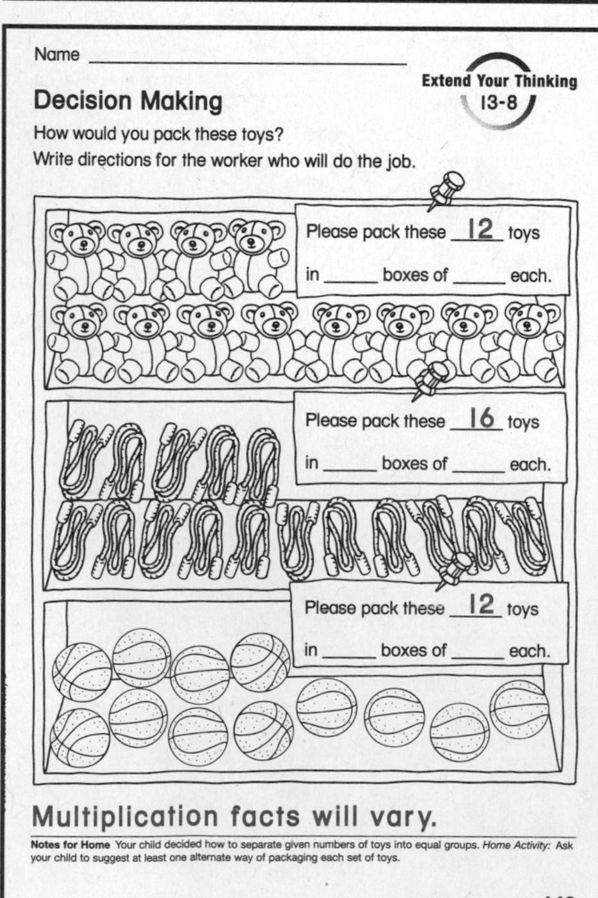
Name ______________________

Extend Your Thinking 13-8

Decision Making

How would you pack these toys?
Write directions for the worker who will do the job.

Please pack these 12 toys in _____ boxes of _____ each.

Please pack these 16 toys in _____ boxes of _____ each.

Please pack these 12 toys in _____ boxes of _____ each.

Multiplication facts will vary.

Notes for Home Your child decided how to separate given numbers of toys into equal groups. *Home Activity:* Ask your child to suggest at least one alternate way of packaging each set of toys.

Use with pages 511–512. **143**

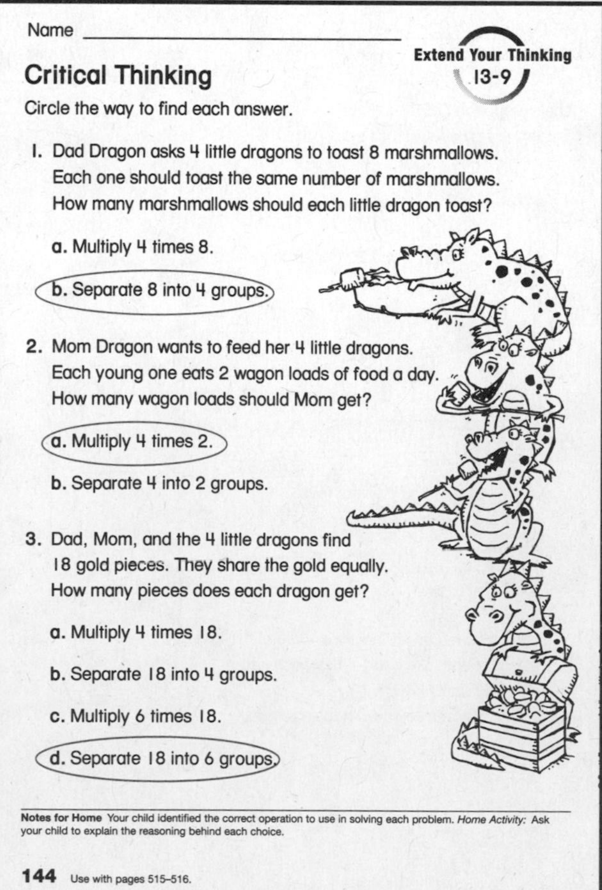
Name ______________________

Extend Your Thinking 13-9

Critical Thinking

Circle the way to find each answer.

1. Dad Dragon asks 4 little dragons to toast 8 marshmallows. Each one should toast the same number of marshmallows. How many marshmallows should each little dragon toast?
   - a. Multiply 4 times 8.
   - b. Separate 8 into 4 groups. (circled)
2. Mom Dragon wants to feed her 4 little dragons. Each young one eats 2 wagon loads of food a day. How many wagon loads should Mom get?
   - a. Multiply 4 times 2. (circled)
   - b. Separate 4 into 2 groups.
3. Dad, Mom, and the 4 little dragons find 18 gold pieces. They share the gold equally. How many pieces does each dragon get?
   - a. Multiply 4 times 18.
   - b. Separate 18 into 4 groups.
   - c. Multiply 6 times 18.
   - d. Separate 18 into 6 groups. (circled)

Notes for Home Your child identified the correct operation to use in solving each problem. *Home Activity:* Ask your child to explain the reasoning behind each choice.

144 Use with pages 515–516.